SHADOW
ON THE
MOUNTAIN

SHADOW
ON THE
MOUNTAIN

A Yazidi Memoir of Terror,
Resistance, and Hope

Shaker Jeffrey
and Katharine Holstein

Da Capo Press

Note to reader: The names of many of the Yazidis and some of the private citizens who appear in this book have been changed for security reasons. The identities of people in public life, as well as the American military veterans who played key roles, are all real.

We have also chosen to use the common Western spelling of Yazidi, rather than the traditional Yezidi, so as not to confuse readers. However, we have elected to use the historic name of Shingal, rather than its more popular counterpart, Sinjar. The region of Shingal in northern Iraq is sacred to the Yazidi people, and as it is also the site of the genocide, we did not feel it should be altered for the telling of this story.

Da Capo Press
Hachette Book Group
1290 Avenue of the Americas, New York, NY 10104
HachetteBooks.com
@HachetteBooks
Twitter.com/HachetteBooks
Instagram.com/HachetteBooks

Printed in the United States of America

First Edition: February 2020

Published by Da Capo Press, an imprint of Perseus Books, LLC, a subsidiary of Hachette Book Group, Inc. The Da Capo Press name and logo is a trademark of the Hachette Book Group.

The Hachette Speakers Bureau provides a wide range of authors for speaking events. To find out more, go to www.hachettespeakersbureau.com or call (866) 376-6591.

The publisher is not responsible for websites (or their content) that are not owned by the publisher.

Print book interior design by Jeff Williams.

Library of Congress Control Number: 2019950503

ISBNs: 978-0-306-92283-1 (hardcover); 978-0-306-92282-4 (e-book)

LSC-C

10 9 8 7 6 5 4 3 2 1

For the lost, taken, and every precious survivor.
Whatever comes, may the Yazidi identity endure.

Contents

Contents

ISIS has made no secret of its intent to destroy the
Yazidis of Sinjar, and that is one of the elements that
allowed us to conclude that their actions amount to
genocide.

UN COMMISSIONER CARLA DEL PONTE,
UN COMMISSION OF INQUIRY ON SYRIA

Come in under the shadow of this red rock . . .
And I will show you fear in a handful of dust

THE WASTE LAND, T. S. ELIOT

The Invasion

THEY CAME FOR US ON THE VERGE OF DAYBREAK IN A LONG LINE of beat-up trucks, dark scarves shrouding their faces. It was August 3, 2014, in the Nineveh Province of northern Iraq. The whole village was slumbering in small gray houses, roosters yet to crow. Sky and ground shared a murky oneness like the vast bottom of an ocean. Into that deep quiet, the air suddenly began to vibrate. I sat up, stared into nothing, and listened. Others were also waking, getting out of beds, moving to windows. It was a heavy sound, full of weight—of both metal and intention. You could feel it in your chest. Then, over the rising hum of those engines and through a wake of exploding dust, we heard the genocidal cries of their holy hatred.

In the just-rising sun, I could see them out there, approaching fast over the plains, shouting and firing off machine-gun rounds. Those crazed men closed in as though they'd poured right out of an apocalyptic gash in the earth. Black flags and a few mortar shells; it didn't take much more than that—we

1

knew exactly who they were and what they wanted. Some people stayed in their shuttered homes, cowering, did all they could to keep the children quiet. Others fled right into the hot morning haze without shoes, without anything whatsoever.

In the end, I was one of those who ran. Ran fast—straight out over the land that was ours long before time. The summer air was filthy; the new sun, blood-red. Suddenly, I didn't know the day, or the hour. None of us did. We didn't even know who we were anymore. But who we were was why we were running—running toward our hallowed mountain that rose in the searing distance like an ark.

As a boy I'd watched my father work that land, his white shirt billowing like a sail as he moved along the cucumber fields. My frail king was long dead and I was alone among the tens of thousands who were with me, a hailstorm of gunfire and the shrieks of women erupting in our stampede of terror. Reduced to a pack of wild animals, we clambered far up the rocky mountainside. Mount Shingal was our only possible refuge now, perched high over the endless wasteland of ISIS-infested desert. Our shrines had stood there for centuries, and we knew that steep terrain as well as we knew ourselves. Better, even. When you came across a bullet-riddled body, you just moved over it and kept going for the top.

Two months earlier, I was a senior in high school studying for final exams, and everyone expected me to be first in my class, as I'd always been in the past. Only I knew that I was in danger of failing—hadn't so much as touched a textbook in years. People said in time it would get better—the nightmares, daymares, and the tremors—but a farmer's son doesn't peel off a whole war like a Band-Aid.

At barely seventeen, I'd run away to sign up as a combat interpreter in Mosul, the most terrorist-infested city in the nation. It was the post-9/11 age of occupation and insurgency, the

West's War on Terror in full swing. Now, I look back on that era as the cataract of a monstrous and unyielding storm.

Over the next four years, I went out in full fatigues, supporting American brigade teams as they hunted down terrorist networks across a massive web that spanned the country and stretched over its borders. I was shot at—more than once, I was hit; saw members of my team killed right in front of me. The huge entanglements of radicals we were after didn't seem to have an end, and as far as I knew, didn't have a beginning either. When you got rid of one viral cell, twenty more came back with a vengeance.

Through it all, I made lifelong friends: Texans and Californians, New Yorkers and Idaho boys who'd come there just like I had, straight out of a dust bowl. After the Western forces withdrew, I went back to my village fluent in American slang, met the girl I wanted more than anything to marry. Believed the worst was over.

I was wrong.

The very beast the West had tried to Shock and Awe and annihilate was after me now, out of its cage and making chase across the rocky plains of Shingal. Under one name or another, they'd hunted my people for a thousand years.

I kept my eyes fixed to the mountain now, and the multitude moving toward it, their combined chaos stirring up massive clouds of earth that clogged the air. Several times, I had to stop and cough up mud.

Over 100,000 of us made it to the summit. Up there, on a vast and desolate shelf that seemed to hover in the colorless sky, all you could see was that helpless horde, pressed into a single form, moaning under a crush of baking heat. No trees for shade. No water. No food. People sagged and shivered from thirst in the dirt; the elderly wished out loud to die. It was 120 degrees Fahrenheit. Every infant lay silent in the arms that held it.

ON AN AFTERNOON after the first week, as I slumped over my bed of ground, a faint noise plucked at the stilled air. Slowly, the sound rose and the scores around me draped on the rocks stirred a little. So tired, I peered into the listless void; the world far below enveloped our high refuge like a brown sea. In the faraway haze, I caught a moving form and sat up.

Suddenly, people were on their feet, hoisting children to their shoulders and racing forward. The air above us began to rage and the ground seethed. Then, as though out of a dream, helicopter blades beat the gritty sunlight over me. Glinting things began to fall all around us—water. The pandemonium was immediate. You knew there were never going to be enough bottles, not for all of us. Even now, that splintering chorus of pleas, so weak against the tidal rush of air, haunts me.

As the helicopter moved in closer, people began to grab at the landing skids, their frantic weight pulling the flying machine off-kilter. Some clamored to force themselves in. Others pitched screaming children through the open doors. I saw the silhouette of a cameraman appear at the hatch, aim his lens as a journalist in a dress shirt and body armor next to him pointed at us.

The chopper banked sideways, began to lift away toward the boundless sky. At once in the violent wind, thousands of Yazidi hands went up through torrents of sand, reaching out for their departing hope together.

I stood in the melee half-mad and shouting, sand beating into my eyes. I looked around me at all of them, at that forest of wizened limbs. I couldn't hear a thing anymore, not a single entreaty or the dissipating rotors. Suddenly I was seeing us all from above, saw my own wild and spattered face, parched mouth wide open. And I rose higher still, way up into the ether; what was left of me below diminished until I was nothing more than a shadow on the mountain.

4

All over the surrounding terrain, rabid soldiers of the Islamic State swarmed the plains and foothills, taking our women and girls as sex slaves—mine included—and massacring the rest. They sat in trucks, pointed their weapons, and waited for the rest of us to come down.

And I did go down, crossed enemy lines and even infiltrated their ranks in disguise to rescue the taken. Ever since, I've been on the run from ISIS. They've tried many times to kill me—but they'll have to catch me first.

Chapter One

The Spring Baghdad Fell

IN THE LOW LIGHT OF LATE AFTERNOON, A BOY AND A MAN raced up a sloped field in the Shingal region of northern Iraq. Arms pumping, they dashed between tight rows of sprouting onions: soft new leaves ankle high, the ground hard and the gusting air cool. All around them, the cultivated land stretched on for acres and acres, planted rows like a multitude of rail tracks running into a wavering atmosphere of flickering sun and falling mist. The sky was as pale as an empty canvas, and crested larks cut across it, their birdsong loud and high. In the faraway distance, gentle foothills rippled out like great folds in the boundless blanket of earth spread before the blunt summit of Shingal, which rose like a vision right across it. It was past those soft peaks somewhere, my father had told me, that the first man was born.

Haji ran hard, towering like a dark-haired giant, shirt flashing. Only the big brown satchel strapped to his side held him back. I was the boy a pace or two ahead of him, mismatched sneakers, long-limbed and thin, laughing out loud as I sprinted. I could always feel Haji thudding just behind me like a heavy shadow; at twelve years old, I was a full seventeen years his junior. For all my youth and speed, I was always methodical in my stride—never took a step that wasn't planned well in advance.

Reaching the crest of the field, we stopped and turned, and I leaned into the steady wind that spat bits of dry soil in my face. Even over the howling air, I thought I could hear the lambs baying in their pens. At the foot of the slope, in a small spooned-out dip in the endless plains, I saw all that we were. Our little house, a lonely thatched shoebox, front door wide open. Farm buildings scattered like crates between crippled wooden fences, a mess of dirt roads that seemed to lay strewn like dirty ropes. The farmstead stood as though it had sprouted from the very ground out of which we'd built it. And from that simple snapshot of tranquility that I can see even now in minute detail, I felt the full embrace of home—it didn't really matter what was happening anywhere else.

OVER FOUR HUNDRED miles south of our heedless wasteland, a line of tanks, Humvees, and armored personnel carriers of the 3rd Battalion, 4th Marines pulled out of the gates of their base and thundered across the flat heart of ancient Mesopotamia. They were on a two-lane paved road and headed in a steady beeline for the battered capital. As the contingent roared over the floodplains, my fellow countrymen, watching from ditches and pockets of marshland along the way, gasped. Some in wonder. Others in terror.

Once the procession was out of view, those people rushed back to their state-owned concrete houses. By nightfall, the details would spread mouth to ear again and again, thousands of times over, in endangered whispers, from one impoverished town to the next. Not a single satellite television for a hundred square miles around my speck-of-dust village—that was how we got the news. Never before, in its long history of wrath, had our battle-seasoned country borne a military force of such capable and colossal ferocity. Entering the main drag of the city, the 3/4 Battalion moved slowly. It was April 9, 2003, and America with all her might was on the ground in Baghdad.

Exhalations from the Tigris river drifted along the jumbled streets, cooling the choked air mere moments before dissolving into a hot shroud of carbon and soot. Mighty twin of the slow Euphrates, the current had flowed over a thousand miles from the Taurus Mountains of Turkey to get there, winding down through the arid alluvial plains of Iraq, cutting gorges out of bedrock and rushing past forests of pistachio. It had snaked by sheep farms and mud-hut villages, great dams and military bunkers, flashed under the gaze of falcons and long-abandoned gods, before splitting into the river delta of Shatt al-Arab, whose tangled tributaries once cleaved whole tribes and set realms to war, even before they'd divided Iraq from Iran—all in a never-ending race for the blue sweep of the Persian Gulf. Those mythical waters once irrigated the first civilization of Sumerians and had witnessed the many invasions of Mongols and the six-hundred-year rise and fall of the Ottoman Empire; its rushing current carried vessels of the ancient Greeks and, well before then, had gently rocked the cradle of humanity.

The bombed-out capital now rose right from those muddy banks, buildings still smoldering and sending up furious columns of black smoke. Trapped in swirls of current, clumps of garbage accumulated and then floated lazily along like small ramshackle rafts. In that very place, human beings had lived and thrived for millennia, and the marble palace of fallen Arabian kings—and later our once indomitable dictator, Saddam Hussein, now in hiding—sat looted and empty.

WORLDS AWAY AND looking over the plain face of our house, I could see the window that always stood wide open like a small door into a dream. Past the sill and unseen, my old father was fast asleep, alone in his bed. Those days he slept far more than he did anything else. In the morning, I shaved his face as he lay back against the pillows. The skin of his face slackened, eyes set deep inside their caves, the lids half-open and flickering. Those noble blues that he said had witnessed a whole lifetime before I was born, just so he could teach me, were dimming under cataracts. I combed his hair, carefully changed his clothes. When he moved with my touch, I could feel those old bones slip and clack under his paper-thin skin. After that, I brought him spiced chai and a soft-boiled egg. Sometimes I'd feed the egg to him slowly, sometimes just wait there if he was strong enough that day to use the spoon himself. From time to time, he'd look over at me sitting against the wall, and shrug. I'd look back and give him a faint smile. We were exchanging a sure knowledge about the pointlessness of any sorrow and the brevity of all things. Then he'd drain the last of his cup and close his eyes awhile.

We also talked in that room, for small stretches through the day, like crossing a line of stepping-stones over his endless river of sleep. He had no sense of the time anymore, which seemed to stop and hold its breath between those walls. My mother said that in his dreams he spoke with the Seven Angels, one God-given to us for each day of the week.

Past the house, on a fifteen-mile concrete plate poured over the open moonscape, stood our village of Khanasor, meaning "the Red Bar," some said for the Yazidis' appreciation of watering holes and wine. It was but one of dozens of planned villages the central government constructed in the 1970s and built for the same purpose as all the others across the province: to contain and control the mountain-dwelling and nomadic people.

Not long after taking power, Saddam Hussein rounded up the Yazidi tribes and forced them down from their tiny huts on sacred Shingal and into soulless towns erected at its feet.

Over thirty-five thousand people, including a handful of Sunni Muslims who taught at our government schools, all packed into cinderblock homes, each one exactly like the next: just enough to keep us warm, but not enough to fill our heads with bad ideas—like expecting free elections, for one. Still, in Saddam's dream of a homogeneous Arabized nation, we were just a hangnail among cancers of Shia, Christians, and Kurds.

Yazidi people have never asked for much, except to be left alone to live off the land they've inhabited since the days of Adam, from whom they believe they are the first descendants. Their beliefs are both ancient and guileless: no saviors or prophets—they worship one god, and the sun and angels, especially the Peacock Angel, Tawusi Melek, who is the deity through which God attends to the infinite universe. Because the Peacock Angel was once said to have fallen from heaven, many have mistaken him for a devil, and Yazidis as devil-worshippers. It is this confusion alone that has made us targets for millennia—over seventy genocides so far, and counting.

Above all things, the Yazidi are pacifists—never wantonly killing a soul—and no matter what anyone did to us, we would only bow our heads and pray for peace. It's the Achilles' heel our enemies have always counted on, and one of the reasons why there are so few of us left. In eight thousand years we'd gone from 8 million to 650,000. In a half a blink, we'd be gone.

Still sitting on the hill next to my brother, Haji, I held a hand up against the desolate horizon and blotted Khanasor out.

MEANWHILE, THE GUTS of Baghdad burned and car horns blared. Later, people said you could hear the wild glee of gangs looting government buildings of tacky furnishings. Marble lamps and velvet curtains. Boys ran out from the narrow alleys and along the sides of the road to watch the parade of approaching invaders. The column lumbered toward the city center. Some people cheered and jumped on the banks of the river. Others only stared as they stood in their torn and dirty clothes. In most parts of the city there was no running water, and electricity was scarce. Everywhere the stench of gasoline and smoke seemed to have set fire to the air that shimmered in the bone-dry heat. There was an atmosphere of a carnival, but with an unmistakable knife-edge. After all, this was a war.

Smiling Baghdadis rushed out of crumbling buildings to offer the Marines cups of chai and slices of sweet cakes. Many wept openly, hands on knees or holding up the photos of loved ones: mostly fresh-faced young men and women captured in their hopeful prime and never seen again. Since taking power in a coup d'état in 1975, Saddam Hussein and his Baathists had ordered targeted arrests and killings by the hundreds of thousands, whether in secret underground prisons or in summary executions out in the desert. On more than one occasion, he ordered the gassing of whole villages of Kurdish people, the bodies simply left to decompose right where they fell.

At one end of Firdos Square, the massive bronze statue of Saddam, an open hand beckoning the city and a bird perched on his shoulder, rose sixty-seven feet into a polluted sky. Erected to commemorate his birthday, the statue cast a long blade of shadow over the paved ground. Within plain view of the seventeen-story Palestine Hotel that flanked the open space, a crowd of Iraqis was swarming the statue. Heads thrown back, they shrieked and ranted at the molded face. Already demoted from dictator to fugitive, the actual man was long gone.

STILL STANDING NEXT to me, and out of breath, Haji let his clinking bag of tools drop. Rummaging around in that old satchel, he was like a magician planning his next trick. Haji could make anything from the things he kept in there, and my family was never really sure how. My father often said that if Haji didn't hurry up and find himself a blue-eyed Yazidi bride, then he should just get out his kit and make one out of the earth.

As soon as we sat on the lip of the hill, Haji would hand me things that he would need: a hammer or tin of oil. We'd talk about my day at school: the books I was reading or which kids gave the teacher trouble, and how to stay well out of it myself. On that day, our talk turned to the war and the strange and perilous times we were living in—no fighter planes overhead, no bombs, but whole platoons of rumors. In school I was taught that terrified American soldiers were blowing themselves up at the gates of Baghdad, but somehow Haji knew it wasn't true. All around us for miles under a thin reef of cloud, the world stood still, not a soul in sight.

A HULKING BAGHDADI figure stepped up to the statue. Wielding a sledgehammer borrowed from an American soldier, he set to work at pummeling the solid concrete plinth. All sweaty in his muscle top, his hairy arms were like cinderblocks. I learned much later, in one of the countless stories people told again and again, that he was a national champion wrestler. Even he could do no more than crack the surface.

Finally, an American soldier helped to tie a metal cable like a noose around Saddam's neck, and hooked that to a Hercules M88 crane that was used for towing armored vehicles across the fields of battle. Chanting and clapping sounds rose over the mounting drone of the crane's engines.

One tug from the Hercules, and the statue of Saddam Hussein slid against the base and toppled over like a toy soldier. Once it heaved to the pavement, the crowd instantly fell onto it with the frenzy of savage animals before a kill. Hurling shoes, kicking and screaming bloody murder. It didn't seem to matter that nothing they could do would bring back the innocent legions of dead. Somehow, the horde separated Saddam's big head from the torso, and by a rope fastened around his neck, they hauled the thing through the streets like a sled. Men and boys took turns riding on it.

From the balconies and windows of the Palestine Hotel, the scores of Western journalists occupying its three hundred rooms captured that unfolding historic scene in real time, and projected it around the world. Photographs of the toppled statue covered front pages of newspapers from one end of the planet to the other. So many believed that the war that had only just begun twenty-one days before was all but over. Still, the spring Baghdad fell, we Yazidis were the last to know.

YEARS AGO, AFTER too many crops were lost to drought, my brothers dug down, two tall men deep, until they hit precious mud. Together under the bright broil of June, they built walls of brick up from the well bottom, and then they carved out a tiny pump room next to it. Finally, in that little subterranean space, Haji assembled a mechanical hand pump as though he'd done it before ten thousand times—and saved us.

"Here it comes!" Haji always hollered.

Seconds later, in a gift that kept our family of seven sons and three daughters clothed and fed through the bitter rainless months, a fusillade of cold water burst from the pipe and splashed into a man-made canal. The faucet gushing, I jumped barefoot into the trench and the rising waterline crept like a chill up to my knees before overflowing the lip and rushing straight down the sloped field.

When Haji came back up, he stood, clothes dripping and his brow splotched red, and watched the progress of the stream he'd muscled and drawn up from its cavern. Within minutes, the resurrected soil turned to a rich dark mud. In that moment, I watched and worshipped my brother, and yet he just stood there on the crest, Shingal rising far behind him, not saying a word. His water was enough.

Then, I dropped down and floated in the drink cold as stone. Buoyed on my back, I stared way up into the bright and endless sky, listening to the chitter of the larks and the gentle splash of the spill, and felt a perfect calm on the water that held me. I didn't even know yet that that afternoon we'd all been set free.

AFTER SUPPER, WHILE the others went about their business in the house, I stepped out into the farmyard and gazed over the purpling slope of our land. All was tranquil. My brother's hoo-kah smoke wandered past from the front room; and I heard his low voice as he spoke to our mother. She didn't want to hear what he was telling her; she didn't like to hear anything about the senseless happenings beyond Khanasor, and she hushed him.

Haji laughed at her: "Only you would be afraid of good news, Daki!"

"News is like fresh fruit, Haji. Eventually, it always goes bad."

I shut the door softly and made my way across the empty yard. Before me, the silhouette of the barn stood out like a tall ship anchored to the starry night. With a tired hand on the wooden latch, I listened a moment to the muted bawling of the lambs.

Inside, the ewes that knew me bayed loudly as I made my rounds; the newborns only stared as though I were some prophet walking by. In a back pen, I found one pushed up against the wall, alone, black markings like ink stains over her dust-covered fleece. She'd been my first ewe mother and I called her just that—"Daki." Digging at the ground, she heaved her backside into the wall in distress and I could tell that she was too tired for much more. A tiny pair of hoofs poked out from the birth canal—everything in its proper order, no breech. We'd been through this before many times, she and I, and I'd grown an in-stinct to know when to step in and pull, and when to stand back and wait. As much as you could, you let the mothers look after things themselves. But something was different now. When she shook out a high call from deep inside her throat, I knew it for what it was and went to her fast. Taking the quarter-born babe by its flimsy shanks, I yanked the animal right out over the ground and wiped the film away from its passages.

Then I got down with the mother, who could move no more. I sensed the working of a second labor like a separate beast within, there only to take what was left of her. I quickly put my hand in—the animal inside was twisted the wrong way. The sack of amniotic water and dark clots of blood gushed down my arms as I pulled hard, and the scent made me gag. Finally, the unborn tore away from the canal covered in a mess of plasma. One quick look and I tossed the thing down. It was already long past dead.

On the ground, the ewe was doing nothing; I put a bloodied hand on her head and felt my skin steal the last of her warmth. Then her eyes left all things behind and she was gone. There was nothing more to be done. A long time ago, my father warned me that it wasn't good to come to love a living creature that was destined for the slaughter.

And I remember well how Haji, standing behind him like a shadow, had cackled without smiling and said:

"That's a very odd thing, Babo, to teach a Yazidi."

Chapter Two

After the Torchlight

THE ONLY GOOD THING SADDAM HUSSEIN EVER GAVE US WAS our school, a cluster of three concrete buildings rising like giant cinderblocks from the eastern rim of Khanasor. Painted in a bright mural of green grass, blue sky, and flowers as big as my head, a high wall surrounded the grim-looking courtyard. Every time I walked through the doors and felt our stalwart Madam tap my head, an instant peace overcame me. I never noticed the stained plaster or crumbling ceiling tiles that wept sour-smelling water over my desk. Within those walls I listened to poetic tales of Arabian kings and studied the mechanics of the universe. I found out that the world was round, clouds were made of water vapor, and that the tide comes in and goes out again because of gravity. We read from our history books and recited aloud the forged history of the nation, in which our fearless ruler vanquished every enemy—Americans, Persians, the Zionists, and NATO.

Gracing the central corridor, a massive painting of a smiling Saddam Hussein sat in a gilt wood frame: white dove perched on his elaborate epaulet, glinting sword at his side. I routinely bowed my head, but I never paid him much mind. And when his effigy in oils disappeared and just the dirty outline of its frame remained, the fact went largely unremarked. A few shards of glass on the floor told us many things—mostly that the rumors sneaking around Khanasor were true.

When we got to class, every child stood in unison to greet our Madam and then sat as she read aloud from one of her many religious Arabic texts. We all listened with guarded solemnity to the words our pious teacher uttered, but I had no idea what she was saying or why. Sometimes, Madam could sense the shallows of our passions. After all, these quiet children, some of them as pale as porcelain creatures hewn in a kiln, were not of the Huma, "the Book"—which was worse than being a Shia, or even a Christian. All of us were simply of Adam, and the earth.

Indoctrination and propaganda aside, we were lucky to be there: over thirty wide-eyed Yazidi kids, the progeny of ancient nomads and so-called heretics, sons and daughters of laborers and co-op farmers, all of us living happily in varying degrees of concrete poverty, and the unsuspecting beneficiaries of "Compulsory Free Education in Iraq." Underground, Saddam Hussein had hacked out bunkers, secret prisons, and state-of-the-art torture chambers; aboveground he'd erected marble palaces, bronze statues, and brick-and-mortar temples to higher learning. Between ethnic cleansings, wars of attrition, and arbitrary hangings, Saddam achieved the unprecedented in the Middle East: a near 100 percent literacy rate. By the time the Coalition Forces started to clear the catastrophic heaps of rubble, it was the dawn of 2004, and I was a twelve-year-old student in middle school, reading books of ancient Arabic proverbs, practicing my penmanship, and learning to speak conversational English:

"Hello, my name is Shaker. I am a boy."

OFTEN IN LATE spring, mud coated my shoes—the same pair of tired sneakers for two, maybe three years. Threadbare socks, if any at all, covered my callused feet. Most of the time, I had to roll my patchwork pants up at the cuff. When you have an army of older brothers, there's never a shortage of hand-me-downs, but nothing ever quite fits. It didn't matter much; we had what we had, and things were just things. It was impossible to covet what none of us even knew existed. In time, that would change.

When I started primary school at the age of six, my father taught me about being fastidious: "Hair as smooth as a raven's wing," he'd say through a gloom of tobacco smoke. In those days, Babo was never without a cigarette smoldering between his long, earth-scarred fingers, and every word he uttered came out dragging hot puffs of Baghdad King Size tobacco with it. As a child, I believed he must have a flame burning in his throat, and that God had put it there for some special reason, perhaps to secret it away from Seytan, the sultan of devils.

To the Yazidi, every element—earth, wind, water, sunlight, and fire—is hallowed, and we revere each one in turn. But above all, feeling the sun's rays is to stand before the eye of God's first angel, Tawusi Melek. Even now, and despite everything that's happened to us, my Daki still wakes each morning to worship the dawn. My father said she prayed enough for them both, but I could always see stars flickering within his dull cataracts and believed God had placed those there, too—every time Babo cast his torch-lit gaze over me, I felt the gift.

Trekking the six village blocks to school from my cousin Khairi Aezdeen's house in spring was like wading a narrow riverbed. Sometimes it rained seven days straight, and chutes of water poured from the spouts draining the flat rooftops. Flanking the streets like a grim cliff face, long strips of single-story dwell-ings stood all linked together under a grid of limp electrical wires. Every now and again, you'd encounter a facade of color to indicate that there was a business inside.

During the school week, I often lived at my uncle's four-room house located in the center of town, so that I could sleep more and walk less. Khairi always welcomed me, his open hands ready to give whatever he had, even when times were hard. Nothing that happened to us afterward would rob my cousin of that virtue. Often, my brother Samir, who was just two years older, came there with me. In the morning, we all got up from our shared mattress on the floor and slipped on our socks, not bothering to check whose were whose. I still remember how clean that house was, but also how spare: music from the tran-sistor radio on a shelf over the hot plate; the melody of a sitar, beat of a drum. A tambour guitar tucked in the corner. Floor mats. Khairi's constant laugh.

In the cool blur of daybreak, I reached for my shirt and sensed Samir doing the same. Then we waited our turns at the bathroom sink, behind eight cousins, all standing in a row like chattering birds on wire, always right next to Khairi with his big eyes full of lashes, blinking.

Crammed satchels strapped to our backs, we made for the open threshold. Sometimes my grandma, Dapîra, would be wandering the courtyard in her blue shawl, feeding the birds and offering soft prayers to the sun. As I walked out, she'd reach up and tousle my hair, laughing. Seconds later, I stepped into the unpaved street, felt the squish of fresh mud, and remem-bered to be grateful for the rain.

Up the road and one by one, other children came out of their cement boxes, as though each door was part of a strange factory that disgorged Yazidi schoolchildren every morning. Some kids loped along still in a disheveled state of half sleep, puffy-eyed and tucking in their shirts, the voices of their mothers calling after them. Usually after a few blocks, we joined up with my crew: Barzan, Saïd, and Tarfan. Tethered to me by blood, Samir remained a pace or two ahead, glancing back every now and again.

Out flew Barzan, furtive glances left to right, and an all-knowing crooked grin. Filthy coughs of molten smog and the metallic sounds of machinery at work always trailed him into the street, as though some mechanism had only just melded his sturdy limbs together. Of us all, he often had the best shoes, but once he stepped in the mud that fact was quickly forgotten. The proud son of a successful welder, Barzan had more money than any of us. Each Friday, he would come leaping out of his house with a small packet of dinars held high. Sure enough, before the first bell rang, he'd already doled out a little cash to each of us.

Up another block, Saïd took his time making an appearance. He'd stand awhile in the doorframe in his wayward shoes, hand holding out a half-eaten stub of cucumber or whatever he could scrounge from his father's unreliable co-op. Then by some tacit arrangement, Barzan or another one of us asked him to get down to business:

"Tell us a joke, Saïd."

Mouth full of breakfast, Saïd stopped in his tracks and held court in the muck; it never mattered if we'd heard the gag many times before.

TEACHER: Children, what does the chicken give you?
KIDS: Eggs!
TEACHER: Very good! Now what does the goat give you?
KIDS: Meat!
TEACHER: Yes! And what does the fat cow give you?
KIDS: Homework!

Rounds of belly laughs, and we continued on our way.

No matter the weather, under his white shirt Saïd was always clad in a red jersey for the English soccer team Arsenal, and when he wasn't proffering punch lines, he was talking soccer and making up teams for afternoon matches.

"Who's in?" he'd say and point his cleft chin at us. "After school."

"I have to go back to the farm. My father is unwell," was my routine answer, though it pained me to miss a game. My father frowned at my playing: *Bury yourself in knowledge while you have the chance, Shaker, not in the dirt. The dirt will always give itself to you.*

"Who listened to the game last night?" Saïd would inevitably want to know, his brown eyes going big. "I don't even know which teams were up—couldn't get a signal, made me crazy."

"Electricity's been out for two days from here to Mosul. We've got the generator going nonstop," Barzan told us.

We all believed that some natural event was the cause: the Tigris flooding its banks or a lighting strike. The elements in Iraq could be as capricious as the politics.

"Nothing to do with the weather. And a lot more to do with bombs," Samir called back. It was the first we'd heard of it.

"What do you know about bombs, philosopher Samir?" laughed my cousin Khairi. No one believed it.

But Samir had turned away with a look on his face that told me he'd stopped listening. Standing still now, he tilted his head, and a flat hand went up over his brow. Saying nothing, he searched the bright distance. His lips cleaved and let out a breath.

Out there, a bird of prey sailed the high winds over the plain and we heard a single screech reverberate down over Shingal. As the dark form swept lower on the zephyr, the curvature of his eyes sharpened—and now that bare gaze seemed to stalk me. For a moment, there was nothing else.

"I would do anything for my slingshot," someone whispered. "Look at his wingspan."

I told them the bird was too far out. "And it's a sin to kill such a creature for sport."

As we all stood there watching the wavering falcon, the atmosphere around us began to quiver. And somehow I could feel what was coming like an omen. At once, the ancient air surrendered to a shock of sound and a pair of fighter jets ripped through the heavens, cutting away right over us. All the boys jumped up in their filthy shoes and screamed. The first sight and sound of those mighty planes tore open our psyches and awakened something slumbering deep within us—the primal instinct we all had for war and its colossal machinery.

"See!" Samir yelled and pointed. "*See!*"

And the riptide of sound dissipated to a low thunder.

Then a breathless voice called out, and we looked over to see Tarfan running wild. People were streaming out of their houses. Panting before us, Tarfan stopped, beat-up satchel in hand, the contents of paperwork and pens spilling out.

"Who were they?" we all asked the sky that seemed so empty now.

Eyes bulging, Tarfan looked at us like a boy who'd swallowed his own heart. He dropped his tattered bag in the mud. "I'll bet it's the Americans—who else?"

When I came home, there wasn't any talk of war whatsoever. There were no sounds in the house, except of my mother's sighs and my father's breathing, which you could hear rattle and heave no matter which room you went to. All through the season, I held vigil with my dad, all of us taking our turn like supplicants to the ticking hours, which had become his alone in their waning.

"Sing," he'd whisper to the candle flame.

And I would for a while, taking up my tambour.

22

Sometimes, his knuckles would gently lift and fall as though his fingertips had joined mine on the strings, or he'd reach out to be sure I was there.

"I've spent my packet, boy," he muttered just once, and we let it go.

Other times, he'd jerk an elbow toward the stacks of volumes lined up on the sill.

"Read some."

"Yes, Babo." And I'd open a book. It never mattered which one.

Every hour or two, and only while he slept, we'd move Babo from one side to the other, using a long drawing sheet—me at one end, a grim-faced sibling at the other.

"Death comes up through the feet," my oldest brother, Naïf, told me when the skin on Babo's legs started to mottle. And I wanted to shame him for his careless talk. The day I saw Babo's nails going blue, I felt something fragile in me slip and shatter. I coated my father's dry lips in ointment, kissed his brow where he was still warm with blood, though the rest of him was as cool as night. Somehow, I took what I could get and made it what it wasn't—time.

The early summer morning came like every other, but that time I found my Babo sitting up against the pillows. The window open, a glass of water held in his hand.

"Hello," he said and looked right at me.

I collapsed into his gaze and watched dumbstruck, as he got up unaided from his bed. He moved slowly forward and touched me on the shoulder; his eyes were like glass.

"I'll have an egg," he said. "Some *naan*. Milk. How I've missed it." Then, for the first time in half a year, he went to the bathroom alone and turned on the taps. Loud and clear, I could hear him singing.

In a jubilant state of my own second-coming as a boy, I went right to the kitchen, fired up the hot plate, and cracked the eggs into butter, thinking of all the smug things I would say to my know-it-all-brothers.

When my father came out smelling of soap and smiling, I passed him his full plate of food. We talked while he ate—a mile a minute. He asked about each of my friends, my grades, and said I might as well play a game of football now and again to keep my body healthy.

"Not too much, mind you, Shaker. Not too much of anything, but love," he said. It was a thing he'd told me many times. We didn't go near what had been happening to him—it seemed the strange spell of atrophy had broken at last. Finally, he instructed me to run down to my uncle's house and bring everyone back to see him.

"Hurry now, Shaker, and tell them I'm here waiting."

OUR ACRES OF farmland were hushed, the dirt road empty. I felt the sun heat my back when I ran and kept going until I was dripping. In the distance, the edge of town took shape and I heard an infant bawling like a calf. There would be a wedding that week and my mother was busy helping prepare the food well ahead of time. Yazidis celebrate all feasts together as one, because as dwindling members of humankind, that's all we are. The bride and groom were so often cousins, and if not, would at least be Yazidis of the same tribal line—which is almost the same thing.

When my father married my mother, it was his second marriage. His first wife had died giving birth to Naïf, as often happened. One year later almost to the day, my mother's mother offered up her seventeen-year-old daughter's matrimonial hand to my Babo—a man with a good plot of land, a healthy boy she would make her own, and a solid house to tend to. So Naïf got a new daki, a year later a brother; and the rest of us came, year after year. Our mother used to say that marrying a man old enough to be her father was not such a bad thing: he'd made all his foolish mistakes long before she was born, and at least he was handsome.

When I got to my uncle's house, they were all inside talking. Aunts, uncles, cousins, and a few other men were crowded around a brass hookah, which sat between them on the floor like a bejeweled octopus. Each man took small sucks from a long tentacle and held in the sweet-smelling fog.

When Daki saw my shadow flood the open doorway, she put her knife down on the board and clapped fresh thyme from her hands. Then she took in the patches of sweat on my shirt.

"What is it?" she said. "Babo?"

"Of course it is, girl." Dapîra's old soft face poked out from behind my mother. I will never forget the certainty in her gaze.

Looking back on it now, I can remember everything that happened in that room with a crystalline clarity: sets of eyes on me blinking, and the hot rush of blood roaring though my chest. I told them all, so proud of my news, that my dad was wide-awake, what he'd eaten, that he was wearing a clean shirt, and that he needed them to come right away.

Without a word, they all raced for the door. In a moment, I heard my uncle's pickup revving to life and watched my mother rush into the passenger side, holding the embroidered edge of her shawl up over her face. My grandma glanced at me for a moment before getting in. Then uncles and aunts crammed into the flatbed and the truck lurched forward, rows of hands holding on as the vehicle barreled hard up the street. There was no room for me in the back of the pickup, and it was understood that I'd be making my own way home. Young legs had to earn their rest—my father had always told me that.

And they didn't believe me, anyway. That's what I thought, and I kicked a stone down the road a few paces.

NAÏF WAS IN the doorway when I got back, smoking one of my father's stale Baghdads, contemplating the glowing tip. He looked at me as I passed by, and I saw his torment, which was hard to figure: why he'd be so upset at mistakenly thinking the end had come for Babo. He should have been rejoicing instead.

All along the walls of our house my kin stood silent, lowering their heads as I passed by. Even now, I can feel each step down the narrow hall to Babo's room. The smell of soap was strong in the heavy air, and I was sure he was waiting for me to bring him a cup of chai, sing a little. I was going to tell him how not one of them had believed me.

Inside, several neighbors stood by as my mother, grandmother, and two of my sisters sat weeping around the bed. A sheet was already pulled up over the form of my Babo, leaving just his caved-in face exposed. Someone had already placed two silver coins that flashed over his lids.

When my Daki looked me over as I got close, I could see the girl in her shining through her grief, and she reached to pry open my clenched fist. She spoke to me softly and for a long time. I'd been mistaken all along, and it would take time for me to forgive myself, and the angels who'd played a trick on me.

"You were the one standing with him in the space between worlds, Shaker," she told me. "It was his gift to you. In time, you'll know what it means."

It didn't help me much, not right then, with him lying there. I placed both palms on his rigid form—all the marrow had seeped from his bones, the last living breath long gone. My old king was dead; I could live to be a thousand, and there would never be another.

Chapter Three

The Cruelest Month

WHEN THE MAN CAME TO OUR DOOR, HE HAD A CLEAN AK-47 strapped to his back and a stained paper bag full of fruit in his hands. Figs. Bruised apricots, flies hovering. Two other men lingered outside, smoking cigarettes and wandering the courtyard like old dogs kicking up dirt. Mopping her wet brow with the edge of her shawl, Daki quietly took the fruit, uttered a quick thank-you—*yaho*—and looked down.

Then the man, who lived on the land next to ours, crossed the threshold, bringing his long shadow with him like a cool sentry. He wore the scent of gun oil like cologne. Slowly, he slid off his weapon and cradled the barrel, appraising the small house Babo had built with his bare hands, where thirteen newborns had drawn their first breaths, and two their last. Not much to see in there: threadbare rugs, a couple of tambours in an open cabinet, the faded picture of my father as a young man, staring out from under his army cap with those blue eyes full of hope.

Since we buried my father a few months before, I'd seen that particular neighbor several times, watching from a distance as I planted and plowed under the desert sun. But he didn't even glance at me now as I stood panting next to my mother, hair dripping.

"Shaker," Daki said, without raising her eyes. Hard to tell from her flat voice what she was thinking. "Go and get your brother."

I didn't bother to ask her which one.

NAÏF STOOD ALONE on the crest of the hill, shirt hanging like a rag from his hand. His glazed back was a bare cliff of bone and muscle. Stronger than the rest of us, he had wide hands that could uproot trees and hoist boulders. He was back from working the construction sites in Tal Afar, to fix the well that had suddenly gone dry. Haji had tinkered and sweet-talked his contraption to no avail. The trouble wasn't the pump, but the desiccated earth that had given us all that it had left. A builder by trade, Naïf knew there was nothing to be done. When I got to him at last, he motioned to the dry basin.

"Miracles were not meant to last, little brother." It's what Babo had always told us—and with those words, somehow I knew our time on that land was coming to an end.

In a blubbering rush, I reported about the neighbor with the fruit and assault rifle, the two others outside, and my mother left all alone. Wide-eyed, I pointed down at the house. Just then, a small convoy of old sedans was snaking along the road toward the farm. The trucks stopped just past the gates to our farmyard, engines idling. A few men got out; one stopped in the cucumber field to take a piss.

Naïf told me not to worry, that no one would lay a hand on Daki. Then he gestured with his chin in the direction of Khanasor. How that vista had evolved since Saddam was caught in a spider hole, blinking and covered in lice, and mere yards from one of his favorite palaces. Right across our village and on every other rooftop, satellite dishes had popped up like mushrooms. In the blurry distance, military helicopters hovered over the foothills. Rumor had it the Coalition Forces were building a base from the ruins of a high Ottoman citadel that had a good vantage all the way to Syria. Not far beyond the village and out along the open plain, a long white tent sat over the flat dirt like a forgotten game piece. Fires were already blazing, and shoals of smoke spread out over the barren valley. When you saw the *jevat* tent, you knew there was either a wedding, a funeral, or trouble to settle in the tribe. They would come for us in time.

Our family had always been in a deadlock over who had the right to farm our fields. Yazidis didn't actually own anything, even if they'd paid for it. Under a homicidal dictatorship, no one did. If a person had connections in the ruling Baathist party, they could have more than others; just a whisper in the right ear would grant whatever was coveted. Even another's land. My father had no meaningful connections—he'd held his fertile ground by virtue of reputation alone. Now that Saddam and Babo were both long gone, things were getting heated—without Babo, our family had no muscle.

Naïf and Haji explained that nothing would happen quickly. Both tribes had to agree on a course of action, and that could take months. They were right. The tent went up and down again and again, men came to the door with guns and offerings, and like everyone else we implored the angels for rain. And every night, my mother sent up wishes for steady work and fine brides for her sons.

WHEN I WAS still very little, I remember asking my father how a man set about finding a wife.

"I didn't find mine," he said. "They found me. And then I went and got them—it was the same both times. Love is like a river, Shaker, flowing two ways at once. You just have to jump in and let it take you."

His answer made no sense to me, and I told him so. And then he told us the story.

ONCE THE TWO families from the Jeffria tribe agreed that widowed Babo would marry young Daki, my father bought a white horse and a saddle. Then he put on his officer's uniform and rode into her village with a ring tucked in his pocket. Not quite a full woman, Daki waited on the dirt track, her family clustered about her, singing. A small sack of clothes in her hands, she wore a red sash, tied according to our tradition, three times about her waist.

When my mother glimpsed her betrothed riding that elegant beast down the steep hill through a wash of spring mist, a gurgling baby boy she'd love at first sight strapped to his lap, she knew she was seeing far ahead into time. And it was good. Daki gave a shy nod and her father smiled up at his new son-in-law. Had my mother shaken her head just once, or mouthed a "na," the family would have led her back into the house—no questions asked. That was our way.

THE DAY I came in from shepherding and found Haji talking a mile a minute to my mother and saying a girl's name over and over again like the refrain from a love song, I knew he'd jumped into the river at last. Her name was Kamila and her family was waiting.

On the way to Kamila's family home to settle the wedding, my mother sat ramrod straight in the front seat, her mouth forming a silent, jubilant prayer. Our mother had bought so many gifts, we'd had to reload the car twice. It was the custom, she kept telling us as we packed box after box of sweet cakes, candies, bolts of fabric, and dresses. Daki had taken the obligatory extravagance to a new level.

When we pulled up to the bride's simple concrete house, her entire family emerged in a long parade of smiles; tambours played as we greeted one another, arms entwined as kin. I watched as Haji gently led my mother to Kamila's father and she passed him the sack of dinars, worth the equivalent of seventy-five grams of solid gold. Our spiritual leader, Baba Sheikh, had long ago set the dowry price. Every bill and coin was hard to come by, and we'd had to sell more than a thing or two: several sheep, chickens, and one of Babo's hunting rifles, just for a start. Still, not one of us begrudged the expense. Love was a precious gift and you never worried about its material cost.

After the traditional exchange of offerings, we ate and drank for hours, everyone talking at once. Then, in the steady kerosene light, Haji stood with his bride and placed a polished gold band on her finger. The hint of a tremble, Kamila did the same, sewing the first thread between them, fast and forever.

WITHIN A MONTH and according to Yazidi tradition, our family held an elaborate village feast spanning three days. Up until then the bride had still lived in her family home. Right from the start, Daki planned every detail—and so our real trouble began.

"We can't spare any expense, or Kamila's family will not think that we respect them. Pay no mind. Pay no mind. This is about family blood." I must have heard her say that a thousand times.

Yazidi wedding feasts were massive operations. Pouring in from villages all around sacred Shingal, most anyone who shared our way and our clan's blood had received an elaborate invitation. Over 1,600 hungry guests expected to be well fed, and we had to pay for all of it: invitations, musicians, photographer, wedding clothes, flowers, food. To forget a single soul was to forget ourselves. For us, there was an illusion of safety in numbers—I found that out before I could even read.

In 1995, my parents brought us all to work a co-op farm in Rabia, a small town on the border crossing into Yaarabiya, Syria. Out there under a seamless desert sky, my people worked sunup to sundown. In that drought year before the salvation of Haji's water pump, my family was lucky to have such work. At night-fall, the laborers filed back to the communal compound to eat, and then wandered back out exhausted to their sleeping huts. Dozens of poor Yazidis crammed into close quarters with our tambours, songs, and homemade wine; people got to know each other well. One giant family, that was how my Babo put it.

Halfway through that season, a pair of young men, all of sixteen and from the other side of Shingal, stayed in our hut. Daki made a good space for them in a corner. Right from the start, those boys gave us easy smiles, calling me *brako*, brother, and patting me on the back. My father had taught me the word *orphan*, and I understood it meant that they had no one else but us. Every so often, they drew pieces of candy shaped like min-iature lemons from sacks in their pockets, handing them to me like secret messages. Those tiny sweets were the first I'd ever tasted, and I sucked on them so slowly, savoring the thrilling sourness that coated my tongue.

The day I walked into the hut barefoot and alone was my last in Rabia. My mother had sent me back for a rest, and the walk from the fields under the desolate sun was long and lonely. No one around in the compound.

From the first step into the dim room, I knew something was different. The smell was sweet and warm and I stopped to check for the candy in my pocket. Not sure why, but that's when I saw him. Body slumped a few feet away from me like a grain sack on the floor. Face down. Eyes closed. Two raw cra-ters blown out from his back. Bits of bone. Blood all over. And I stood there staring, mouth hanging open for a long time. Not sure what to do. I might have been holding my breath, but he did not move.

Everywhere in the small room, you could see evidence of a wild fight for survival. Dark footprints stamped over the floor. Still wet. A scattering of candies like bright beads. Upended furniture. Shattered oil lamp. Gaping holes in the walls. Looking around, I took it all in. Maybe there was a sound, I don't remember now, but some other thing drew me further inside.

Heaped in a darkened corner, I found the other boy sitting up against the wall, eyes wide open. Dark holes the size of coins pierced his bare chest like fang marks. By now, my limbs had started shaking and I fell fast to my knees, too afraid to cry out loud. Across that stained floor, a pale half-departed gaze reached mine. I knew that person well. Heard him snore while he slept. Sometimes, he gave me his naan. But he wasn't doing anything now. Then he blinked, eyelids fluttering, and a hand twitched in his lap.

Alive. Barely.

And I could not move.

Trying hard to speak now, he heaved wet hisses of air from deep inside that ruptured chest. Gushes of blood poured out over his mouth and down his chin. All he could manage was a slurred "*Brako, brako,*" before his eyes rolled way back in their sockets.

That's when I ran.

By the time Babo came back with me, both of us panting, the second one was also dead.

Later, someone explained that the brothers had fomented some mortal dispute between themselves and the powerful Arab al-Sharram tribe that held dominion in the region. The word *rabia* means "four"—the boys had been killed with four bullets total, two each right to the heart—and as it happened, I was four years old at the time. My mother had told me so just the day before and held up her hand, slowly counting fingers.

No matter what anyone said to me afterward, I'd learned a new fact the moment I'd walked into that room, and that knowledge would never leave me: the human body is material. Destructible. It doesn't take much to tear right through it—a bullet will do just fine. It was the first of many lessons I would be taught about conflict: always take the road to peace whatever the cost—there's no price too high to pay for staying alive.

BY THE TIME of the next *jevat*, Naïf and my other brothers had few choices left. Khudida had announced his own engagement to a girl named Markaz, and the whole matrimonial parade of parties and expenses started up again. Daki had already spent almost every spare dinar we had, and there wasn't much else coming in.

All this on his shoulders, Naïf climbed up to the high pasture, where I was shepherding the few sheep we had left. The land of our father spread out as far as the eye could see, we stood there together, talking.

"They offered a small payment," Naïf told me. It was enough to get us a place in the village, but not much more than that.

"And you all agreed?"

"Truth is, Shaker, one day, they'd just decide to get in those trucks and come take what they want. It can come to that. And when it's all said and done, we aren't this property. It's just dirt. No one thing makes us who we are. Not even our skin. It's what our parents taught us and we have to live it now."

"It's because of the man with the AK, isn't it?" I said at last.

Naïf shrugged and stared way out. "This might be God's land, but it's still bloody."

Chapter Four

Sergeant White

OUR NEW HOUSE WAS MADE UP OF EIGHT CONCRETE ROOMS LIKE cells all stuck together. No doors between them, courtyard in the middle. A single patch of dead dirt. Right away, I went to work at the scrap of yard: poured out mounds of soil, planted vegetables. A row of flowers for my mother. Haji suspended chains of tiny lights from the downspouts, giving us stars, and set up a cooking grill. I shared a room off the yard with my mother and three sisters. At first, we slept on mats positioned over the floor like thin rafts and hung old sheets for screens. My married brothers took rooms with their wives where they covered the sad walls in wedding photos. Leftover siblings divvied up the rest and made what they could of it. Most every evening we gathered in the front room next to the kitchen to prepare meals, sing, and mull over the long day.

Now that there was no more land to labor, I was free to wander the village that winter of 2003, looking for my cast of schoolmates and a pick-up game. Sometimes, we just sat around shooting the hot breeze and tossing rocks, or played tag around the scatterings of boulders and scrub. Other times we simply roamed the untouched, ancient-looking earth like the sons of Adam that we were.

We'd gathered on a massive shelf of bedrock the size of a football field, great caverns hatcheted into the blunt cliffs looming on one side. Way up there, the gritty summer wind blowing sideways into our parched faces felt like being on the deck of a huge ship. It never even occurred to us we needed better props—poor boys who want for everything can imagine just about anything.

Standing the ground like our captain in his red Arsenal jersey, Saïd was always the first to offer up whatever he had, and the last to ask for anything. Without a word, he proffered one of his socks, and on cue we peeled off our T-shirts, tossing them into a dingy pile. It was always the same routine. We grabbed a couple shirts, bunched them together, and stuffed it all into a long sock. Knotting the end, Saïd squished the mass around, shaping it as best he could. Meanwhile, my cousin Khairi and I took the other tops and jogged along the shelf, dropping them to mark out goal posts. Somehow, we always fell into neat teams without argument and took our places. The thing was to play and forget that we hadn't eaten lunch, or maybe even breakfast; or that my mother had just sold our last lamb. Or that we didn't even have a real ball.

And that's just what we were doing when we heard it: a steady foreign thrum plucking at our stillness. *Wap-wap. Wap-wap. Wap-wap. Wap-wap.* At once, we all sat up, peered across the brown void below, and then squinted into the hot eye of the just descending sun. Veering away from the horizon, two dark specks moved like prehistoric insects over the ground, their rising hum amplifying as we watched, low and coming straight for us. Then the air began to beat, quickening the atmosphere and my blood. Our reactions were all the same.

Every boy leapt up, catapulted off the rock, and tore out across the hot desert sand, hollering.

TWO FAT CHOPPERS; twin horizontal rotors front and back. Chinooks. American. I'd seen them on the TV at Barzan's house. So, I raced the ground in Babo's shredded sandals as though every breath depended on it; eyes locked dead ahead, arms pumping. Fast and steady. By now, the whole sky was pulsing like a drum and people were climbing rooftops and pointing. All around me the loose ground rose to a dry boil, and I kept on going right through the first wild torrents of dust.

Parting the desert floor as they pounded down, the Chinooks soon disappeared into churning explosions of sand. Suddenly, I was stone blind in the grit. Then I heard high whining sounds overtake the rotors, felt the earth quiver under me, and I waited, eyes closed against the convulsing sands. When it all stopped, I hunched down and made for the rear ramp, mouth parted and full of mud—first on the scene, by far.

A soldier stepped off the back of the giant chopper, hauling a rucksack over his back. Right away and as though he knew I'd be waiting there, he handed me a plastic bottle full of cool red liquid.

In a stupor of awe, I moved back a few yards, tongue lolling in my mouth.

When the boys caught up and glimpsed the bright new thing in my hands, their savagery was instant. Before I knew it, we were all on the ground in a wild free-for-all. Kicking. Punching. Clawing. Anything to get at what the flying man had given me.

Not one of us even knew what was in that bottle, but it had unleashed some dormant predatory gene into our collective blood. I held the thing fast like my own soul. Then Nawaf, who sat next to me in school and whom I'd known all my life as a loyal friend, grabbed a rock from the ground and smacked it into my forehead. With the shock of pain, I felt the bottle slide out from my surrendering grip. A mess of blood and hot tears smeared my face.

A moment later, a pair of hands hoisted my pathetic form up by the armpits, dragging me, feet leaving tracks in the ground, right out of the dirty melee. Set down by a Chinook, other soldiers were suddenly all around me, talking. Someone poured cold water over my head.

The soldier who'd given me the bottle apologized, wiped down my cheeks, and told me not to worry, that there was plenty of Gatorade to go around.

Standing there, chest heaving, I got my bearings back: before me was a flesh-and-blood all-American soldier. Over six feet tall for sure—star-spangled grin, so big and bleach-paper white. Skin like I'd never seen before in my life: dark as the smooth tar we used to fix the roof. Never seen a black man, or even a white one. Never seen any kind of man but our own. Never even held a plastic bottle of Gatorade. Never—so many things at once.

"Hello," I stammered, trying out my English, grateful for my language teacher, a diabetic Sunni named Jassim. He was famous all over Shingal for producing the best English speakers in the province. And I was first in my class. "My name is Shaker. I am a boy."

"Dang," he said. "You Yazidi kids are smart. Good to meet you, Shaker, I'm White."

"No," I said, shaking my head. "No white. It is black."

When he laughed, that man roared, head flying way back, and I thought I saw a gold tooth flash in his mouth. Right from the start, I believed those men who came down to earth in a raging sky were gods.

"No, no," he said, and pointed at the name printed over the breast of his fatigues. There was an American flag patch on his shoulder. "My *name* is White. And I am a man."

Our shared laughter that afternoon sealed a kind of covenant. Without a doubt, I knew we were going to be friends.

THE NEXT MORNING, I shot up, ran across the yard, and begged my brother Naïf, who'd just opened a barber shop a few blocks away, for a few dinars. He scolded me for turning into a Yankee-Doodle so quickly, dropping a few coins in my hand before I raced off again.

I bought two cold bottles of Coke from a small local shop that had a cooler, and stuffed them into my school satchel before making my way to the water complex. The US Army Civil Affairs office was building a makeshift base around the tower to protect it. Holding over eighty thousand liters of clean drinking water, the tower was critical to village life—and a twenty-story-high target. Thirsty desert populations were the most vulnerable to al-Qaeda blackmail: whoever had the water wielded the power. By the time I got to the front gates, walls of sandbags were up, and soldiers sat at their posts looking out over barrels, trigger-ready.

Didn't take long for someone to see me: scrawny kid shuffling around the dirt lot at the front gate. Within minutes, White showed up and someone stepped out to check me over. Pulling the Cokes out of my satchel, still cold, he said, "Look what he brought you, Sergeant. Glass bottles, too."

"Nothing like a Coca-Cola out of a glass bottle," White said when I walked inside. He patted me on the back.

Nothing much to that outpost, just three ugly government buildings circa 1975 that had been used to man the tower, and a few army tents. Still, I felt like I'd just stepped into the kingdom of heaven. Soldiers in fatigues milling around all smiled when they saw me. A few walked over, tousled my hair, and we slapped out high fives. It was 110 degrees, and when the other soldiers saw my drinks, they all asked if I could get more.

Knowing the Americans were coming in any day, the shop-keeper had stocked his shelves. Sergeant White negotiated my pick-up and delivery fee and helped me take orders: Pepsi, Fanta, Diet Cokes. The list got so long that White had to find me a wheelbarrow. Before I knew it, there was real money going into my frayed pockets. I'd already made enough to buy my mother all we needed for a good dinner. Then White and I sat in two metal chairs by the perimeter fence. He opened our bottles and showed me how to toast saying "cheers." From then on, I'd say it every time I had anything to drink, even milk.

"Wow, that's good, Shaker," White said, putting a leg over his knee, and he took a long loud gulp. He had an Adam's apple the size of a walnut. "What's the word for 'thank you' in Kurdish?"

"*Na!*" Maybe I said it a little too loud. White looked a bit startled. "No Kurdish," I told him. For centuries, Arabs of every creed and tribe had told Yazidis they were Kurds. "Yazidis talk Kurmanji. We are not a Kurd."

"Kurmanji, I got it. Back where I'm from, people call my kind of people the wrong kinds of names all the time. So, you teach me your words. And I'll teach you mine. Deal?"

"*Yaho*," I said, sipping my cola. "Means, thank you."

"*Yaho*, Shaker. Now, you go get those drinks, and then come back here with your friends. Get as many of 'em as you can. Looks to me like a good day for a game."

As I left the compound, change jangling in my pocket, I turned and gave White a salute; and all the way to the gate, his thundering laugh was right behind me. I have relived that moment ten thousand times since.

LONG BEFORE SHOCK and Awe, and especially after it, we were taught at school to despise all Westerners and America as the ground zero of infidels, or nonbelievers. Soon after the war started, our teachers, still under directives from the ministry in Baghdad, had scrawled out "Death to America" in Arabic on the board, and we all had to chant it. Later, we copied out "We want America to fail" on pieces of notepaper, and were sent outside to toss them into the air. A wasteful exercise that baffled us, but we did as we were told. After a lifetime of propaganda, our

40

young brains should have been washed clean of any chance at kinship with those friendly invaders. The trouble was, as Yazidis, our own country had labeled us as the worst infidels in Iraq. So, when those Chinooks delivered Sergeant White and his battalion to Khanasor in a fanfare of dust, they'd brought us both our saviors and our brothers.

"What in the heck is this?" White asked, turning over Saïd's stuffed sock in his hands as more than a dozen bony bare-chested boys were lingering mute behind the gate.

"Ball?" I said, with a shrug.

"*Nah*, first things first: this thing goes bye-bye." Every time White spoke to me, I held on to each word like treasure.

Shaking his head, White told us all to put our shirts back on and wait for him to return from Mosul.

A few days later, the Chinooks were back, beating up the air over Khanasor. More soldiers exited the hatch and started unloading supplies. White was right there in his body armor and shades. Soon as I got to him, he told me to get a team together and meet in the big lot on the other side of town. Right away, I tore through the streets, eyes peeled, grabbing boys from their doorsteps, beds, a barber's chair, down from trees, and out of their mothers' aromatic kitchens.

THE COPPERED GROUND out there was as hard as granite and in full view of blocks of houses and a large public courtyard. Someone had dug up fresh mounds of dirt and positioned markers like seat cushions to form a large diamond shape over the ground. Beyond a stretch of rolling dunes, the craggy heights of Mount Shingal shimmered soft pink in the summer heat. People were on their rooftops drinking beer, smoking hookahs, and hanging laundry on the lines. Others unfurled blankets over the cooling pools of mulberry shade, children hanging in the branches, old men leaning half-asleep against the trunks. Someone had started up a cooking fire, and the warm, meat-roasted air swelled. I was wearing Haji's gargantuan sneakers and stuffed the toes with wads of cloth. White had already split us into mixed teams, using a simple number system: even on one side, odd on the other.

It seemed like the whole contingent was there milling around: army shorts and baseball caps, dog tags hanging down. Some threaded their way into the groups of chattering kids lingering on the periphery to hand out Life Savers and lollipops. The children cupped their tiny hands into bowls and squealed.

Then White stepped up to me carting a massive duffel bag, dropped it hard at my feet, and addressed the gathering. "No girls want to play?"

"Shy," I said.

"OK, I get it. So, listen up," he hollered to the ramshackle assembly of boys. "Today we are gonna teach you our great American pastime—baseball." Then he looked over to a man named Hadir, who was their military interpreter and a Yazidi from our village. Hadir repeated every word in Kurmanji—it was already the best English lesson of our lives.

White explained the basics: "You need three things to play the game: a bat, a ball, and a glove. And you only need to know how to run, hit, and throw." Then he directed me to open the big duffel bag.

On my knees, inside a wall of wide-eyed kids, I yanked at the long zipper. The bulging sides pulled way open, spilling bright colors and newness out into my hands. In the space of one second, my farm-boy eyes spanned ten thousand miles, right across the desert, propelling far over ranges and crossing whole sweeps of ocean—and every village boy came with me. None of us knew a thing about baseball, but it didn't matter—that stuff was real, bought in a store in America. Leather mitts, balls, and several bats. T-shirts, stacks of them. Bags of white tube socks. This time, we boys kept our cool, and waited.

Then each soldier found a kid from their team, and we all fanned out in our brand-new clothes over the makeshift diamond. Starting in pairs, simple games of catch. For a moment, I had to stop to watch what was happening and take that miracle in. Then I slipped on my mitt.

"Looks just like Arizona," I heard one of the soldiers say. Later, I would search it up on a map.

White was with me on the plain, yelling out instructions, dark arms full of veins bulging like cannons under his shirt. The first toss sucker-punched my glove, and I fell right back into the dirt. Then I leapt into the air for another catch, leaving my empty shoes behind. I can still see Sergeant White standing out there under a great wing of blue desert sky, smile meeting mine like a second sun, the echoes of his laughter taking flight and filling up the ancient Arabian air.

WHEN WE ORGANIZED our teams over the playing field, I was first up to hit. White walked behind me with the bat. Standing over my thin shoulders, he brought the bat around and told me just how to hold it. Maybe he knew I was nervous, all eyes on me. He took his time. Deep voice in my ear, he placed those big hands right over mine. Through the warm sureness of his grip, I could feel his pulse beating. We practiced though several slow empty swings.

"Take it easy now, Shaker. Breathe. You have to feel the hit in your gut."

Even now, his voice is as clear to me as my own. Sun on its way to the other side of the world, it was suddenly just the two of us, standing together on the plate. I looked out as the last gold ray melted into the ridgeline, and could feel us slipping into twilight like a pool of cool water. The air went blue.

When I hit the ball, a lightning crack splintered out for miles, careening in a great arch way into the ozone. People shouted.

White hollered, "Run, Shaker!" and I bolted—fast around the bases, lost those shoes, and kept on going all the way home.

THROUGH THE CALM seasons of 2004, the soldiers from what was called "the Khanasor Water Project" held regular games—football, soccer, baseball—and their routines, patrols, perimeter checks, and drills seemed to braid into the rhythm of our village life. Soon, whenever a game was on, it seemed like half our town showed up to watch and cheer. Families set up grills, played music over speakers, and brought out plates of food. By far, it was one of the happiest times of my childhood, despite the loss of my father and the farm. We were doing all right now on that dull slab of concrete. Saddam was gone. I was learning real English. An American soldier was my best friend.

After school I went right to the base, delivered drinks and junk food. White always made a little time for me. More than once he brought his team to my house to share a meal with my family. At first, his interpreter tagged along, but as my English steadily improved, I took over. We'd linger in the courtyard under Haji's winking stars, teaching each other words and talking about anything that came to mind. White had a kind and casual way about him, always came to us with gifts of food that we needed—my Daki said he was all good, right down to his toes.

White also told me that I could make good money as an interpreter working for the army if the war was still going on when I came of age, and then I could apply for a special visa to live in the United States. The military was going to pay for him to study at an American university, and he promised that he'd help me do the same.

"We look after our own." He said it to me many times.

And the meager borders of my mind stretched far past Shingal and our crumbling little school. White told me that's what being an American was about—getting rid of the bad guys and letting the good people win. And I believed that for a long time after.

WHEN WHITE AND his small team of ten men set off on missions into Mosul, he didn't tell me first. Never did. The soldiers couldn't risk disclosing their comings and goings. Mosul was the capital of our province, and there was trouble brewing there. As far as terrorists went, some said it was the evil eye of the storm. Despite all the superior foreign firepower and promises, the war wasn't going the way anyone expected. Soon, you could feel a certain unease rise to a simmer like a change in air pressure. Sometimes when the Chinooks flew in, Apache gunships flanked them the whole way.

I WAS ON the roof when Naïf told me he heard the sound I was longing for; Daki always said he had the hearing of a bat. I raced into the street, ran past the base and the looming tower, and flew out over the empty field to wait for my friend. Coke in one hand, football tucked close. I was wearing a clean T-shirt and a new pair of shoes. I'd been rinsing out the socks White gave me every single night. Nothing moved over the desolate plain, and I waited low to the ground, ears cocked.

As soon as I heard that familiar thunder, I was on my feet, hands up to my face waiting for the onslaught of dirty wind. The thrill of those choppers coming into view never lessened, and my heart seemed to beat in time with the rotors as the beasts whined down.

No one said a word when the hatches opened, and they took their time unhooking their gear from the center line. I waited as I always did, a few yards back and holding my breath. Often the soldiers were as tired as zombies when they came back. Too late for a game tonight, but we'd get out there first thing the next day after school.

When the team came up to me, walking slowly in the bruised light, they cradled their helmets like empty bowls in their hands. No one had to say a word. The hatches were all empty. The rotors silent.

Palms on my shoulders now, which started shaking. No way to stop it. My body knew the truth before I did, and I fell to my knees in the dirt. The ball and bottle of Coke left my hands, but I couldn't feel a thing. Instantly, all of them were down there with me in a huddle, uttering soft words for hard things—words like *IED* and *MEDEVAC* that would have to be explained much later. For now, the only ones that made any sense were *bomb* and *dead*.

IN THE MORNING I got up well before the others, long before any living thing for miles, and went into the slumbering hills where we kept our temple. The day we buried my Babo way up there had been the worst of my life. This was the second. So tired from crying and lack of sleep, I searched the earth for a good stone, and held it, offering up a prayer of gratitude. In my culture we left circles of stones around the graves of the dead before leaving, and no other marker. In the cool darkness, I shut my eyes and somehow felt those strong American hands slip over mine again. A warm pulse beat out endless time into my palms, and I stood there a long while. And then I looked way up and let White go.

We were at war.

I knew that now.

Chapter Five

Mosul

Lumbering bumper to bumper, a convoy of loaded fuel tankers and several cars made their way into the bustling Yazidi towns of Kahtaniyah and Jazeera, joining the lazy flow of evening traffic. Inside each rusted-out sedan sat a lone male driver peering over the wheel, more than a thousand pounds of explosives packed all around him. A boy standing at the side of the road as they slowly cruised by said the men appeared dizzy, but had grinned at him, mocking—though he only realized it afterward.

Then, at precisely 7:20 P.M. on that bright August day in 2007, just as whole families were sitting down to eat, the vehicles came to a simultaneous stop. The crazed drivers shouted out incomprehensibly. A moment later, the convoy erupted into a towering inferno that consumed four straight blocks. At the epicenter, the living turned instantly to vapor.

For several minutes after the explosion, there was nothing but an eerie and airless silence. Then a few children hurled clear of the blast wandered half-alive and blind from the ash cloud. Those who could still speak called out for their mothers. One of them held a severed arm in her hands like a doll. The sky had torn off the world, she said. And five hundred Yazidis went with it. More than one thousand more were mutilated.

Over fifty miles south, I was at home in the courtyard drinking a Coke, which always made me think of Sergeant White. I didn't know my people had just suffered their own 9/11. Our Baba Sheikh declared a month of mourning while my people dug the bodies from cataclysmic piles of rubble. Sometimes, all we found was a crushed torso or foot; a ringed finger, an ear. For the most part, dead infants came out intact, but charred black as though they'd been dipped in corrosive paint. I gave God thirty days of my silence to pray—hard—and then, at just sixteen, I was in the fight.

DAKI STOOD ALONE by the kitchen window when I walked in, dark exhaust from the stove drifting, resurrecting stale bread in oil. Another debt collector had just stopped by for empty promises; no money coming in, we were still trying to pay off the weddings. Our cupboards had become an abyss of want. During the war a fresh egg was a jewel to be savored. Sometimes, the hunger was like a fist to the gut.

In those days honest work was hard to come by, and the Americans paid their combat interpreters well. Always a step ahead, after White was killed in action, Daki had appropriated my Iraqi identification card, desperate to keep her son from fighting in someone else's war. Military and police checkpoints were going up all over the province, and I couldn't go anywhere or do anything without it. Over the last year, Nineveh Province had become a sanctuary for regrouping insurgents, and we were now square in the eye of al-Qaeda.

When the conflict veered sideways into a full-blown insurgency, the American government implemented a massive troop surge to put a lid on the apocalypse of bombs. "The New Way Forward 2007" extended the deployments of soldiers already in-country, and twenty thousand more troops were sent to secure the raging capital and blood-soaked Al-Anbar Province. Squeezed clean out of Baghdad, al-Qaeda in Iraq (AQI) had been forced north into the Za'ab triangle, toward Syria. Once there, they counted on a well-established rat-line, the clandestine route used to move illicit weapons and rabid fighters across the border. Now they were right on our doorstep. While we stood in our kitchen jabbering, AQI cells were congregating in the terrain all around us.

At night, we could hear military convoys pound by; occasional gunfire flashed like falling stars over the hills. Insurgents roamed the desert no-man's-land disguised as shepherds and nomads, keeping tabs on the traffic, moving arsenals, and waiting for orders. Their leader, al-Masri, "The Egyptian," had taken over in 2006 when his predecessor, Abu Musab al-Zarqawi, was killed in a US missile strike.

As far as I could tell in the months I'd spent feverously studying the war, al-Masri was well equipped to handle the challenge ahead—outwitting and outlasting "the infidels." He'd had a hand in founding the first AQI cell in Baghdad, fought in the battle of Fallujah, and had run a steady circuit of suicide bombers out of Syria right down the Euphrates river valley. In his most infamous act, he was said to have ambushed two American soldiers, killing them both with his bare hands. His minions had already infiltrated the Iraqi military and police forces and were securing loyalties among the occupation-weary tribes—just biding their time.

By the fall of 2007, my brothers and I saw the writing on the wall: if the Coalition failed to secure Iraq, we Yazidis were sitting ducks. There was no room for us in Nineveh: Kurds wanted their own country in the north; the Sunnis just wanted everything.

By the spring of 2008, I could no longer wait to come of age. At first, my idea was to sign up in Mosul. One year, maybe two—in and out. Pay off our loans and go back to school, and eventually apply for a visa to the USA. Thanks to the teaching skills of Jassim, dozens of young men from our village had already left for military interpreter jobs on bases all over Iraq; they all came back to visit and bought new televisions and cars. They also returned with a high price on their heads—but that was nothing new to a Yazidi.

THE MAN DRIVING the smuggler's cab had taken the road to Mosul many times; bullet holes stitched across the back doors on one side, the back windshield blown all the way out. His thick moustache quivered when he talked, but those gunpowdered hands were steady; he kept one assault rifle on the floor next to him and a handgun in his vest. To him, I'm sure I was exactly like every Yazidi boy who'd come before me— fresh bait. He snickered when he saw my clean shirt and pants, and spat out the window. I gave him the twenty-five thousand dinars Naïf had lent me, and promised the rest when we got to the front gates of Camp Marez, the airfield and army base on the edge of Mosul. My appointment with the woman from Global Linguistics Solutions (GLS) was in four hours. It was just before 6:00 A.M.; the transaction, like my trip, had been planned well in advance.

THE WEEK BEFORE—CHICKEN bones boiling on the stove, the hunger for meat almost unbearable—Naïf figured out how to get my identity card off of Daki. She kept it on her at all times like a secreted diamond. All I needed was thirty seconds with my ID and a borrowed scanner in Naïf's room. We recruited Markaz, our reluctant sister-in-law, and in a swiftly executed operation that involved splashing Daki with tea, profuse apologies, and an exchange of aprons, it was done. From there, the forgery was easy—Iraqi IDs were crude documents. Within an hour, I was officially eighteen years old.

THE THREE-HOUR DRIVE would take us east across the high northern edge of Mount Shingal, skimming villages that sat on the valley like strewn cardboard boxes, and then slightly south as we joined the road winding toward Tal Afar: home to once-complacent Turkomans and Sunnis, and now a cauldron of embittered insurgents. We didn't make it more than a couple miles before we hit the first police checkpoint; we handed over our IDs and never had to get out of the car. Simple. After that I eased into the seat, put my head back, and rested an arm along the open window frame. Sheep grazed the fields for a stretch before we hit the grim factory lands and I fell into my old daydreams of the farm.

"Only dead men take this road asleep," the driver said, rib-jabbing me hard out of my stupor.

My job was to keep both eyes out for IEDs littering the roads, disguised to look like garbage.

At the next checkpoint, there was a larger contingent of Iraqi officers, all of them patrolling the lanes of increasing traffic. A line of trucks and caravans sat idling along the margins, backs open, waiting to be searched. My driver slipped a callused hand into his pocket, pulled out a small wad of folded-over bills, and held the cash out the window like a parking stub. The officer, who was also smoking a cigarette, grabbed it between drags and slipped it into his front pocket. Then we shifted routes and were off on a tear.

MOSUL IS ALL of Iraq, distilled down into a city of wrath. Two hundred and fifty miles north of Baghdad, on the banks of the Tigris, it sits on an active fault line of intersecting ethnic, religious, tribal, and sectarian groups. Nearly three-quarters disgruntled Sunnis, and just under one-quarter Kurds, it was a teeming battleground for their ongoing competition. By the time I got there, the city could be divided right down the middle between its eastern and western flanks, sprawling out into dense roadways and tight alleys, some as ancient as the sand on which they were built.

The insurgents and Arab nationals had their mean grip on the west; the Kurdish political entities and military forces controlled the east. Before the invasion of 2003, Mosul had been the headquarters of the Baathist party and a critical military center. The fight taking place for dominion there now was in many ways a mirror to the overall fight for the country itself. We were headed toward the airfield just south of the city, but well within its sights. Mosul used to be known for oil and marble; now it was known only for bombs.

When I saw black towers of smoke rising in the distance, and the trash accumulating into larger and larger piles on the side of the roads, I knew we were closing in. Every mile we hit a military or police checkpoint. Forward Operating Base (FOB) Marez, known as the al-Ghizlani camp to Iraqis, was attached to the airfields of Mosul Airport and a massive military base called Diamondback. We made our approach slowly via a long straight road. The great stretch of the city, all dreary tower blocks, rusted domes, and minarets, rose up past the military barriers. Once or twice, I heard the *thud-thud* of a blast echo out, and I peered through the dull morning haze into what looked like ten thousand Khanasors lined up in a row. Half the province, over one and a half million people, eked out a living in that ancient urban jungle—the hatreds therein ran deep.

What you couldn't see of the scorched city, you could hear: wailing sirens and pounding choppers. No trees, no grass, not a bird in flight that wasn't made of metal. If there was ever a moment when I second-guessed my decision, it was then—Mosul was the citadel of the devil. The air outside was acrid.

Fifty yards from the gate, the driver stopped.

"Two Arab-looking guys in an old car driving up to a military gate? No way," he said as though to himself. Then he explained that sometimes the less experienced guards would just shoot and check later.

"You mean you want me to walk now?" I didn't move. All I could see out the window were cement walls and razor wire. A sparse wasteland on one side, grim skeletons of the city in the distance on the other.

"Yes. Get out."

I handed him the other half of his payment; much of the first had gone to appease renegade patrols along the way, and before I'd walked ten feet on the trampled dirt road, he was already well out of sight.

FOB MAREZ SAT next to Camp Diamondback, which was a huge military city made up of large white tents and Containerized Housing Units called CHUs, or "cans," running the length of the airfield and far out into surrounding territory—barbed wire, hulking barriers, gates, and lookout towers. It was a twenty-first-century fortress designed to contain the human and material instruments of a military superpower, while keeping the ancient war raging past its walls from getting in.

Hyperactive cells of insurgents were right next door, and every now and again lobbed mortars into the fields, sniped at platoons going out on missions, or sent along a drugged-up suicide bomber. On December 22, 2004, during the lunch-hour rush, a 122mm rocket careened at 1,500 miles per hour right through the roof of the large, soft-sided white tent of the dining facility, detonating into three thousand fragments over a radius of more than eighty feet, and plunging into everything in its path. The mortal carnage in the aftermath was catastrophic—twenty-two dead and over sixty wounded in a jumble of food, bloody trays, and searing shrapnel.

Security there was ironclad and aggressive, nothing like the gentle pat down and casual high fives the soldiers had given me at the Khanasor water tower. All I had on me were a few crumpled dinars and my fake ID card, but the guards still checked me head to toe with a metal detector. Right away, I glimpsed a big American flag and the Airborne eagle insignia hanging under the guard tower, saw the flash of a star-spangled grin, heard a roar of laughter, and thought of White. He'd been through those very gates, walked the gravel roads. And he'd died in pieces under that stinging sky. It never occurred to me that I might be signing up for the same fatal destiny. All I could think about was sending my first pay-packet home, and I imagined what Daki could do with it: pay bills, buy meat, maybe even new shoes. Live a little, at last.

A pair of soldiers flanked me across the compound and pointed to a windowless building like all the others.

"You wait right here in this CHU now, and don't go wandering."

I didn't dare go outside. Didn't dare do a thing except breathe inside that tank under ranks of cold electric lights. A few hours in, a man brought me a plate of wings, showed me to a latrine. Maybe I thought it was a test of will, as my whole life so far had been, and so I sat—nine hours straight or more.

At 18:00, two female MPs came to escort me out; no sign of the woman from GLS.

They escorted me all the way to the gate. No eye contact. Hands on their weapons. Told me not to talk so much when I rambled.

"If you had a legit appointment, someone would be here."

Then they sent me back out, gates slowly closing.

THE SUN HAD arched westward across the sky and over the banks of the winding Tigris, where the dark heart of Mosul beat. I was out on an empty gravel road headed for the wrong side of town—wrong side of anywhere. No choice, I walked alone for about a mile, the lights of the nearby airfield ablaze like small fires, the city just beginning to twinkle. I was on the lookout for a safe place to hunker down and hatch a temporary survival plan, but there was nothing whatsoever in that military no-go zone. For a moment, I stopped and just stared way out: somewhere in the east lay the tumbled ruins of the ancient city of Nineveh, which had once held dominion on the flourishing river highway between the Mediterranean Sea and Indian Ocean. In that wrecked place of crumbling urban blocks full of siren wails and the *clack-clack* of gunfire once stood the largest and most prosperous city in the world.

Now, all was still in the land of the ancient Assyrians. Women in cramped city houses were making supper, their men were making bombs, and children of war were trying for a childhood. The base spread out behind me was the biggest target in Nineveh Province, but even there in its shadow and among the lingering souls of the ancients, I felt like the second-biggest: a poor Yazidi boy offering his services to the infidels for something as fleeting as dinars. If I got caught wandering out there, my purpose would be instantly clear, and so would the consequence—decapitation or a bullet to the head. Of course, they would beat me first; maybe sever a finger to send back to my mother.

Then the muezzin call swelled over the terrifying rise of my first Mosul night, and I stood on a ribbon of tamped dirt listening to its soporific whine, and the city beyond seemed to surrender, going full quiet as it folded into its own spell. I stood there as though on a tightrope—my chances of surviving the night out there were slim.

The guards up ahead peered at me under their helmets, and beams of light hit my eyes. Stunned like prey, arms held out and ready to run, all I could think of was to yell out:

"Help!"

And then a simple phrase uttered through the bleak air bridged the chasm of fear my mind had just fallen into.

"*Cawani basi ti ib xer hati*"—hello and welcome.

"Yazidi?" I called out, and ran straight for the sounds as though to arms held open.

The men lowered their barrels and laughed.

"Knew you were Yazidi when you didn't kneel down to pray," one of them said. "Let me guess. Did GLS forget you?"

THEY GAVE ME a CHU with a bunk, and by morning I was in a room taking the interpreter test. One hundred multiple-choice questions covering Iraqi history, politics, and geography, and I only had to get half of them right. I passed with flying colors, got my badge, and waited in another CHU with four other "virginterps," three Kurds and a Sunni—in Iraq, that's how countrymen identified one another. We were all eating from plates of fried eggs and talking about the test when a man came in and stood before us, clipboard in his hand. He looked right at me.

"Write this down on this piece of paper: *There are three hundred people in that building with concrete walls.* Write it in English and then write it in Arabic."

"What about Kurdish and Kurmanji?" I said, scribbling.

"You speak all those and write in all those?"

"Yes, sir. I do." Still writing.

When I handed the clipboard back to him, he looked it over and grinned.

"You a badass, son?"

"What's that, sir?"

"You are a badass, son—and I need one good badass this morning. Come with me."

On our way across the compound, a line of Humvees thundering past to yet another CHU, Sergeant Cook gave me the rundown. Boots crunching the ground, he walked fast and stopped several times to check his clipboard. He was gnawing on his cheek like it was gum, licked his lips again and again. The air outside was hot.

"I'm assigning you to a small team. Ten guys or so. All highly skilled. You'll be embedding with an Iraqi army unit stationed out here in Mosul—7th Brigade, 2nd Division, under Colonel Dildar Jamel Mohammed; you'll do just fine. The teams rotate in and out of COPs—those are combat outposts located in hostile areas. In fact, you guys are scheduled to go out tomorrow morning. Your job will be to interpret between the Iraqi army and our guys, back and forth. So anytime they need to talk to each other in person, or via radio channels, or among the locals out on patrol, you're on. So get to know the comms people really well. You get that?"

Keeping up my pace, I just nodded, taking in what I could.

"And one other thing. We give all terps new names. You look like a Michael to me—like the archangel. Yazidis believe in angels, right? Think that should do it."

WHEN SERGEANT COOK opened the door, a group of men were sitting around in shorts playing video games and shouting out plays in front of a small television set. *Madden NFL*, I'd learn later. The airless tank reeked of sweat and fruit juice; a large fan was sending out a useless breeze from the corner. The men all stopped and looked over, handing me their easy smiles like cards from a deck.

"You guys welcome your new terp," Cook said from the open door. "This is Michael, fresh off the boat. Practically speaks in tongues. Mikey—this is Team Shady."

I went down the line shaking sweaty hands, hearing ranks and names rise up that I'd never remember: Captain Christopher, gunner; Captain Randy Agnew, logistics officer and gunner; Sergeant José Solis, medic from Puerto Rico. The three other terps stood against the wall, sizing me up, nodded half-friendly, and then looked back to the screen. In a moment, the game was on again and they were right back to it. There was a lone man in the corner reading. Flaxen-haired and wide-shouldered, he was deep into his book, mouth working. Carefully, he finished his page, dog-eared a corner, got right out of his chair, and came over to me, hand out, eyes straight ahead.

"Ronald Bowers, Sergeant. Communications. From Idaho. You'll be riding along with me tomorrow—up in the first MRAP."

When I shook his hand, his blue eyes met me straight on, and I recognized the unflinching goodness my mother talked about that you could see in a man when he greeted you. He had an easy smile and was young—apple pie American to the core. I looked down at the book he was reading.

"Bible," he said. "Never leave home without it."

"My book is in here," I said, and pointed at my temple.

"I get that." Then he looked over at the other terps and back at me. "Let's get you over to the DFAC—that's the dining facility. We can talk things over in there. Fill you in on tomorrow's drill. You missed the morning meeting."

On the other side of the door, Ron stopped and put a hand on my shoulder. "Those other terps in there are good men. Solid. Just do yourself one little favor to get along—"

"Never talk about being Yazidi," I cut in, matter-of-fact. "Don't worry, I've lived my whole life not talking about it."

Chapter Six

A Farewell to Angels

WHEN THE MINE RESISTANT AMBUSH PROTECTED (MRAP) vehicle left the wire, ground beneath the chassis surrendered as her deep treads chewed trenches through the gravel. Titanic slabs of steel cloaked the mammoth, nine-foot-high body. Every time those trucks powered up in the lot, they sounded like monsters gorging their way out of the earth. Inside the V-shaped hull, I flew out of my jump chair; hands pushed me back and strapped me in. Fully kitted up in fatigues and body armor, with two metal plates stuffed into deep pockets front and back that could stop bullets from an AK-47. I blended right in.

Helmet sitting in my lap, I put it back on after the team went out to the dirt pile past the gate and test-fired their weapons. Each hot discharge cracked the air to pieces, sending wild echoes right through my bones, and I held in a breath. We were about to traverse terrorist-infested Mosul and I should have been nervous, maybe even terrified, but I wasn't. Adolescent adrenaline had kicked in, overtaking every impulse and coursing through me like a street drug. Before leaving, I'd lingered in the lot while Bowers sat behind the wheels to check things over. He was in charge of all four vehicles: signals, encryption codes, upgrades, and regular maintenance. Every now and again he called out to me, asking if I had this and that. New sand-colored boots laced up tight over a fresh pair of socks, I sauntered like a bullfighter around the metal mammoth I'd heard one of the guys call "Princess," as she groaned in her patient idling.

WE STRADDLED THE western edge of the city and headed north at a lumbering pace, and nothing much happened. Mayhem is all every fresh recruit expects when crossing the jowls of war, but the heavy drive along the two-lane thoroughfare was eerily uneventful. The team told me it was that way most days lately, and it felt to them like we were being baited into a lethal form of combat lethargy. Mosul had a primal force all its own; when it wanted to kill, it did so with a sudden and unrelenting savagery.

IEDs littered the grid, just waiting to go off, and even though we were riding in a beast designed to eat bombs, every soldier in that vehicle was primed for a death match. If the convoy went by the same pile of trash several days in a row, the enemy might conclude it was a good place to sneak in an explosive device. Every now and then we'd stop while something up front was checked; a suspicious parked car, or a possible sniper's nest. What I could see through the MRAP's front armored glass was dismal: squalid blocks of walled buildings and streams of black water running along the disintegrating gutters.

"They hardly ever shoot at us when we go out," Bowers called back. "But they're always watching."

"Hell yeah," one of the guys shouted. "Hell yeah."

COP HOTEL WAS named for the once luxurious and now ransacked Hotel Mosul, which sat high on a bluff like a modern-day pyramid looming over the outpost and fast-flowing Tigris. Smack in the middle of downtown, it was the perfect location for a garrison designed to engage in tight-block operations all over the city. Saddam Hussein had built a villa for his brother fronting the river, complete with a now barren pear orchard; colorful patches of the elaborate flower gardens remained, though unattended and weed-choked. The tacky villa with its European-inspired columns housed Colonel Dildar, commander of the 7th Brigade, and his mostly Kurdish division. Team Shady was one of many advisory support teams rotating out from COPs all over the country, as part of the "Iraq in the Lead" program and the long-term exit strategy of letting Iraq fight for Iraq.

Conditions were sparse: no showers or flushing toilets; plenty of boxed cereal and strawberry-flavored milk. Nestled in an open green space near the riverbank, the terps shared rooms in the building with the rest of the team. I set up my bunk, blankets, and kit. As far as precious possessions went, all I had to my borrowed name were the *shamag*, a Middle Eastern scarf, and shades Bowers had given me as part of the "not getting shot at for being Yazidi" strategy. Whatever their ethnicity, Arabic-speaking combat interpreters were targets, but Yazidi terps were prized kills. I half wondered if my Shia and Kurdish counterparts had welcomed me into the fold only because my presence made them marginally safer.

Bowers found me sitting on my bunk and taking in the magazine pictures of women dressed in string bikinis festooning the back wall. Earlier, I'd had a reassuring back-and-forth with my fellow terps, who'd given me a couple *Sports Illustrated* swimsuit issues before taking me down to meet Colonel Dildar and Major Jonathan Howell at the villa. Both those men were approachable and took time to greet me with pleasant promises of a soldier's education and an open door policy. I'd be seeing a lot of them in the coming weeks. Tomorrow morning we were heading into the city again, this time out of our moving bunker and on foot, right into the concrete guts.

Amused, Bowers cackled as I peeled my farm boy eyes from the machismo décor. I looked at him and tried out a shrug, but my face was radiating heat like a hot plate. Sergeant José, the medic, stood behind Bowers popping open a soda, affable Latin grin widening under his gold-framed Ray-Bans. Then he raised his bottle to the wall in a mock toast and took a sip.

"We all figured it was high time you were initiated properly into the Team," Bowers said. "Come on outside."

Freed of armor and with sweat patches already reeking on our shirts, we made our way to the outdoor latrines: two plywood closets in a walled yard—several bullet holes caught my attention. Ten feet away, men were hanging around shooting the breeze and looking on as two fifty-gallon drums cut down into big foot-high bowls sat in the lot, their vile contents smoldering. It didn't take more than one inhale to register what was going on. The hot stench of excrement was sickening. Walking over, I felt a pool of bile stir in my gut and then burn up past my throat.

One of the men sauntered up to me with a long, stained stick. "Here you go, Mikey, it's your turn to stir the team stew."

Natural Waste Ordinance Disposal, otherwise known as shit-burning. Shoving the stick into the drum, I dug around the black sizzling mess, all the men singing "Stir it up," over and over again. And I did. Putrid gases rose up to greet me like a sucker punch. I laughed until I gagged and fell back into the yard.

"Welcome to Mosul, Mikey."

Later, Bowers arranged a quick call to my frantic mother before taking me up to the hotel roof for an antenna check. When I told her I was having the time of my life, it wasn't a lie.

The man-made islands of trash floating lazily along the river delivered a rank smell in the gloomy morning hours, and I stood on the polluted banks, listening to the muezzin lure its faithful. Week after week, it was always the same: slow drive out into the labyrinth, alleys like slits and abandoned warehouses offering ample nooks and crannies for doped-up fanatics to hide in. Searches and interrogations. A chaos of bullets and filth.

Soldiers poured out into the streets. Clumps of black garbage bags lay scattered like charred skins over the roads and stuck to the spires of fences. Shaking hands with our weary neighbors. Handing out leaflets about safety checks. At first, Mosul seemed like nothing more than a sinister maze of irredeemable urban poverty. None of what I saw was all that striking to me, a denizen of mud-hut villages. But the sheer scale was suffocating. When you were mired down inside her maw, Mosul seemed to have no beginning and no end.

Still, there were fleeting moments of beauty: children in ill-matched clothes, a mishmash of washed-out colors, often ran out unafraid, arms flapping to greet the soldiers. In their upturned faces and lit-up eyes you saw what was left of decency in that ruined part of the world, and it gave me hope. When he wasn't in the truck standing on overwatch, Bowers always stopped for those eager gaggles, kneeling way down to pass around lollipops, taking his time. I'd interpret his good wishes in Arabic, all of us laughing in that moment as though there wasn't really a war going on. Bowers had a wife named Angie and seven children under five waiting for him at home, all counting the days like rosary beads; you could see the longing slip over his eyes.

I usually walked a pace behind Colonel Dildar and Major Howell, who operated as counterparts: Howell, his face pale and hairless; Dildar silver-eyed and ruddy. Sometimes Captain Christopher Faulkner, our SO2, or intelligence officer, would have passed on information of suspicious activity in a particular location. Other times, we were investigating complaints about power outages, or criminal activities, and a civil affairs contingent of the Iraqi police would charge in. Colonel Dildar was always the lead, asking questions that I relayed to the citizens: Who worked in the location? Why were there trucks going back and forth in the middle of the night? It was also my job to offer cultural insights—only a Middle Eastern man could spot a Middle Eastern liar—and I did so, many times. When uncoordinated bursts of gunshots rained down, I learned the drill fast: hit the deck and roll for cover. Bowers always jumped right on me—the shy kid without a gun earning a bimonthly wage.

THE SPRING MORNING we went into the Tammuz 17 quarter of torn-up western Mosul, I didn't know we wouldn't be coming back that night. Fresh intelligence had come in about weapons caches, and active insurgent cells operating out of civilian homes in a particular trellis of blocs known already to harbor a full web of aggressive AQI as well as other odious guerrilla forces, all fighting for that crumbling piece of city turf. All through 2008, the Iraqi army (IA) ordered regular "cordon and search" operations running several blocks that sometimes lasted for weeks, giving them names like "Lion's Paw," "Iron Harvest," or "New Hope."

Sometimes insurgents kidnapped the children of families living in homes they wished to use, and we'd have to stay there longer to try to wrangle out even partial truths. Having the child meant having control—a wall of silence no officer, no matter how intrepid, could breach. The army ran full methodical sweeps, flooding blocks with soldiers, opening every door, checking each room, under floors, boring into walls—sometimes we went eighteen hours straight. When you got out of there for a break, you didn't know which way was up or down anymore.

When we heaved into the back of the MRAP, exhausted, no one spoke. Radio going wild. Engine groaning. Bowers nodded at Major Marvin Iavecchia, the operations officer, and just drove. Minutes later, we pulled into a flour mill. The fenced-in lot was empty and the warehouse, with its blown-out windows, loomed—our home for the night.

After no water or food for hours, we stepped through the mill doors to a waft of stale air so dry every inhalation clawed down my throat. Our team of several men moved methodically in tight formation along the narrow halls, looking for the owner of the property.

A havoc of broken glass in several places, upended metal chairs, scattered papers. We found the man in an office standing under a dim fluorescent bulb that was hanging lopsided from a pair of twisted cables. The light oscillated and hummed and a strange gray sheath covered it like grime. The air up there grew dank and sour and motes of dust caked over my nostrils. I translated while the men exchanged polite greetings, and then Colonel Dildar explained that the army needed to take over the building. Somewhere behind me I could hear Bowers coughing. Apart from the one man, there was no one else in the building. Standing there, I caught sight of my reflection through a small cracked mirror next to the desk; in the hot malevolent light my face looked wan and aged. I turned away from myself to the filthy linoleum floor, and the buzzing of the mill seemed to intensify. For a moment, I thought I might be going mad.

Then I heard Bowers breathing hard behind me, felt him lean in and whisper:

"Mikey, look up at the light."

The long bulb hanging down rocked slightly against the loose ceiling wires. My eyes held the image for a moment: the strange gray sheath; the filthy lambent glow. And then my gaze shifted involuntarily, casting over the walls and the peculiar raised pattern covering it. I turned back to Bowers, who had his chin held in tight and seemed to be swaying in his dirty boots.

"Flies," Bowers whispered, and I could hear him gagging. "Flies on top of flies."

Hundreds of thousands—maybe millions of them—creeping over each other and every surface, enough to coat each man in there.

A moment later, no one saying a word about the infestation, we were told to set up camp over the floor in the main warehouse. We filed out fast and down the stairs again.

Bowers slept in a body bag that night, zipped up tight.

THREE-THIRTY IN THE morning. We were back in the MRAP, stomachs full on MREs (Meals Ready-to-Eat) and moving through the dead quiet to a gas station just up the block. No one asked what we were doing there—you were told what you needed to know, when you needed to know it. We all spread out over the pavement and milled around. Past the gate I could see a makeshift soccer field tamped over a patch of dirt; the old goal posts stood askew and showed through the gloom like bent straws. I was walking back to the MRAP when I felt it— that empty beat of time right before an attack.

A rocket-propelled grenade (RPG) hissed down from one of the tall adjacent buildings and slammed into the back wall, tearing out chunks of brick and mortar. I turned toward the MRAP and watched Bowers scurry up to the gun turret; he looked over at me and mouthed something I couldn't decipher. Then a second RPG came down and took out the front wall and sent me to the deck, face pinned to one side, cheek crushed against the ground. Through the near pitch, I could see a blur of moving boots and heard shouting without words. My ears were ringing, but I knew not to move, not yet. I just waited to hear a call for José the medic. Nothing—so far, no one hit. Time moved through water, blood in my mouth—I'd bit into my tongue. Then the first bullets rained down, sewing a path of sparks right across the lot. A mess of machine-gun fire, no direction to it. One after the other, angry bees kissed past my ears. I closed my eyes and rolled over again and again to the

MRAP and then crawled behind it. We were taking long bursts of plunging fire from several stories up, and every soldier took to their rifles and returned what they got. And then, just as randomly as it began, it all stopped.

Sounds of footsteps in the alley. Bowers stood poised in the turret, drawing down on two people racing along the fence line; you could see their dark figures flickering through the posts. When they came around and passed the open gate right in front of us, he bit his lip and I knew he had them in his sights: two people, bare feet, running wild.

"I don't know," Bowers said, and we all heard him.

One of our men hurled out an expletive, but Bowers just stood there eyeing the runners, his barrel still lined up as they tore across the road and fled into the soccer field. One move of his finger was all it would take, and we waited for it. The team watched; some of them were ready to do it themselves, and drew up their rifles. Then the figures jumped the gutter into a thin shaft of street light beaming down and we saw them for what they were—small, holding nothing but each other's hands.

"Those are kids," Bowers said, "kids running away."

Then he went down into the MRAP and called for air support. A few minutes later, a pair of helos crisscrossed the sky over us, conducting thermal scans. After several passes, they didn't find a single living thing. Soon after, we were told to head back out.

"Damn," Bowers kept saying. "Damn."

THE HOUSE IN question was like all the others, a stucco facade rising behind stained walls and clanking gates. You could hear the uproar of the ongoing raid echoing out: staticky radio chatter, soldiers shouting in Arabic or Kurdish. The barking of dogs, wild jabber of distraught wives and wails of children as husbands, fathers, or brothers were hauled into the street for questioning. The IA was heavier-handed then their Western counterparts, tossing prisoners around like sacks of flour. The Americans' task was to stand back and offer support.

When they burst into the last house, I was called up front among the break-in team to translate. The woman inside wouldn't open the bullet-riddled door. When they bored in past the threshold like a human battering ram, it was to the loud shrieks of a toddler crawling around inside, and a wife alone with her other two sons, sobbing as she cowered in a black hijab.

No one spoke to her as the team moved inside, according to a well-practiced choreography of swift and fluid movements, AK-47s held close in case there was a knife-wielding grabber by the door. Moving over the floor of the simple front room, they spread out over the house, scattering like one man multiplying into many, all shouting as they went up the stairs to turn out the upper floors.

It never took long; in a bedroom cabinet, curled up in a fetal ball, they discovered the suspect, took him by the hair and hauled him out. No shots fired, the men called out their big catch—Abu al-Who-Knows-What, leader of yet another cell of homicidal thugs. To me they had all become different heads on the body of the same relentless beast. Arms locked around the man's thick neck, his eyes bulged like black grapes in their dark sockets, and he hissed wet air as they dragged him like a flaccid deadweight, legs thumping down the stairs to the front door.

The children all began to wail and shake against their mother's clothes, the television in a corner still whispering light. The youngest kept shifting his eyes back to the screen: an Arabic cartoon played on, sound muted. He giggled once and then looked at me wide-eyed, catching himself.

I was about to go out to translate for Colonel Dildar as they interrogated the suspect, but Major Howell said to wait in the room a few minutes. This was an HVT (high-value target) and they'd probably transport him right out to Diamondback.

The dim little house smelled warm: roasted meat and pounded spices, lamb, garlic, and coriander, and for just one ephemeral moment in that controlled melee, I thought of my father's farm. When a transient image offered itself, I accepted it like a balm: Daki's soft pale hands, spice-coated fingers working the mortar and pestle as she gazed out the window; baying lambs in their pens, wind murmuring along the tilled rows of greenery.

No one spoke in the house. The children could see their father surrounded in the courtyard: zip ties around his wrist, his raw mouth like a gash hurling Arabic epithets. I shut the door. Then, just as it closed, a small marking no larger than a fingerprint embedded into the top panel showed itself to me like a prophecy. I peered in close: tiny peacock carved into the clay. The air seemed to thin as though time had stretched it, and I took a quick breath before turning, resolute.

"Hello," I said to the woman in Kurmanji. "What is your name?"

And as I uttered the words in our precious ancient tongue, her eyes flickered through the slit in her veil. Then, as though invisible hands were on her, the sarcophagus of fabric quivered and fell away from her small moon face: wide almond eyes, all of Shingal shining in their big clear domes—and I knew right away she was one of mine.

"What are you doing here?" I said to her. "Are these little ones all yours?"

But she came right up to me, touching the full length of my forearm, hands, and fingers, and stared at the mouth that had delivered that miracle as though I were a phantom.

"They grabbed me and dragged me out from the field by my feet when I was picking onions. Just like I was nothing—a lamb to be slaughtered. They tossed me into the back of a truck. Married me to him here in Mosul. These are our children. That was 2003. It's been over five years. I was fourteen."

A vortex of questions raced through me, and I wanted to take her and her children right there and then, back to the base, and all the way home. Her home and mine. We could be there by first light. "You must come with me now. Don't be afraid. I will help you."

"No. I can never set a foot in Shingal again."

"You must. This is your chance. Pack a small bag for the children, and all of you come with me."

"And the others who are watching right now from their windows would find out, send their fighters down from the foothills into the village, and slit my throat. My whole family would be murdered, maybe even my neighbors. And they'd pick up his sons, bring them right back here with my severed head. You know this already."

The children were all listening, mouths gaping and silent, not understanding the strange melodic language pouring out of their frantic mother.

"Tell me who your family is, even the village. You were born a Yazidi daughter, always will be."

"No," she whispered. "I have become a thing of shame. Not a person. There are others like me here. On this street. On the next street. All over—hiding."

"Take me to them. I'll tell the base commander. No one can touch you now. You see what's happening out there. Look outside. Their day is over."

Then she let out a strange laugh, high-pitched and desperate, and brought a hand to her flushed cheek. "What they want they take, or destroy if they can't get it. If you think this war will end on this street today or any other day, you're a fool. Leave here and forget as I have been forgotten. To speak out now would only be uttering my death sentence. My boys still need their mother."

Then I looked down into the eyes of her young son, no more than five years old, who was staring up at me now, and I saw a thin gleam of malice lurking in his volcanic gaze—we had taken his father; infidels burst in and dragged him out like trash. The fact would not be forgotten. Suddenly, I knew without a doubt that I would have to leave her in her robes, rice on the stove and lamb's blood pooled on the counter—and not say a word to anyone.

The soldiers were moving back down the stairs with hauls of evidence—stacks of paperwork and crate after crate of ordnance: an RPG, ammo, and piles of rifles. As their loaded-down shadows filed by, I did the only thing I could do in that desolate room, and offered up a small prayer to our faraway angels. Not one verse in, she stepped clear to face the wall as though each syllable had delivered a blow, and buried her face once again in her scarves. The children all watching us intently, their mouths and eyes round; I only looked away.

"You and I are dead already, we all are," the lost Yazidi breathed behind her veil, head bowed low into the corner. "You just don't know it. I let my angels go a long time ago. It's the only way. There is no room for them here."

Chapter Seven

Riding the Surge

First sighting of the August crescent moon, planted in an Iraqi sky full of stars and spite, declared the holy month of Ramadan, and the great canon of the devout took its place over the mindless cacophony of war. And at another call to prayer, I could feel the veil of holy fervor seep down over the city like clear mist. For the moment: not a sound in the east, or murmur in the simmering west. Sunrise to sunset into the late summer, the antipathy of time stood in wait like a sharpened blade over the disintegrating streets. The faithful fasted in their deepening convictions, uttering the poetry of millennia-old prayers in a unison that eclipsed all else.

If I closed my eyes, I thought I could hear them, folded over their frayed silken mats in that city of hatreds. Who has a bomb that can destroy this particular and indomitable Allah, who'd vanquished armies from every corner of the globe and now, at his melodic call, stilled the furies of Mosul? These days, he was simply playing cat and mouse against the might of superpowers and using nothing more than a few cells of crazed lunatics, and bombs they detonated using gutted Nokia cell phones. The Coalition called it Operation Iraqi Freedom, but really, they were mired neck-deep fighting an all-out jihad. And in between muezzin calls, we braced ourselves for a holy bloodbath. It was the fall of 2008, and in the last two days alone, scores had died.

First, two roadside bombs killed eight in Baghdad and Diyala Province. Then mounds of TNT detonated in a single car among bags of nails, razor blades, and screws, shredding thirty people and maiming forty-seven others who were breaking their fasts along the market streets in Dujail, in Salahuddin Province.

I was alone in my canvas bunk when Major Howell called me into the main compound building for a rapid-fire meeting with Colonel Dildar—I knew from the radio chatter that a new mission was in play. Several times now, I'd been invited to translate in sensitive meetings with the chiefs, and felt a certain pride in that fact. Even Saddam, who used my people as close-quarter guards, knew that we Yazidis were loyal to our core. So far, I'd proven myself in the turbid thick of operations all over the city, getting shot at, routinely RPG'd, and doused in shrapnel, but always slipping my boots right back on. Still, the wage was good—Daki had her new shoes, paid the bills, and the family back home had meat.

Fan whirring in a corner, the television was set to Mosul's popular Sharqiya News, sound blaring in Arabic. I took my place by the screen to translate the story that had been unfolding since the early hours in one dramatic segment after the next. On the morning of September 13, 2008, several members of Sharqiya News—Farida Adil, a female journalist known for her in-your-face Western attire, plus two cameramen, their driver, and the Mosul bureau chief—were filming a popular show in the bustling Zanjilly neighborhood, barely a mile from COP Hotel.

Breaking Your Fast Is on Us was one of the most popular shows in Iraq at the time. In each episode all through the month of Ramadan, a camera crew would surprise down-and-out Iraqi families (as if there were another kind in those days) with sumptuous food and extravagant gifts: washing machines, computers, new stoves. Many Iraqis dreamed of making it on the show. Sharqiya News had been in enemy crosshairs since 2004 for airing advertisements condemning terrorists and for heralding the age of peace and cooperation with American and Coalition Forces.

The abduction of three crew members occurred as Farida Adil waited inside the modest living room of the family that was about to be filmed. The rest of the news staff had just pulled along the block to the nearby thud of a bomb blast and the racket of machine-gun fire. A sea of adoring crowds had gathered in the street, and nestled like barbs among the throng were a number of radicals, coolly counting down the ticking seconds. At some silent signal, they stepped forward drawing weapons, made holy proclamations, and hauled away three of the crew.

Still inside rehearsing, Farida Adil had no idea anything had gone awry until someone burst in to tell her. At the time, she was wearing a tight pink blazer and ponytail—both haram in the eyes of extremists. Quickly, she donned a veil and fled the house to safety.

Kidnappings and ransom demands, murders, and armed robberies were routine all over Iraq, but that aggressive celebrity abduction was big news, and was now the main concern in the COP meeting room. AQI had developed a taste for more impudent assaults—the latest attack had happened in full daylight and before a large crowd of witnesses. Our SO2 had just gotten word that the abductors were lurking around in the industrial part of Al Zirai, in the Shifa region, the nefarious quarter abutting Zanjilly. Major Howell told the team to be ready to move out at first light.

HEAT LIGHTNING OVER Alshohada Bridge, not a cloud in sight; it wouldn't rain here until October. By the time I strapped into the jump seat of the MRAP, I was already dripping hot. We hauled out fast, headed north—it wouldn't take long for the watchers to clock our movements and dial them in. The three-vehicle convoy slid into an empty car lot near the mark; we pushed down the stair ramp, everyone watching their six. Beyond the carcasses of a few shelled buildings, it was as quiet as a still shot.

Nothing moved, not even the air.

Pepsi's trademarked insignias crowned the top of the factory—an absurdity among absurdities you only find within the ruined bowels of an urban war. I'd seen the surrounding pulverized streets in the mock-up laid out over a table in the meeting room, and I knew we were headed to the alley. No more than rubble in places, every blown-out window was a vengeful eye, snipers lining the team up in their scopes and considering. Life or death for one of us might depend on nothing more than his mood; the next prayer; a chai break. Everywhere you went, the capriciousness of fate stalked your mortal paces. From the start, I knew that that long measured walk would end in a perilous place.

More than once, we'd been called out to meet the Iraqi police to investigate and remove corpses from that district. If the bodies had stayed out baking, you needed to bring a shovel and sheets. Major Howell's radio crackled as he moved to confer with Colonel Dildar. I stood at the mouth of the alley, staring it down like a bad day. Right over me, a lazy flock of blackbirds shed altitude, some congregating like a jury over the Pepsi insignia.

That's when I saw it: a gray blanket spread out over the ground. For a moment, I thought I glimpsed movement, but it was just the breeze buffeting the fabric, which had stains and small tears all over it. Two feet away, a bird watched me approach, stretching its dark wings, its beak gulping at the air, claws scratching at the pavement. I looked down to the covering: a dress shoe turned in at a strange angle and the blackened tip of a finger showed under the fringe. Then I did what I should not have, and pulled back the blood-soaked fabric.

They say headless bodies have no souls—but the souls are always there, lingering near their vacated shells. There were two men from Sharqiya News: a cameraman—light meter still tucked into his pocket—and the fit-looking bureau chief, wearing prosperous city clothes. I took in the ruined collar of a fine dress shirt, no doubt ironed just that morning. And along the raw stub of neck: butchered vertebrae, ragged veins. The carotid still wet, coagulating blood already soaked my boots. On one of the hands, I saw a gold ring; every one of these details spoke to me only of life.

I'd seen the dead many times, helped to wash their spent bodies for the funeral rites. Took a turn kissing my own father's cold brow before we wed him to the earth—but not this way. Not this way.

"Bodies," I finally called out. "Bodies."

Major Howell and Colonel Dildar followed procedure to the letter, commanding the scene and my own nervous system. I stood by, translating between east and west; others took pictures, jotted down notes. Several people searched the vicinity for missing body parts and the other kidnapped crew member, whom they would never find. Sometimes the insurgents hammered severed heads onto fence posts or tossed them like ruined balls into residential streets to scare the residents. Rumor had it that the skulls of the most blatant heathens were fed to pigs.

But I could not stop myself from wondering how the militants executed the killings: knife or sword. Before or after a bullet to the brain. Despite every admonishment I lived by—to shield who I was and wanted to remain—my rookie Khanasor eyes stole glimpses of those terrifying stubs of raw flesh. Finally, I turned heavenward, watching the birds, all congregating now in the eaves along the Pepsi factory, just waiting for us to move away from their dinner. I peered down at my own feet, blood- and filth-spattered, and then glimpsed the bodies again. A contagion entered my veins, as it infiltrated every soldier in their time. Suddenly, I was disconnected and drained clean of the living essence that made me feel anything at all.

Then Major Howell touched me on the shoulder, our eyes meeting over the oblivious dead: "Stop looking, Michael."

I was only inviting it in.

THE LONG-WASTED TRACK running parallel to the river just north of COP Hotel was known as Death Road, because IEDs went off there every day. Bowers had taught me how to patrol that deadly street like a pro. But I'd said good-bye to Bowers at Thanksgiving dinner in the DFAC at Diamondback—had my first taste of turkey meat and stuffing—and learned the heavy cost of a soldier's farewell. Hard to know if you'd ever see the friend who'd walked the line by your side, kept you alive, sane, faithful to God—ever again. Not likely. By then, I'd seen more than a few detonations in my time. Right out on the grid, José the medic had used a numbing cream and tweezers in the back of the MRAP to pull bits of shrapnel the size of nail heads from my shins.

Now we were out again conducting a cleanup-op near Divil 1 and 2, by Death Road, trawling out the trash. For New Year's 2009, I'd grown a full goatee and shaved my head. When Sergeant Cook saw me on a day off back at Camp Marez, where we took showers, naps, and did our laundry, he came up to me with a back slap:

"Well, well, well, badass—now you even look the part."

Maybe I believed it.

I watched as Captain Faulkner stood in front of a plywood board with a can of spray paint and used the full span of his long arm to scrawl out his name and cell phone number. An insurgent gang had been working Death Road hard, and Faulkner was compelling the enchained residents to come forward with information to shut the group down. On offer: prosperity, a future. But in those days fewer and fewer civilians were, as Bowers put it, drinking the Kool-Aid.

Another mound of garbage sitting there oozing along the culvert like a vagrant, and I slipped on plastic gloves, considering where to begin among the cracked bits of plastic, bricks, rusted metal sheets, and tossed rocks. Even months later, I was still dragging around the absence of Bowers, or maybe I was just tired. Sleep was getting harder to find. Still, I should have been looking where I planted my boots; out on patrol your feet were the enemy's best trigger. And if it hadn't been for the hiss of Faulkner's spray paint, I wouldn't have stopped midstride and seen the thing that would have done us all in. Quarter of an inch, that's how far my heel was from the detonator—I jerked back my boot fast—

"Bomb!"

The device had enough TNT packed in it to tear a gash out of the whole block and suck us all up with it. Boom—there and gone. They would have sent me home to Daki in a small lined box, along with those used copies of *Sports Illustrated* and my death pay.

Who knows why that moment did it, but standing there in the aftermath of the controlled explosion, my nervous system began to collapse. I'd survived, by some nonsensical roll of the dice. And now I couldn't stop my mind from racing back and forth, combing over every minute detail: the precise angle of my boot over the detonator, the hiss of Faulkner's paint can, my eyes' foolish skim of the lethal trash heap. And out there in the alley, leaning against a rusted gate, my whole body fell into a wild gallop, limbs shaking from the inside out. Then I slithered all the way down as though I were deflating.

"You OK, Michael?" I heard Major Howell call out, and felt hands on my back pulling.

"Yes, yes," I said again and again, like some broken thing, as they led me to the MRAP.

When I asked for water, someone gave it, and I thought I was all right.

WE LEFT THE wire again after midnight under the thin gloam of a waning moon. Four vehicles: MRAPs and Humvees. Operation New Hope, launched in February 2009, had morphed into several joint US and Iraqi sub-ops throughout Mosul, all designed to degrade al-Qaeda and their capabilities in the region. For the entire month, it was boots on the ground: carrying out search and raid missions, following up on arrest warrants, destroying enemy munitions caches, and setting up a holding force to prevent re-infiltration. We all joked that we couldn't remember the last time we'd changed our socks. Still, it seemed like the minute you got rid of one cell, another would come right down the line on a relentless conveyor belt carrying fighters out of Syria, the ranges of Nineveh, or just up the street a few blocks.

Captain Faulkner's brainchild of handing out his cell phone number paid dividends when a ten-year-old kid called in first, and then just showed up at the COP gates, a plastic bag full of empty Pepsi bottles in his bony hand.

"One brave kid," Faulkner said when he called me in to translate.

The cemetery of the thirteenth-century Mar Thoma church sat nestled like a secret castle deep within a subdued residential area, behind huge stone walls. The boy who'd called Faulkner lived in the vicinity and, like most children of war, had turned out to be a proficient spy. Night after night, at 23:00, he'd watched from his fragile perch in a persimmon tree as Arabic-speaking men showed up in a convoy of old sedans. He heard shoveling and saw crates of munitions of all varieties. He listed each one to us like an expert: IEDs, detonation devices, explosive belts.

Then he walked over to the map tacked to the whiteboard and put his finger right on the spot. When Faulkner asked him why he was there, putting his life at risk, the boy turned slowly in his shredded Nikes. He pulled in his lips under the fluorescent lights; his face went dark.

"They killed my brother and my father—and now you will kill *them*."

I will never forget the grim resignation in his war-torn voice.

AS WE PULLED along the church lane, the walls stood to one side like a cliff rising up into the dead of night. Moving through the gates, the vehicles lumbered between a dense lattice of grave markers displaying large photographs of the departed, faces illuminated as beams of searchlights were cast over the flat terrain. Right away, several soldiers went to work digging. No one liked being there: the shovels themselves were a desecration, but cemeteries were good hiding spots for munitions caches—I'd been through this routine before all over Mosul. It wouldn't take long. Two feet down in a fake tomb, we found the first crate and hauled it out. Then another and another. It was as though there were no corpses there, only things used to make them: rockets, explosive belts and barrels, IEDs by the dozens. It would take hours to pull it all out, categorize and document each one. The long night was still and quiet.

But the enemy had been waiting for us, having taken up positions along the high walls. The first group opened with RPGs and machine-gun fire. Every soldier dropped. Prone near a grave marker, I tried to get a bearing as more shots poured down from every side. All around, men low-crawled the ground like heavy shadows. I could see a church spire rising like the head of a spear and watched muzzle flashes light up the perimeter. A deafening blur now, men hollered, returning fire. A foot away, an Iraqi soldier turned to look at me, his wide-eyed face frozen in terror—then a bullet sheared off the back of his skull and he fell away. I rolled from useless cover to useless cover as figures went down like dominoes. I shouted for the medic, but the fury of combat engulfed my voice. Impotent, I waited.

Because you often don't feel a hit, we'd all been trained to check for holes, and I found mine as my hands crawled down my calf. The accompanying burn was diabolical, but I still believed it was just a graze—within seconds, my pant leg was soaking wet. All I could do was lie there, mouthing the name José into the raging gun-powdered air. A long time later, I saw a face emerge as though from dark water, but by now I was losing so much blood that it was hard to tell figments from reality.

A memory rushed in: the time José stitched up my forehead back at COP. We'd been told to keep our feet clear of the river that served as a fertile breeding ground for swarms of bloodthirsty insects. I hadn't heeded the warning and the fly that bit my face took out a chunk of flesh. José showed up with his magic numbing cream, gauze, and huge Puerto Rican grin. "No big deal," he'd said, and I picked up the phrase like a dropped coin.

"No big deal," I heard myself saying now, as my severed veins gushed.

Then some other medic crawled over, holding up a syringe, and I was no longer sure that José had been there at all. Flashes twinkled all around the blur like the Christmas lights the teams strung across the base in December.

And then in that stupor, I was sitting behind Bowers on a motorcycle riding fast between the pear trees in the barren orchard, both of us laughing, the others all calling out, "Happy Birthday, Abu Jacob." Father of Jacob, the name the Iraqis had given him as a sign of respect, and for one of the sons he had waiting back in Idaho.

More rounds buzzed past my head, but I couldn't hear a thing, and I saw another form go down, legs twitching.

And Bowers was with me again at the gates of Diamondback when my brother Samir showed up dressed in new fatigues. He was signing on to be an interpreter.

Go back to Daki, I'd said to him, and handed over my full pay packet. Then I held him hard by his thin farm-worked shoulders. *Get rid of that army gear they gave you. Get out . . .*

"Get out of here," I said to the medic. "This is no place—this is no place for angels." Even as I heard myself say it, I knew I was teetering over the edge of mortality.

A soothing voice told me to settle down, and somehow, I knew just then my situation was grave. And yet I didn't feel a thing anymore. I was fading now; slipping in and out of places like a boat sailing pleasant waves.

That's when I peered into that enveloping nothingness and caught sight of my Babo on his white horse, riding the fog and hellfire between the grave markers. Then my shallow heartbeats and laboring breaths seemed to give way, and I heard my mother whisper:

You were the one standing with him in the space between worlds, Shaker. . . . In time, you'll know what it means.

And Babo was right there in his uniform, gold ring on his finger, glinting. Those pale lodestar eyes on mine, and he held out his long arm. So grateful, I raised my hand.

The medic told me to stop moving—he didn't see what I did.

But Babo had pulled me right up to his saddle, and we were riding away fast through the mist.

"Have you spent your packet already, boy?" he looked back and asked me.

"Maybe so, Babo, I don't know."

Someone hushed me.

But I was long gone.

Chapter Eight

The Fortress

WHITE LIGHT GLEAMED OFF THE WALLS—LIKE COMING TO, DEEP inside a sugar cube. Moments later, an onslaught of odors: melting plastic, peroxide, iodine, urine—blood. Blurred views of people moving about as though through water; fatigues and face masks. The slaps of latex gloves peeled off. On the stretcher next to me, a human form writhed under its thin covering like a pupa working its way out of a cocoon. When the movement stilled, I turned away. Moments later, a fire of agony erupted within the mangled sinews of my leg, and all on its own my voice released a long primal moan. Suddenly, fingers tugged, and I could feel the wraith-like shadows of people hovering over me. A downdraft buffeted my hair and IV lines dripped like leaky faucets into my arm. Then, as though a sorcerer's hand had waved it off, the sensation of pain lifted, all feeling itself emptying into a cyclopean void, and I ran an impassive gaze along the room.

Other damaged shapes keened on gurneys; some sitting up and staring out, their stumps already bandaged, the latest products in what I would come to think of as a factory of missing limbs. I was in the military hospital at Camp Diamondback, where the 1st Medical Detachment Forward Surgical Team treated my wounds. Hard to know if the staff had tagged me as dead or alive—they used their own secret ranking system in there. The dying were always the last to know it.

Groggy, I slowly moved my deadweight hands for a quick corpus-roster: face, arms, every finger, and then I surveyed the full lengths of both legs, one covered in thick bandages. My body had taken in two bullets: foot and calf—same side. I exhaled and closed my eyes, relieved. But behind my lids, a slow film played out of the frenzied minutes just before I was shot: checking the man who went down next to me in the graveyard and battling to stop eruptions of blood. I plugged a finger deep inside a gaping hole, and warm flesh squeezed around my digit like an infant's wet mouth suckling. The medic appeared and applied compression bandages; he administered a shot and slithered back into the pitch and carnage.

On my right, an American soldier talked about going to see a guy named Walter Reed. It would be years before I learned that Walter Reed was a military hospital in the United States, where some of the most broken soldiers went. All things considered, I was lucky—after surgery I'd be back on the front line in a matter of weeks.

Acid stirred in my gut, and I held it down, pressing a cheek into the pillow. The raw truth of that endless war lay in waste all around me. So hot now, my temples throbbed, and I longed for Haji's well: clear water flowing from the spigot. Cucumbers flourishing in a desert. A game of baseball in the shadow of Shingal. Small miracles of home—all that had been sacrificed already could not be for nothing.

Cheating death was an amphetamine. As soon as I walked out of the unit, battle-scarred and several notches above alive, I returned thicker-skinned to the gladiator ring for another long round. Back with my crew and ensconced in the bunk at COP, singing in the back of the MRAP, shooting the breeze in the yard. The Coalition Forces had to succeed in dragging my beleaguered Iraq to her feet—I knew that now more than ever. There was no going home to Daki and the concrete house with its new satellite TV and pretending we were not ensnared in a battle for survival. Babo had carried me through the Armageddon, and I truly believed it was to fight for what could be, not what had been.

Team Shady disbanded, and in the early spring days of 2009, I was out in the dirt and on base in my getup: *shamag*, shades, tambour in my hands. I leaned against a blast barrier like a dog of war, watching a plane hurtle along the runway out of Diamondback. Inside, many of my band of brothers ascended over the city that had almost eaten us alive, before their metal bird pushed into a gauze of cloud and was gone. I tried to imagine what they were going back to: farms in Iowa, fishing towns in Maine, apartments in the city, base housing in Miramar; college, babies, discount malls, and grocery stores—peace. I couldn't envision any of it. Team Shady was already a dream of a dream. The sun would never shine on us all at the same time again.

Weeks earlier, I'd been standing near the very same place to a different view, when a CH47 carrying the new MiTT (Military Transition Team) Spider descended in great updrafts of dust. Captain Robert Brownsword was the first one to saunter off, carrying a rucksack in one hand and an unlit cigar dangling in the other. Blue-eyed, white-teethed, and tanned in his grinning prime—all of America distilled into one young man. He had a thin Clark Gable moustache and ready grin. Not too far behind, a bullet-shaped Lieutenant Colonel Jay Migone walked down the ramp in meaty strides, eyes roving the terrain. Grabbing the cigar from Brownsword, he punched him in the arm. In unison, they both looked way over at me and smiled.

"What the hell kind of guitar is that?" Migone called out when he saw my tambour.

I told him that I liked to sing to pass the time. Daki had sent me the instrument after my surgery, believing I'd undergone some minor procedure unrelated to my violent line of work. Migone was lighting the cigar and sending out clouds of smoke. He and Brownsword were making their way over, almost as though they'd been expecting to find me right there, right then—Spider's new terp. Back in the bird, the others were pulling gear off the center line and dumping it out the back.

"Sing about what?" Migone said through a warm shroud.

I smiled and strummed a quick chord. "About loving women, drinking beer, and hunting terrorists—I'm Yazidi." In those days, I also felt like a bona fide fighter—death had made a try for me, and I'd won.

Brownsword, his stubbled face so bronzed it was more freckles than skin, brought his earnest East Coast eyes in close, talking to his own cool reflection in my shades.

"Got the lingo and the look—been around the block already, haven't you, Yazidi? Oldest religion in the world, right? Original sons of Adam." He nodded. "I've studied your people."

"Yes, sir. But I don't believe in magic," I said, raising a finger. Word had it that a number of Yazidis had gone missing and then turned up dead all over Nineveh; above all else, most of them had been accused of witchcraft.

"Who cares?" Migone laughed. "Believe whatever you want. This base might as well be Tucson, Arizona. You're free as an eagle inside these walls."

Brownsword looked over. "Yazidis believe in seven angels, and one of them, Tawusi Melek, fell to earth. Some of his

Muslim countrymen think that means they worship the devil and magic. Magic is against the law."

"What kind of law is that?"

"The kind that lands you in chop-chop square. Like in Saudi Arabia. Over here, I guess they pick 'em off one at a time," Brownsword said. "Let's go down to our CHU and settle in. You come on too, Mikey. Basim is here—he's Yazidi. Pretty much all our terps are."

TEAM SPIDER WAS a different animal altogether. Ten soldiers, five terps—Gus the Turkoman, James, Basim from my village, Hussein, and me. We got tight, fast. They swaggered around base like some new kind of twenty-first-century Wild West posse, dressed in fatigues and armed to the hilt: handguns and knives strapped to their legs, fingers spread, reflex-ready to duke out the war. Their crew of terps could always be found right at their side: in the DFAC eating, in a CHU watching movies, in the back lot playing cards. For the next six months to a year, we'd be base-hopping all over the northern provinces, looking for bad guys along the rat-line and trying to get the IA and border police in shape.

MRAPS IN THE city, but Humvees in the desert, on patrols I usually sat in the lead truck with Captain Brownsword, who was also the gunner. In Team Spider, every soldier wore three hats, and responsibilities were tethered to abilities, well before rank. The first time we went out in the sand, I watched him lug .50-caliber ammo belts and the machine gun out of his CHU and prop it up in the turret.

"I sleep with my baby every night," he said. "Always be ready to go."

A few minutes later the operations officer, Major Iavecchia, a welcome leftover from Shady, strolled over, talking about the food on offer in the DFAC: pancakes, eggs, bacon—chicken noodle soup was my favorite. Soon we were all out in the lot, filing into trucks and heading out over the hot sea of dunes.

Our four Humvees pulled out of the gates and joined a convoy of vehicles from the IA's 10th Brigade, 2nd Division, which included a number of Ford pickup trucks courtesy of the American government. We were on our way to FOB Sykes, a US Army forward operating base located just south of Tal Afar. Brownsword explained that the top brass in the IA liked to use the pickups even though they weren't armored, because there was air conditioning inside, and out in the desert oven, staying cool ranked slightly higher than staying in one piece.

A section of FOB Sykes known as PAD 2, which I was told was short for "lily pad," was almost empty, so we each got our own CHUs. After five minutes to unpack in my container, I stepped out to a waft of coal smoke—we had enough red meat in the deep freeze to last until kingdom come. I found the team setting up lawn chairs and strings of Christmas lights, and flipping burgers over a barbecue. Iavecchia put country music on the loudspeaker and wandered around belting out every tune.

By sundown, I was lying back next to Migone in an armchair, chewing on rib bones between taking deep sucks on my hookah pipe. Migone turned to me, smoke pouring from his nostrils.

"What do you call what we're doing right here—in your lingo?"

"We are smoking *shisha*, sir. It's good. No funny business in it." As I drew on the pipe's long tentacle, lying back under the purple hue of an Ottoman sundown, part of me had forgotten we were even on a sterile military base—sitting ducks in a desert crawling with terrorists. Even the weather here, like the war, could change on a dime. I'd been told FOB Sykes was called a "no frills" outpost, but I'd never felt closer to being right in the middle of America—and I liked it.

OUT ON THE rat-line, the convoy cruised vast tides of sand, IA vehicles on one side, Team Spider's some distance away on the other. We were out there to check on the fledgling border patrol units, whose job it was to form a tight net to stem the malicious flow of fighters and weapons perpetually sneaking over the line. Sometimes, we'd set up a perimeter of vehicles and just wait, idling, observing. More often than not, we'd watch as a ragtag group in an old van would come careening across the flats and an Iraqi contingent would dive in like a lasso. On some days, we could sit out there twelve hours or more, just picking border crawlers off. They were like cockroaches—every time you got one, you'd loose ten more.

Often there was a wild firefight, but small guerrilla groups could not hope to overcome the hard-boiled firepower of a battle-hungry Iraqi brigade-in-training, keen on lobbing mortar shells like a candy dispenser. Most of those guys used their machine guns as though they were garden hoses. The Iraqis were also known to be merciless with their catches.

"We keep a good eye on them out here, but who knows what the hell they do after they ship them out to the detention centers," Brownsword said. "What the heck can we say after Abu Ghraib, though, right? It's their country. And some might say we had a bit of a hand in fucking it up."

"Are they doing good enough, sir?"

Those days, I was always asking. Rumor had it the Coalition was leaving sooner rather than later, but the borders were still hemorrhaging guerrillas, and the tribes were weary of living dirt poor in a war zone. Under Saddam they'd had a tacit agreement: see no evil, hear no evil—and plenty to eat. Lately, they were running out of reasons to make deals.

"Half the time, Mikey, I don't know what they're doing. But, believe it or not, the border units are doing better than they were. The powers that be fired the whole Iraqi army, and we had to start over from the bottom of the barrel."

We looked over the bands of sand shifting like veils, overlapping back and forth in the gathering winds. An Iraqi soldier was firing his AK-47 into the air and hollering at the empty heavens. All around him, the others laughed as a line of prisoners was led to a waiting truck; hands bound in zip ties, their caches of contraband lined up on the ground. A soldier walked up and kicked one of the captives in the groin. No reason. We could see Migone barking and wagging a finger. When I looked over at Brownsword, he was walking the other way, back to the Humvee for his turn in the turret.

ONCE AGAIN IN the truck, I sat behind Iavecchia, who was chewing on a day-old piece of Juicy Fruit gum and manning the Blue Force Tracker, a GPS-enabled mapping device. We all had our team radio headsets on to an encrypted frequency that only our small crew could hear. Migone, who was in the lead vehicle with Basim, was relaying information over from the IA battalion about linking up with another contingent after we were done with our patrol. We coasted over a burnished sea following the IA convoy—no sign of any roads, just those rolling mounds of sand stretching like time from horizon to horizon.

"What the hell is going on here?" Migone sputtered over the radio. We'd been wandering the desert for over three hours, and he was certain the IA were lost. Migone went quiet for a few minutes, and we carried on making plans for dinner. Steak, again. Team meeting right after, then a Van Damme movie—my turn to choose.

Up ahead the convoy came to a full stop and Migone hopped out of his Humvee and came to ask Iavecchia just how far off we were. Iavecchia studied his computer screen and waited a few beats before looking up.

"How about Syria, sir?"

Gripping the sides of the open door, Migone looked down at his boots and up again. "You telling me we crossed the border and this sand I'm standing on right now is Syrian, Iavecchia?"

"Yes, sir, I am—and you are."

Brownsword laughed. "So much for movie night, boys."

And all I could think was: *My country is starting to look like a lost cause.*

SUMMONED INTO THE meeting CHU: a mock-up of northwestern Iraq—from Syria right across the great outwash of desert—was laid out over a table like a makeshift toy model. Dixie cups labeled with the names of bases, army divisions, and landmarks punctuated the beige paper terrain: FOB Sykes, Turkish Castle 10th BDE, COP Destroyer, Garry Owen, Kisik Division HQ, Diamondback, Marez, and the furthest point south, COP Nimur. In my time, I'd see them all. A rock for Mount Shingal. I took a fingertip and planted it north of the stone, just where Khanasor would be.

"That's where I was born," I said.

"And that's me too," Basim said, smiling, touching the same spot. "The other side of the village from you."

"Basim's little brother was in my class," I told the others. "He got all the brains."

"Hey, you guys are Yazidi?" a brand-new terp said from the threshold. He closed the door behind him and came over to the table. We knew him only as "RPG," an acronym he'd acquired as a moniker while working with another team. We assumed he was Kurdish, but he never said—and we would not think to ask, though he seemed friendly enough when playing cards and eating candy bars in the CHUs.

"Yes, we are."

Right away, I wished I hadn't said it, though in time, the fact would become obvious enough.

RPG grinned, showing both decks of his gleaming teeth, and patted me on the back. "It's OK, Michael," he said. "Chill."

Then he picked up the stone marked "Mt. Shingal," tossed it about in his palm, and let a laugh out through his nostrils.

A moment later, Captain Brownsword stood over the table model, pen held out as a pointer; Team Spider converged all around like football players in a huddle.

"Welcome to Upper Mesopotamia, heartland of the ancient Assyrians—territory of genocides, prophets, and warring empires as old as time," he said, sweeping his hand over the long folding table. "Since the Arab Islamic conquest of the seventh century, this blood-soaked desert has been known by the Arabic name of Al-Jazeera—and it is now our area of responsibility."

Then he took his ballpoint and stabbed a lone black square sitting over the beige surface between COP Kisik to the north, and our FOB to its south. A small strip of paper marked it simply: The Fortress.

We'd be pulling out at first light.

"Their battalion commander wants us to give their units a good once-over. He has some concerns. You know the drill."

A "HABOOB" STORM crossed the Al-Jazeera at dawn and a thousand-foot wall of wind-driven sand descended from all sides like a giant blindfold. The enfeebled sun went red-eyed and the raging desert turned the day to night. For hours, we languished in our CHUs, shuffling cards and writing letters home, while seething onslaughts of orange grit lashed the metal walls. Nothing to do but wait for the lull that would come as suddenly as sleep.

When the current finally dispersed, an eerie calm followed and we ventured out like sleepwalkers into the dead-silent aftermath. Dirt blanketed every material thing. Surveying the scene, you suddenly understood humankind's lonesome place in the blind infinity of time: From one end of my country to the other, the ruins of lost empires were buried. Centuries from now, I thought, an excavation will find our spent mortar shells and razor wire entombed among barbecues and army helmets. What history would write about our season on this land—where thousands of wars had already been lost, or won and long forgotten—was far from determined.

Late in the day, the convoy headed north into the hinterland of Al-Jazeera that we'd seen in the mock-up. Through the dusk, a somber facade came into view, rising like a black ship anchored to the desert. Swirls of choked air rushed over the ramparts and the massive turrets, each three stories high and set into corners from which high-caliber guns sat waiting. Our small armada poured over the flat sea of sand, kicking up a long dry wake that made our approach impossible to conceal. An Iraqi flag fluttered, and silhouetted figures positioned along the bulwark watched our steady approach. Brownsword gave us a quick history on the Fortress, one of Saddam's old POW prisons converted to an Iraqi army base.

Someone in the back called out, "Creepy as fuck."

No one else said a word.

GOING IN WAS like entering an unholy cave; the walled-in air was rank. Along each of the four stories were rows of darkened medieval cells set behind bars, and at the end of each corridor stood locked gates at which a mute Iraqi soldier stood sentry in his uniform, weapon poised and face shaded in the vague light. From the outset, there were no niceties here, as though the grim atmosphere of the building and its dark history had infected the current inhabitants, who numbered in the hundreds.

Team Spider took over half a row of cells on the second and third floors, and one corner turret. We hauled in our kits, each member taking a small chamber for a room. I lay down in mine a moment and rested; my deep breaths echoed into the windowless void as though they were not my own. In that cool quiet, the hollowed-out souls of the men who'd been imprisoned there before me seemed to stir. I shuddered and sat straight up.

Minutes later, Migone and Brownsword and the full team passed by and gave me a silent signal to follow. We made our way to a narrow staircase, and went down. All around us, the clanking of gates reverberated through the prison, as our feet whispered against the smooth stones. Brownsword made his way along the stairs first, eyes clocking the shadows that swallowed us like fog.

"Saddam usually had his torture chambers in the basements," he told us. "Makes you wonder about the men who went down these steps before us and what happened to them. Saddam was bad enough to his own, but he held the Iranian POWs here. I can almost feel it. Can't you guys?"

"What, sir?" I said. I had my eyes on the back of his head, which kept going back and forth, back and forth like a gun on a turret.

"Their screams, Mikey. Extreme pain like that, en masse so to speak, it takes over the air of a place. Saddam's son, Uday, liked to hang prisoners upside down from cables and electrocute their genitals. Maybe rip off the fingernails, hack limbs off one at a time, starting with the hands. Or put a cigarette out against an eyeball."

"Will you shut up, Professor Brownsword," Migone said. "You're scaring the kids."

"I'm not scared, sir. This is my country—I know what happened." And I did.

"All right, Mikey," Migone said. "Our host, the battalion commander, has summoned us for a little private chat. There's going to be a reason he wanted it underground. Let's concentrate on that."

When our team squeezed into the low antechamber that was hewn out of the subterranean rock, we knew right away there was trouble. The battalion commander, who was at the helm of the facility and its numerous occupants, stood alone and alabaster pale against the wall, waiting for us. When we walked in, his deputy and two officers stepped forward from a shadowed corner. The commander said nothing and gestured to the entrance, a sheen of sweat over his brow. I swung the door gently, clicking it shut.

"Gentlemen," he began, and I interpreted. "This entire outfit has been infiltrated by al-Qaeda—top to bottom."

"OK. How many?" Migone asked.

"Many—we are overrun. Other divisions are encountering the same problem. It's getting harder and harder to smoke them out. For now, we have to keep up the routines as if we know nothing. We can run a few drills before you leave."

"Overrun—as in outnumbered?"

"Possibly, Lieutenant Colonel. Yes. We don't know how many. The fact is—I don't trust my soldiers."

"In other words, Commander?"

"In other words, sir . . ." The lone Iraqi chief swallowed hard and then looked over each man in the room. "None of you are safe. Not even me. You're here to take a look, make your presence known."

"There are ten of us, and you have just these three?" Migone said. "I don't like that balance."

"Without you, sir, there is just one of me."

IN THE CORRIDOR before making our way back up, Brownsword turned to me. "Mikey, you get your gear and set up in my cell. They'll slit your throat in your sleep if they can. You go nowhere alone. Kapish?"

"Yes, sir," I said. "I got it. Is he for real, sir?" I'd heard of infiltrators in the IA, and even among the terps, but had thought it was an anomaly or one of the many war myths that swirled around the bases, usually in the DFACs or over mindless card games.

"Oh, he's for real all right. We're fighting a cancer over here—and it has *metastasized*."

BACK IN OUR fetid section, under the silent gaze of the IA soldiers who'd taken up positions at either end, I grabbed my kit and carted it right over to Brownsword's cell. Already, he and Migone were bringing in sheets of plywood and tacking them to the gates, masking the guards' lethal views.

"We're gonna sleep in shifts and make sure we are hard targets," Brownsword said. "Mikey, you don't move from this cell unless I tell ya."

Then he pulled out his full arsenal and kitted up: M240 Bravo with two hundred rounds of ammo propped behind a sandbag at one end of the hallway—in case the terrorists thought about mounting an attack or lobbing in a grenade—jumpmaster blade strapped to the outside of his leg, pistols, combat knife, all in full view. Then he found a set of brass knuckles and slid them over his fingers and clenched his fist.

"Right now, I'm going to have myself a nice little tour of this rat's nest," he said.

"OK, sir," I said from the end of the bunk, and could feel my neck pulsing. The cell was cold, but the air was strangely oppressive. Like prey, I could sense our predicament with every living breath. Inside those bleak walls, we were trapped—only one way out.

"You know, Mikey," Brownsword said, checking his armor before leaving. "When I was in training stateside, they taught us to build trust by stripping off our gear, putting away our weapons—as a sign of good faith. But the reality is, this is the Middle East, not California. And right here, right now, we are sleeping in enemy territory. In this part of the world, you gotta display your strength full throttle. I know you Yazidi are pacifists, but you gotta let these guys know if they decide to fuck with you,

you won't hold back. Maybe even let them think you're a little bit crazy. You got that?"

"I got it, sir."

"I know it may go against your beliefs, but this is something you'll need to come to terms with soon. If our situation here is any indication of what's coming, and I think it is, you're going to need to remember what I'm telling you."

Then Captain Brownsword stepped into the hall and looked both ways as though he was checking the traffic. He cleared his throat and sauntered up and down the passage, conferring with the others before going out past the plywood-covered gates.

"You and your guys can scram," I heard him say to the Iraqi guards, and then he went whistling down the stairs.

DEEP INTO THE long night, the prison seemed to hold me in its jaws, considering. Every few minutes, I heard muted sounds reverberate as though we were in the vacant cavity of a prehistoric beast. I tried not to imagine the barbarism that had played out within those walls, but Captain Brownsword was right—they seemed to weep their cruel history.

Between restless waking dreams, I heard a noise and looked up to see a silhouette standing in the corridor before me, obscuring the bars.

"Who's there?" I called into the pitch, and felt the thunder of my heart.

But there was no answer and I sat up to peer into the heavy gloom.

I made out the wet sound of lips parting and could just see a dull light reflecting off teeth. The warm scent of fresh shisha reached me like a curse.

"RPG," I said to the darkness. "What is it?"

No answer. No movement whatsoever. The outline of the man stood stock still, looking in as though he saw right through the darkness and all the way into my skin.

Then in the faraway corridors, I could make out the echoes of Brownsword whistling *Yankee Doodle*, and the metallic raps and long clanks of his left hand running those brass knuckles against cell bars, no matter who was slumbering behind them. He'd been up and down every floor, all night long, raking the cells like a madman. Pistol ready in his right hand, half grin slicing his all-American face.

Several times he came back to check on the others and me.

The first time, he said, "The Iraqis have bored holes into the plywood, Mikey."

"Why would they do that, sir?"

"To watch us. If you lean out you can see them."

Now, I heard him making his way back, moving toward the turret. The form before my cell let out a small breath and recoiled. Then he moved slowly back down the hall, feet shuffling. I heard steel bars slide open and shut. Another man coughed into his tank. And I sat in the dark and waited for Brownsword.

Chapter Nine

General Petraeus

WE CRUISED IN THE HUMVEES, EAST ON HIGHWAY 47, PASSING just south of Qaryat al-Ashiq and Badush, known for its cement plant and prison and nothing more. Mile after wasted mile, not a living thing in sight. Then, under the lingering arm of the Tigris, we descended into her undulant colonized valley, skimming the dark viscera of Mosul. Blackbirds circled the carbon haze and trash danced over the road. Parallel to the track, military planes thundered down the runway, taking off against so many odds into a fuel-laced ozone that shimmered like cellophane. The thoroughfare cleaving Camp Marez from Diamondback always seemed like a road back into civilization: the DFAC with its salad bar and buffet lines, PX, and industrial laundry machines. Past wired checkpoints toward the gate in the throng of base traffic, a recent spring rainfall had rinsed the road clean; we slowed way down.

I was in the back, staring out, tired spine resting against the metal. iPod in my lap, headphones blaring. Every muscle, taut while out in the desert scrimmage, suddenly slackened. We'd have a few hours off to get ourselves together: wash our fatigues, eat a good meal, call mom before the next move-out. By now, I'd been through most of the motley outposts and HQs studded across the northern provinces, made a surprise visit to my startled Daki in Khanasor, had dinner with the rest of the team at Basim's house, shaved my head, bulked up lifting weights.

Dump truck at a standstill, idling near the last set of gates, we didn't think anything of it. Base traffic was as relentless as the conflict it fed: deliveries and convoys, food and fuel, coming and going sunup to sundown. We were ten minutes ahead of schedule—*on the nose*, Brownsword would tell me later. Any other day, we'd have made a scheduled pit stop to relieve ourselves, take a smoke, grab a Gatorade—and looking back, not one of us remembers why we just kept going on the 47. Maybe there was no reason at all, and in some ways that makes it harder. In a war, survival often hinges on the infinitesimal—the stupid. If we'd taken our break that day, we'd all be dead.

Moving through the final gate into Marez, we passed another combat advisory team, all fueled up, going out the other way in their convoy. In a standing position behind the "Pig," Brownsword waved and called out a *hello;* blurred faces and hands appeared briefly behind the armored windscreens. Even now, I can see them: the wide hollows of their young eyes, fleeting rise of their palms. How many times I've wished so hard to go back and stop that convoy in its tracks—we all have. In dreams, I run out screaming to no avail. Other times, I just watch them go again and again and again, finally waking tangled in the layers of my own sweaty sorrow. Our team knew that team, even if just on sight—every living soldier and terp. All of us, together, and so far from home.

Pulling into the motor pool, the hatch came down and I had my mind on one thing—a nice bowl of chicken noodle soup.

Saltine crackers on the side. I'd already asked the Filipino cook to show me how to make it. Boots on the ground in the lot, body armor and helmet still on, ear buds dangling; before I'd walked two paces, a mortal fault line suddenly cracked open across oblivion and called in its marker.

The ear-splitting explosion slashed the sky, pushed me sideways, and shook the earth. Every head in the lot went straight up. We all knew what to expect, and it all came: tower of smoke, a rush of hot wind from the ensuing fire, and then people running, running, running—mouths open, but soundless. Sirens blared. My ears were ringing. And I just stood there, watching the acrid smoke drive a black channel straight into heaven. Six soldiers vaporized. Two children standing on the side of the road erased from the world. Dozens wounded in diabolical ways. You could smell it.

Then I ran fast with my team and huddled against concrete barriers, where we waited coated in grime like sewer rats until the all-clear. Migone had his hands folded over his lap and stared into them as though into a chasm. Brownsword sat next to him doing the same. For a long time, none of us said a word, but we all shared the same thoughts, passing them between us like breaking bread together.

It was probably a fertilizer bomb—maybe a few thousand pounds. Brownsword thought he heard shots fired as we were pulling in; the soldiers must have known.

"This one is gonna stick, isn't it?" Migone said.

"Yeah, it is." When he spoke, it looked like Brownsword was moving a sharp stone around in his mouth.

It was Good Friday, April 10, 2009, and we'd just missed the deadliest attack against American forces in over a year, and the second in Mosul in months. Not because we were smarter or better equipped or saved for some predetermined purpose. Ten minutes—six hundred extra seconds on the clock—had bought us our lives. And all because not one of us had to get out and take a piss.

UNDER STRINGS OF Christmas lights and paper lanterns, sweaty bodies packed the dance floor set up in the yard. Music blared, voices crooned, and the lights overhead twinkled against a backdrop of spiraling streamers: all red, white, and blue. Even now, every Fourth of July, I think back to Ron Bowers, a self-declared man of God and country, who read me verses from the Bible and articles from the Constitution. Bowers taught me everything I knew about the United States of America, starting with "independence," a word I'd heard but never understood that you lived—until now. My country's sovereignty was declared on October 3, 1932, when the British gave up the last yoke of their rule, over 150 years after America split from the same crown. The similarities ended there—and you didn't need a history book to understand how.

Revelers in party hats had come from all over the FOB and other bases. By dusk dozens of soldiers and Iraqi personnel converged on PAD 2 for the barbecue and camaraderie, and to pretend for just a few hours that there wasn't a holy war raging past our doorstep. Migone and Brownsword told me that Spider's parties were always big and notorious. Out in the festooned yard, a sea of smiles, parting only when more food came in on aluminum trays. I could not imagine the time when I had not lived the raw base life and known those two gregarious men—we were brothers-in-arms and kinship, and the fact would be proven to me again and again.

The two of them sat back in folding chairs, with Zina, our new female terp, standing off to one side. Brownsword said we could end this war in no time if we just invited all the tribes and their sheikhs to have a sit-down, fire up the hookah, and make a few deals. It was finally occurring to the higher-ups that the war couldn't be won by bombing everything to smithereens; General David Petraeus wanted his officers in among the people, carving out allegiances.

I had met the general one time at Camp Taji in the sweltering late summer of 2008, while at a training conference for MiTTs. Petraeus was right: the tribes were the ones you have to answer to in Iraq. But if the rumors of a full US withdrawal were true, I wondered how those deals would hold when America was gone. There's no loyalty out in the desert.

The day Zina showed up at FOB Sykes with her long braided hair and lithe gusto, she gave me a sliver of hope for the future—and a female in fatigues to gaze upon like an apparition. If a young Arab woman was working the dirt and still kicking, I thought, things in the wider country must be improving. She also made cordon and search interrogations easier: wives and daughters, who were mute around the males in uniform, gravitated to her readily, and usually with the bitter truth. Married to and divorced from an American officer, desert-wise Zina had returned to the broken land of her birth to do her part to cobble it back together. In some ways, we were in awe of the woman Brownsword called "Zina the Warrior."

"Mikey," she kept asking me, "what are your plans after this? After the Coalition leaves?"

"Zina, they won't *all* leave—ever. The Americans still have bases in Germany and Korea and other places." I was trying to convince myself as much as her. I had seen firsthand what happened to Mosul after Petraeus left—it was what Migone called "a shit-show." But with all we'd been through, Team Spider had taken over my entire worldview. The truth was I could have gone on with them that way for years, and maybe I believed I would.

"If I were you, I'd get my family out and just start over. There's an American special visa program for terps. It's called an SIV. You should start thinking about it." Zina wasn't the first to say as much. "You're Yazidi, and that's even more dangerous than what I am."

"What do you mean—what you are? You're fine. Brownsword says it all the time: that Zina—she's *fine*." And I laughed.

"Don't act stupid, Mikey. I'm a woman—a whore for the West. They'd murder my family and burn down my house. It's already happening to some of us."

RPG had been listening to our conversation. Just then, he stepped in and handed over a new pack of buns, as I worked a dozen beef patties that hissed fat over the coals, flipping them one after the other like cards. "Lambs to the slaughter," he said—I can still hear him say it. I told them both that the worst was almost over, that we had protection now. My youthful optimism no more then a frustration, Zina would hear none of it.

RPG just winked at me.

Hours before, he and several terps had driven a pickup into Tal Afar's market streets to buy the young beast that now dripped its rich fat over a spit in the yard. RPG had been the one to slit the young lamb's throat in the crooked shade of the fence line, where he'd kept it tethered. From a distance, I'd caught sight of the animal's resigned black eyes when it turned its head momentarily and looked at me, just as the blade went down—it knew, and didn't even flinch as the thing was done. I remember still the first slaps of blood splashing over the dry dirt, and one of the others said RPG had used his knife better than a mullah.

I watched Brownsword work the dance floor, eyes half-shut. Migone was sprawled in a chair looking out into the shisha fog of the party in full swing. Even now, it amazes me how they could peel off their body armor in the very heart of the blistering Jazeera and live those hours as though tomorrow we weren't heading out past the wire again. I put more meat over the coals and realized I was doing exactly the same thing—nothing else to do but keep going.

If you didn't come back, you just didn't.

ONE YEAR LATER, in the summer zenith of 2010, I was called from the relative idyll of those northern outposts and down into Iraq's notorious desert bloodbath—Al-Anbar Province, better known as "the Sunni Triangle." The largest "governate" in the country, Anbar's strategic location on the Syrian, Jordanian, and Saudi borders made it the home base of AQI, who'd wrested control over the historic smuggling routes first carved out during the days of the Old Silk Road, back when the East traded culture and materials with the West, and without any carnage. From that solid foothold, AQI's leaders fanned into the villages, recruiting massive numbers of disgruntled, and therefore willing, native insurgents, and co-opted the sheikhs from the most powerful tribes.

Though predominantly Sunni, the insurgency was not monolithic, but was made up of myriad factions: Baathists, Salafi-Jihadi Islamists, and other elements from the ousted regime. Moreover, the insurgency's face changed perpetually like a chameleon, depending on the influence of external forces. In short order, they carried out an onslaught of complex mass-casualty suicide bombings.

I'd run around those merciless sands many times before, as a temporary terp supporting combat teams and officers, trying to put a lid on the mayhem and break up the nefarious enemy cells. The region was swarming with terrorist groups and criminal gangs, and we might as well have been trying to catch them all with plastic spoons. If Mosul was a city of bombs, Anbar was a kingdom of indiscriminate killing.

One man drove a fist through the rampant insurgency, becoming an icon to those who served under him, including me—General David Petraeus, commander of the Multi-National

Forces in Iraq (MNF-I). Under his authority beginning in February 2007, the boiling-over violence gradually tempered. In September 2008, Major General John Kelly had signed over the assumption of responsibility for security of Al-Anbar to Mamoun Rasheed, governor of the province.

The Coalition Forces had already started their withdrawal. Twenty-five thousand troops would remain in Anbar to continue to monitor and advise the Iraqi Security Forces (ISF) as they embarked on their first real attempt to take up the helm of their country. For my remaining time as a terp, I was sent all over the province, eventually spending two months in the terrain around Al Qa'im. General Petraeus had tamed Mosul in his time, but the Triangle was another beast all together. Optimistic casualty statistics aside, in Anbar you had to keep your nerve or you were dead—and now I was right back in the thick of it.

THE DESERT STANK like a sewer and the yellow-tinged air flickered dully as we crossed the empty field. Our convoy parked in a lot outside of Akashat, a small forsaken mining village on the busy smuggling route south of Al Qa'im. The bullet-bitten town walls stood as silent in the July broil as the clay from which they were made, but we knew that barrels were pointed at us from every direction. Those days, commanders of the Iraqi infantry division always made sure I had a loaded 9mm tucked into my belt.

Dogs barked, an infant wailed, cooking fumes rode the breeze—and then all went quiet. The inhabitants knew we were coming, and that we'd be leaving again soon enough.

After weeks patrolling the Anbar-fever, the skin on my face thickened to a dark rawhide, and I let my goatee grow out to a smooth Middle Eastern pelt. Before stepping out of the MRAP, I pulled a black balaclava right over my head and put on my shades. Everyone on the many teams I terped for out there knew me as "Mohammed" and made their assumptions—I kept a well-thumbed copy of the Koran in my kit and pretended to pray to Allah five times a day. If anyone asked, I could recite a whole litany of suras as though they were the poetry of my blood.

In those days, intelligence about high-value targets was gleaned from a growing network of informants within the upper echelons of the tribes. Lately, AQI had been wearing out its welcome, taking over the lucrative smuggling trade, apprehending fuel subsidies to fill their own coffers, imposing draconian Islamic laws and barbaric punishments for simple infractions like smoking tobacco. The elders who resisted often showed up on the side of the road missing their heads. Despite their weakening stranglehold in the region, the terror group still knew how to make an indelible point.

Entering the village, we walked in formation down the empty main drag, grim houses to either side; each window stood open to a dark void. Dozens of eyes were on us; we could all feel it like a shift in the breeze. I translated as the usual suspects of bomb makers, bandits, and smugglers were hauled out. Criminals of every ilk still called the border villages home.

On that particular day, we were after a number of HVTs, and I held each nefarious face in my mind as we entered the first location: a simple mud hut like the one I was born in. Photographs of suspects were tacked to the walls of the Iraqi police HQ, and we were told to study them after each meeting. Same routine—one shiftless town after another. You got used to it: the screaming children and whimpering wives. In short order, there was a line of terrorists standing by the trash-filled gutter, hands zip-tied and an IA officer draping black hoods over their bowed heads. I watched as one man wet his pants, the urine pooling at his bare feet. He didn't so much as move a toe.

"Look at those motherfuckers," the American team sergeant said into my ear.

On the way back to the lot, I could hear several men fulminating about the heat and talking about getting some Gatorades out of the cooler. When I pulled back the sweat-soaked balaclava, a torrent of my own rancid breath escaped, and I gulped the dry-as-a-bone air. Then a boy ran across the lot grinning, arms flailing like a mad bird, and several others chased after him. They didn't even glance at us. We all stopped at once, and swallowed our hearts, checking each kid over for the telltale lumps of suicide vests. Weapons poised—nothing. You could see the indentations of their ribs though their careworn shirts. A bird of prey sailed over the village walls and hovered. I looked at it awhile, thinking of Khanasor, and tugged at my new beard.

Then that silent wink of time splintered as a deafening sound cracked the empty firmament. Several yards away from me, a huge parabola of red-tinged dirt went up like a fountain in the lot. My ears roared as I fell, suddenly blinded. I knew the moment for what it was and waited on my back, head pounding. My pulse and breath quickened together.

Moments later a wet spot on my leg became apparent and I touched it, fumbling for holes, but the torn up skin had gone numb. Reefs of dust fell over me like snow as I gazed up blinking, listening to the cries and pleas of the fallen, who lay strewn all around me. We held our collective breath for the bursts of gunfire that never came. In a moment, I tried to go up on my elbows, and waited, staring out for someone, anyone. Through the miasma of war, I saw nothing but a blurry mayhem: bodies and parts of bodies scattered over the ground, bits of twisted metal, and live soldiers rushing in every direction. I heard the baying of a lamb in the adjacent field and smelled burning meat. Turning to the side, I vomited.

In a moment, a dust-covered medic appeared like a phantom and started cutting away at my pant leg. I could hear the fabric tear and saw him peering in. He slipped on a new pair of latex gloves. Soon, I could feel his fingers prodding around inside me, but no pain, and I wondered if he hadn't already given me the shot.

"Is it that bad?" I said to him. My eyes roved the wounded spread over the field in strange tangles of limbs, under a dirty veil of smoke. "Why aren't you treating them first?"

"Them who?" he said. "They're all cooked. Another medic's working on the captain, but it's not looking good. Just lie down. You're going into shock. Listen, in a second, your leg is gonna burn pretty bad."

Then he tore open a packet and poured the contents of thick white powder like icing sugar all over my hemorrhaging calf. Right then, the naked depth of my pain revealed itself—I'd just dipped my leg into the pit of hell. I started to scream, and before I could stop, my voice seemed to rush back into me. All I saw was a searing white light. Hands dragged me up by the armpits and the world disappeared.

WHEN THEY PULLED me on the stretcher into Camp Taji, a massive military installation seventeen miles north of Baghdad, I stared to one side over the sprawling motor pool and my lids flickered. I heard someone say they were going to send me north to the hospital at Balad. There were incoming wounded everywhere. Doped up on battlefield narcotics, my mind and body cleaved, and each seemed to go about its business independent of the other. I'd been in that nebulous place before. Voices blared from an overhead speaker, and helos beat the hazy air over me. Hundreds of vehicles were parked in the lot like tamed metal beasts, engines still ticking—but I was suddenly there in another time altogether, walking over the ground that seemed to give way under me—under us all. When I opened my eyes, I was in Taji before Akashat, before a lot of things. In my mind it was July 2008, and I was a teenage kid in loose fatigues and full of swagger.

I SAW MYSELF jumping out of a Humvee, kicking up dirt under my boots. High fives to the others; tossing my duffel over one shoulder and shoving a slice of Juicy Fruit gum in my mouth. I'd been invited to Camp Taji to participate at the MiTT academy and a large-scale meeting, headed up by some of the top commanders in the Coalition and ISF. General David Petraeus, the man who had put al-Qaeda on the ropes, was at the helm. During his command in Iraq the general made it a regular event to meet with the MiTT teams at Taji. It had been an honor to be one of the few chosen participants that day, and a testament to my loyalty. I walked that colossal base, a city unto itself, broad-shouldered and sure, feeling for the moment like the man I wished to become.

When General Petraeus strode across the base, you felt America and all her might descend like an Apache gunship. A few seconds of reverent silence, and then cheers erupted. He was dressed as most any other grunt; only the four plain stars stitched to his cap betrayed the breadth of his power. More than anyone, General Petraeus was also the man to whom my fellow citizens and I had pinned our dwindling hopes for a lasting peace.

First and foremost, the general understood that to secure the people, the military had to live among them; clear out the terrorists, excise the criminal elements, hold the area, and rebuild from the bottom up. He had also forged coalitions among the disaffected sheikhs, and sought reconciliations with the alienated Sunni tribes. His doctrine seemed to be taking hold: casualties and car bombs were way down. The fact wasn't surprising: when Petraeus took command of Mosul, he'd reined in her furies—and as soon as he left, they'd all returned with a vengeance.

When I watched the general cross the floor and stand before us, I listened to him in awe and made a simple plan: finish high school and apply to an American university. As long as he was in command of Iraq, I believed I was in charge of my future— and that I even had one.

THEN I WAS back on a gurney in another trauma ward, waiting in a drug-fueled stupor. Part of me moved back and forth between 2008 and 2010 like a pendulum. A nurse leaned down, shined a penlight into my eyes, and I squinted. Someone pushed a line into my arm and fluid started to fill my veins. It wasn't as bad as I thought: I'd heard them talking about shrapnel, razor blades and nails they'd have to pull out before stitching up the wounds. Blood loss. No matter, the drugs were still coursing through me like a spell, and I heard the nurse say, "His name is Shaker Jeffrey, a.k.a. Mohammed. He's in shock. They drugged him up real good."

THEN IT WAS 2008 again, and I was standing out on the airfield straddling Taji, General Petraeus striding toward me—just as it had happened. A warm wind sent papers spiraling across the tarmac, and I watched as several officers chased after them; but the general kept walking with his entourage, eyes dead ahead. Moments later, he was standing right next to me, a hand reaching out and grabbing mine as we fell right into a conversation about Yazidis, Khanasor, and my job as terp. Even now, I still see those few minutes with the general on the airfield as the most thrilling moment of my service to the American military. I told General Petraeus that so far I'd taken bullet wounds to my leg and foot and he asked questions about the injuries. The wind grew stronger out there, sending the flags flapping, and we had to lean in to hear each other.

"Son," the general said, "you are the guys between us and them. We couldn't do our job without you."

"Thank you, sir," I heard myself say, as I'd practiced for hours. "Is it true, General, sir, that you are leaving Iraq?" Even then, I knew that President George W. Bush had appointed the general to head up US Central Command; it was the talk all over the news, and across the bases, that it was time for the United States to get out of that war.

General Petraeus nodded and looked me straight in the eye. "The president gives me my orders. You know how it is."

"Yes, sir. I respect the American president and his decisions, sir."

We talked a while longer about the war and my country, and then he patted my shoulder and said, "Stay safe, son."

Just two months later, on September 16, 2008, General Petraeus signed over command of Iraq to General Raymond T. Odierno and I held my breath.

I SNAPPED OUT of the flashback, and opened my eyes. My head swiveled on the gurney as the corpses were brought in in their black bags, and someone told me they were all Iraqi army, including the captain. Not one American. Hard to tell if it was real or I was dreaming, but I could still feel the gusts from the airfield buffeting my hair and I sensed someone give me another shot; a hand pushed me down, and I slipped back again.

WAR DRUGS TRANSPORTED me to the DFAC at Taji, after the conference had wound up, the top brass long gone. I was eating Taco Bell, junk food stalls all around me, the smell of hot grease. Soldiers and support staff at the next table were arguing about the troop withdrawal and it was getting heated. Violence was going down; too soon to tell if it would hold. Some wanted out of the war now instead of waiting years; others said this whole thing was a disaster—more than half of Americans believed the invasion had been a mistake. I heard the phrase *clusterfuck*, and made a mental note. I was eating alone, thinking about my conversation with the general on the tarmac, and everything I'd learned about at the conference.

"You all right there?" a voice said, and a man sat down next to me. A purple sash was draped around his neck and a gold cross gleamed. He had a steaming cup of coffee in his hand; he took a sip and looked me over as he drank. Finally: "You don't look OK—I saw you out there with the general."

"He's leaving Iraq."

The priest nodded. "Some point, we're all leaving."

"What does that mean for us still living here?"

He glanced down into his cup, as though reading the future from the surface. Leaning in, his voice barely above a whisper: "Don't tell anyone I told you this, but this whole country is going to descend into hell—that's what it means."

"I don't understand," I said.

Then his voice lowered like a boom.

"I'd get out of here well before then. It's going to be a slaughterhouse."

Chapter Ten

Left Behind

I WALKED THE DESOLATE TRACK PAST THE GATE IN A COLLARED shirt and blue jeans and waited for my smuggler's cab home. Same long road, opposite direction this time—December 2011. It had been four years since I arrived. Now at all of twenty-one, I felt a thousand years old. Even my name—Shaker—seemed like a fragment from a faraway time and of another person entirely: a poor farmer's boy in mismatched shoes selling cold sodas to the troops.

Under the dull crown of a just-burgeoning dawn, my tired country seemed comatose in its stilled and forsaken miles. Daily attacks and bombings, though fewer, had persisted—Sunni insurgents and Shiite militias backed by Iran. President Nouri al-Maliki said his fledgling forces had a good grip on the situation, but it was much too soon to tell. I kicked a stone a pace and counted up my stack of cash. Military trucks idled along the barriers; two Iraqi men in uniform limped out of the morning gloom smoking, one of them dragging a goat.

It was the tail end of the military withdrawal that began in December 2007, and the last convoys of American troops were making their way south on Highway 1 toward Kuwait. People stood quietly along the ditches and swells of marshland, watching them go out just as they'd watched them invade eight long years before. This time, anyone could see it all unfold live on television. In army bases across the nation, motor pools sat empty and the catering companies had packed up their elaborate kitchens. No more Taco Bell or Popeye's Chicken. The sovereign state of Iraq was on her own—and so was I.

When the driver pulled up blaring his horn, I dumped my satchel into the trunk; the hookah nestled inside a taped-up box on the back seat. Nothing else to my name. Standing in the patch of grassland next to the airfield, a shepherd boy watched me awhile, spat in the dirt without lowering his eyes, and then turned to his grazing sheep. One after the other, planes soared off the runway, plunging into puffs of cloud that sat like anchored warships against the leaden sky.

Driving in the glut of traffic along the 47 past the shelled-out buildings and stretches of ruined walls, I cracked the window to let in gusts of cooling air. The winter sun was pale and easy with its light. *Shamag* wrapped about my neck, my sunken eyes scanned the freed world outside, and I brushed the 9mm tucked in my waistband—I'd hide it in the duffel as soon as we pulled in to Khanasor. The driver gave me a sideways glance and fingered the radio dial. Static crackled and voices jabbered in Arabic. I didn't like having the pistol, but not having it wasn't an option.

Brownsword's voice rose from the tides of my memory: "Mikey, you pack heat from now on or you'll end up packed under ten feet of sand," he'd said to me in the DFAC before he left. "Who knows which way the winds are gonna blow."

We'd said our good-byes months ago—all back slaps, bear hugs, and swallowed male pride—when the first units disbanded during the gradual two-year withdrawal. Right on schedule, ready or not. All those long farewells to my American brothers and sisters in arms were like a slow bleed.

"And when anyone asks you what you were doing during the occupation?" Brownsword tested me later while checking over his kit. In less than an hour, he'd be thirty thousand feet in the air, heading west to the other side of the world. Another life entirely.

"Construction—in the cities. I got it, sir. No problem."

"Good boy," Migone added, holding out an envelope full of dinars. "Just take that and be quiet about it. Changing cash around here is a son of a bitch. Send it home to mom."

Then Lieutenant Colonel Migone looked me in the eye long and hard, as though seeing a thing buried deep inside me that he didn't want to say out loud. And he turned away without another word, hoisting his duffel and kicking up the dirt next to Brownsword, before ascending the ramp to the chopper. Both men glanced back in their turn, disappearing into the bird as though into the mouth of a cave. I held the image a long time like a comforting hand, and then let the memory go to the carbon fog outside the groaning car, as the driver next to me pumped the gas.

The old sedan was straddling the road next to a trash dump that sprawled like a gangrenous city all its own, and where whole families lived in makeshift dwellings, satellite dishes lashed to the corrugated tin roofs. Children crawled all over the mounds like ants, picking through the stinking heaps searching for scraps of metal to sell at the markets. It was all some of them did all day long. For years, the rash of squalor beyond the bases had seemed so remote, but it hit me hard now.

Mile after slow mile, I stared out at my splintered country through the grimy window—the Iraqi police standing around at the checkpoints talking into their radios or smoking—and saw what others could not: the corruption, infiltrators, and fear.

One night in the Fortress, an afternoon lost in Syria, wannabe soldiers hosing down the desert with bullets. In Mosul alone, I was sure, insurgents could pick them off like sandgrouse.

"A baby doesn't learn to walk from its mother's arms," the driver said to me, as though reading my mind. "All they did was come here and piss all over us."

Maybe some of us pissed all over ourselves, I wanted to say, but offered, "Sure. It will take time," instead.

I still had hope, but was no longer careless with it.

THE CAR VEERED west, away from Tal Afar, and a signpost seemed to hurtle past and right through me: SHINGAL. We were driving over the ancient stretch of desert I'd crisscrossed in the Humvees, and visions of the past came at me like flash cards: arms of the sacred mountain rising like an ark; farm buildings lazing in the spooned-out valley; a water tower in the distance; Sergeant White's hands over mine on the baseball bat. And not long ago, Basim's house on the far side of Khanasor—Team Spider all there, sitting shoulder to shoulder around the long floor mat, steaming plates of fragrant food filling the center: couscous, grilled lamb, cucumbers in yogurt, stacks of fresh naan. We all ate with our fingers until we sagged and had to sit way back. Migone grabbed his belly, exhaled, and called out for mercy, and still Basim's smiling mother brought out more food.

"Is this how they all are?" whispered my brother Samir, sitting next to me, his face flushed with ale.

"Yes," I said to him. "It is."

HOME. THE LAST time I'd been there, I'd brought back small sacks of American candies and taught my mother how to make chicken noodle soup.

"Shaker, tell me how to greet the Americans when they come here to eat," she'd said to me, all excited.

And the next day, as half a dozen soldiers crossed the threshold carrying bags of food from the markets, my mother rushed in from the courtyard, holding out her hands.

"Hello and welcome," she sang out, grabbing them each by the shoulders and squeezing. "Hello and welcome, you sons of bitches!"

And minutes later, the joke revealed, the team all stood there doubled over in their fatigues, tears streaming down their faces, as Daki whipped me hard with a towel and I ran around the room in circles trying to stop myself from laughing.

"You spank your boy good and hard, Mrs. Jeffrey, until his scrawny little butt is nice and raw. Translate that, Mikey, you little shit."

WINDOW OPEN. POTS of herbs on the sill. Smells of good food, the cupboards full—I didn't have to go inside just yet to know it. Instead, I stood in the street looking in as though watching a dream, duffel bag and box at my feet, as my family moved about the front room. My brothers and their wives tore off bites of naan as they stared at the television sitting on a stand in the corner. Dapîra sat wrapped in her blue shawl, dozing. They were watching a show about cooking; a woman decorated delicate pastries that looked like flowers, and I heard my mother let out an *ooh*.

New refrigerator in the corner, the freshly painted walls as white as paper. There was a satellite dish propped to the roof, a water tank with a heater, and colorful dresses and cotton shirts flapped like bright flags from the line. A small hatchback sat in the street, and I ran my hand along the fender. Still warm and ticking. I heard Naïf say he'd taken it to buy bags of coal at market, just as I'd asked. I felt for the roll of cash tucked away in my pocket and thought of my Babo.

"What do you think of me now, I wonder?" I said to the sky.

Then I picked up my things, smiled, and stepped across the threshold and into the warm embrace of home. I'll just begin again, I thought, and went to hug my mother, and kiss the top of Dapîra's head.

STANDING IN THE courtyard over our patch of dirt, I fanned the red coals and tried to remember everything Migone had told me about manning the barbecue. Fat dripped from the cooking chicken skins and I basted the legs in a thick brown sauce. Kraft Hickory—I'd come back with several bottles.

Set up in the corner, the grill sent up puffs of aromatic heat like a lazy afternoon, transporting me right back to FOB Sykes, and I cracked open a cold soda. Haji watched me from one of the lawn chairs on the other side as I sliced open a pack of hot dogs and dropped one on the grill. I explained the importance of the onions, relish, mustard, and ketchup on hot dogs and burgers.

Haji was quiet, looking from me to the main door and back again. He lit up the hookah and took several long deliberate puffs. Coals hissed and tambour music thrummed from an adjacent yard. We could hear Daki moving about in the heart of the house, her voice soft and harmonious and finally freed of all her cares. She was practicing the American movie slang I'd taught her.

"Hey, you want a piece of me?" she said in slow English.

Haji got up, closed the door, and went back to the lawn chair.

"Shaker," he said, sitting on the end, elbows on his knees. He was rubbing his hands together, a nervous habit picked up from our mother.

I crossed the dirt and handed him the dressed up hot dog on a plate. Haji bit a chunk off the end and chewed fast, a round bulge planted in his cheek; mustard pooled at the corner of his mouth. Then he swallowed and waited a moment, considering.

"Weird," he said at last. "But good." And then he paused, weighing his words. "I saw the pistol in your bag."

I knew what was coming, but let him have his say. The smoldering grill kept my hands busy, and I made a show of moving around pieces of meat.

"A translator was murdered on the road to Tal Afar last night."

"I know."

"It's like the tenth one this month. There have been kidnappings, beheadings all over Nineveh. Elsewhere, too. There's a list of you guys, especially the ones who worked for the commanders. They say you worked for lieutenant colonels and met General Petraeus, the American, in Taji. Why would you do that?"

"My job was construction. In the cities."

"It's an execution list, brother."

"Yup," I said. "That's why I have the gun."

"I wish I had known it was going to be this bad. We are grateful, but the price is too high."

Then I put the tongs down and looked up from the grill. For a moment, I held my brother's face in the hard fist of my unwavering gaze. A strange sensation of rage was creeping up from my gut like thin flame and I worked a moment to tamp it down.

"It was the right thing to do for us and for the country, and I don't regret it."

Haji nodded and I knew he understood that the daydreaming little brother floating in the pool of well water and shepherding lambs was long gone. I told him not to worry—I knew the dangers and how to "watch my six." My plan was to finish school and to try and get to America through the Special Immigrant Visa (SIV) program.

Standing in the yard of our concrete house and working the barbecue was disquieting. It was as though no time at all had passed, and yet nothing was the same—starting with me.

BENEATH A MANTLE of stars, all of Shingal slept. But forty miles to the west, disgruntled Sunnis with blood on their minds continued to creep over the rat-line and into our wasteland. Bats slipped in and out of the sky as though through small tears in the sky, and I watched them, wide awake night after night, until sunrise.

Lying on a mat by the wall, I stared at the damp clothes sagging like deflated body parts on the line. The iPod sat in my lap, and I toggled through tunes, each one releasing memories of bases and friends, so far away now. Lately, I had trouble remembering small things about them that I wished to hold on to. Eye color. Middle names. The sound of a laugh. Sometimes, I think I left part of myself back in Mosul and out on the sands, and I thought of all the soldiers I'd seen who'd lost their limbs. I was missing something, but there was nowhere to go—no Walter Reed hospital for souls that would give me a new one. Maybe it was just "Michael"—the name—I was missing.

Gradually, streams of thought coalesced into a drowsy stupor, and I fell into more waking dreams as though into a well. Night after night, it was always the same.

EYES WIDE OPEN, I strained to see through the gloom—winter, 2008. We'd been working the streets for days in a row; my insides churned with tasteless MREs. Bowers and Faulkner had the HVT by the collar, and then the IA officers took over, pushing and kicking him along the corridor. Under a black hood, the man grunted like an animal, his hands working at the ties that clamped his fists together behind his back.

We moved into a small room with a table and chairs, and they shoved him down into a metal seat. Bowers stood back against the wall and Faulkner slid over a chair. All the sounds in the hot room seemed amplified. It felt like being inside a bunker.

Colonel Dildar was already there watching, waiting. Then he gave a signal, and at the rise and fall of his hand, an officer pulled off the black hood. The face underneath was roughed up, hard to tell how badly under the sheen of oily sweat and urban filth. A mess of blood and spit smeared one side of his swollen bug-bitten jowls. He had a belly like a barrel and belched several times; everything he did in there was passive and deliberate. They were all the same. The higher-ups in the terrorist networks always looked nonplussed and well fed.

As soon as Colonel Dildar spoke, I took my position at his side, sitting down between him and the suspect, who stared at the table in his stinking clothes. I concentrated on the words I heard, and those I uttered back and, for the moment, not much else.

"Real name?"

"*Eat shit*," the suspect said to me in Arabic, and spat.

"Try again."

"Screw you."

And it would go on for hours.

When the others went out for a break, Faulkner, Bowers, and I were left alone. The overhead lights went out for a beat and came back on again. A fly buzzed against the ceiling and I exchanged a look with Bowers. Somewhere along the outside hallway, a door slammed shut and I flinched.

That's when the suspect slid his eyes over to me and sniffed at the air. He brought his purple lips together like mating worms.

Faulkner shuffled through papers; Bowers was just looking straight ahead in the shadows.

"*Ya sharmouta*," the man uttered under his breath. "You bitch. Working for these dogs."

I'd been through the same routine before many times, and said nothing.

"Shingal," he said, and clucked his tongue on the roof of his mouth.

I just sat there stock-still.

"Can smell it on you like a dog's shit."

Faulkner slapped down his pen and looked over. "What's he saying, Michael?"

"Just a bunch of nonsense, sir, about the way I smell."

And I shrugged.

A moment later, the militant sat back and chuckled at the ceiling, and then looked back at me like I was an animal he'd cornered.

"Khanasor, I'm thinking. Your English is too good."

I knew the blood that stained his shirt like war paint was not his own; some of the leaders liked to take off the heads themselves, and that's where all this talk was going. But by now, my own blood had stirred, and an ancient call to defend what I held most dear spread out from the very center of my body. When he spoke next, I was ready.

"You filthy devil-worshipping Yazidi pig," he started up again. "Your women were made to be our whores. When these dogs all run home, I'll fuck your sisters and make you watch before I slit your throat."

The open back of my hand flew out like a catapult and clocked him hard. My third finger snapped like a wishbone.

But Faulkner and Bowers already had me in a hold, and were dragging me out kicking and panting.

And before I was all the way out the door, I watched him lean to the side and smear his bleeding nose against his shoulder. Then he offered me a raw impassive gaze in which all the dark hatreds of Mosul stirred.

"See you soon, Michael," he said out loud and laughed.

And I could feel I'd be taking him at his word.

STILL ON THE roof and wide-eyed, I came to, mouth open and dripping. Fresh pain still shot along my finger, and I held my hand up against the full moon. Then I touched the ground all around me: the rough concrete that made up the roof of our house. The sweat-drenched sheets that were stuck to my skin.

Winds had gathered and were gusting, sending the clothes flapping on the line. And I looked over to see Haji's silhouette moving toward me. I filled my lungs. Felt my heartbeat.

"You OK, brother?" Haji said into the night. "We heard you cry out."

"Yes," I whispered, and grabbed the drink he held out to me in the silvered darkness. He tried to convince me that it would get better soon. I drank the water that was so cold and full of moonlight, and then I listened as Haji's footfalls faded, until all I could hear were my own quick breaths and the wild dogs howling along the slumbering hills.

Chapter Eleven

Dil-Mir

A BOOK LAY OPEN BEFORE ME LIKE AN OFFERING ON THE DESK. The big room was bright and empty as a tank and I was all alone in it, waiting for the others to come. Years ago, this had all been a matter of routine: getting up in the morning, boiling an egg, filling my satchel with notebooks and pens, the carefree walk to school along the unswept lanes. I ran a hand over the smooth bleached paper, caressing the surface as though it were new skin, fingers tracing the many lines of black ink. Words. Pages and pages of them stacked into the tens of thousands—a whole world containing worlds, bound to a feeble spine. To me they might as well have been meaningless jumbles of letters. Anyone walking in and seeing my fingertips whispering back and forth across the text would have mistaken me for a blind man. In a way, I was.

As soon as the bell rang, an avalanche descended. The doors flung open and a torrent of warm bodies rushed in, jabbering, laughing, and filling up the vacant rows. The stench of sleep and young sweat was overpowering; I took in a gulp of air through my mouth. A few curious glances thrown in my direction, but I just sat there still as a stone. I kept my eyes tied to the open page and concentrated hard on the first sentence—

—and got no further. The other students were unloading their bags and setting up their desks. Nothing more on their minds than the next break and another tedious day ahead. Hard to believe I'd once been one of them.

When the teacher walked in in her robes, I slipped back my chair and stood among the others, returning her greeting in a monotone unison. Somewhere behind me, a boy fell into a coughing fit. The windows were open and I looked out at the sky. Clouds and electrical wires—everything in its place. A car revved and soft music poured from the adjacent streets. The teacher was calling out the attendance list, but I could barely hear her. Then the sound of her voice intoning my name wrenched me into a sudden panic. I couldn't speak for one full minute, or escape the cyclone of thoughts that seemed to engulf me:

Michael. Mohammed. Mikey.

You look like a badass, and I need one good badass this morning.

Time had splintered into fragments, and I just stood there drowning inside an invisible maelstrom.

She said my name again, and finally I pulled up my hand and nodded.

"Here," I breathed, heaving out the word like a boulder.

But I was not there at all.

IN MY LAST months at FOB Sykes, Iavecchia showed me how to breach time and space in mere nanoseconds.

"You heard about Facebook, Mikey?" he'd said, clacking at the keyboard.

People. Millions of them, all at my fingertips. And now that the war was over, I would need the miracle of that simple gift to sustain me. Little did I know that one day it would also come to save my life.

The first time I typed in the name "Ronald Bowers" and saw his dimpled American face fill up the screen, I felt a thrill of disbelief. Then whole albums of my smiling friend unfolded in vivid color: our time in Iraq, his family and happy-go-lucky life back in Idaho, all delivered at a mere click. Soon a whole population of military friends and schoolmates were at my fingertips. Joining Facebook was like opening a door to a hidden bridge over a chasm.

After returning to Khanasor in 2011, I would sit up late at night, alone and trolling through old faces and photos on my laptop, searching for echoes of the people I'd known and the person I'd been—Michael—sitting in the back of the MRAP with my tambour, manning the BBQ at the FOBs, out on patrol, playing cards. I longed to crawl inside each frame to live it all again for just a while. And then skirting yet another sleepless night of horrors, Bowers sent a message from his side of the world like a flare going up:

"Are you there?"

"Yes, brother," I answered fast.

And my secret living hell was explained.

WHEN OUR TEAMS of warriors disbanded, back to humdrum domestic lives of garbage collections, school runs, and six o'clock dinners, a strange fever of symptoms unleashed itself into our collective blood—rage, hallucinations, full-blown panic. Some days, the future felt as hopeless as a terminal disease and the hours passed away without any meaning. Ron Bowers understood it all and told me about the service members who'd gone home and attempted suicide, were rapidly divorced, had taken to pill popping and drink. And he'd used a single word to describe the malignant sensation that seemed to bind us all like a poisoned strand of DNA—*doom*. The most hardened soldiers wept in their sleep, he said, hollered at their young children, accused strangers of some murderous intent. Sanity had become a flimsy thing, slipping through fingers like the sands over which so many of us had seen men and women let go of their souls.

Not long before the night Bowers reached out into the void, he'd collapsed. And maybe that's why he called on me, on anyone. Together in that void, me on my roof in Khanasor, and him on his sofa in Idaho, it was as though no time at all had passed.

"I don't know what happened," he said. "One minute I'm in the 7-Eleven looking for a loaf of whole wheat, the next thing I know I'm somewhere else, backing into the shelves, cans of food falling all around me, not able to breathe. Might have been a smell, or a sound. But something triggered it. And then this guy, he comes in and grabs hold of me—he just grabbed hold of me, and pulled me close with both his arms. Tight. You know, any other time, I would have slugged that guy. But he was one of us, and somehow he knew—he knew how to bring me back."

"What did he say?" I asked, grazing the concrete ocean with my fingertips.

"He just kept saying: *I got you. I got you. You're here.*"

"Will this thing we have ever go away, brother?"

"I don't know, Mikey, it's just there. But my wife is going to kick me out if I don't get it together. I mean, how do you go back to watching TV next to the missus when you've spent a year dodging bombs in Mosul?"

Bowers never took to calling me by my given name, Shaker. When I talked to the guys, I was forever Mikey, and I liked it that way.

"Maybe in time it will get better," I said. "It's what they say."

"You don't peel off a whole war like a Band-Aid, Mikey—especially not a farm boy like you. That's all I know."

IN THE SPRING, I started the car, my family all packed inside it, trunk stuffed, roof rack teetering, and took the beat-up track toward the foot of our sacred mountain. Back and forth, I made the same drive to and from the villages, ferrying cousins, aunts, and uncles for the annual pilgrimage known as the Cemayî, which we undertook to restore our weather-beaten shrines.

Up on the terraced foothills, the great hull of Mount Shingal sat docked against the vacant azure, sun just burning off the morning haze. The smell of fresh meat was thick in the air, and wood smoke from the early fire pits ambled along the grassy apron. A few first blooms showed on the red rose bushes in the holy gardens, and standing on the cultivated bank I could just make out our old farmlands spread out far below like a long emerald patch. Further up the terraced lengths that stood like a giant's staircase hacked into the rocky hillside, I glimpsed the white spires of our temple with its burnished peak molded into the shape of the sun.

White tents were set up like miniature houses across the leveled fields, and whole tribes crowded inside and outside them: eating, cooking, napping, playing music together. We would all live there, sleeping and rising to celebrate for days, until our monuments were repainted, the temple rooms restored, and the food ran out.

I walked right through that sea of kin that numbered in the thousands, in a bright scene that had played out in peace across Shingal throughout my lifetime, and felt at one with my people and the land we lived on. Up narrow steps made up of cut slabs of ancient rock, I joined the long line to our small temple and waited my turn. Not far from that place, thin canopies of trees shaded the hallowed ground where my father's bones metamorphosed into eternity.

Why did God put the mountain there for us? I heard my young boy's voice say on the tide of wind.

Because he knew we might need it one day. To give our people a place to hide in. The breeze whispered into my ear, and I felt Babo press his hand over mine.

WITHIN THE HEART of the sacred room, dim as a grotto, I knelt over the smooth stone ground. For every wish uttered to God inside the temple, we tied a small knot into the billowing curtain. By the end of the pilgrimage a bright constellation of knotted longings decorated the silks, untied only to make room for others while setting free our secret dreams. Maybe that day I fastened a wish to love, or to find peace in my heart. These were all I ever needed—even now.

When I wandered back to our field and stood along the ledge looking down into the neighboring meadow, I saw her. A few meters from the cemetery yard, she just stood there like a column, as though waiting for my lonesome eyes—so tall, and lithe as a flowering vine. Her white fingers flickered like wings over the black linen of her long skirt, nails lacquered to blood-red petals that matched the shade of her blouse. Closing my eyes this very moment, I can still repaint her in minute detail. And the thing I wish never to forget: her rich tresses worn *por vekeri*—open hair. Those heavy strands poured in midnight streams down her back. Five feet from the stones over my father's grave, she was alone.

Guitars played and people danced in wild circles. Groups of girls flitted about. Some had their faces buried in small mirrors, smearing on lipstick and dabbing their cheeks. Not her. She wore her alabaster skin like her gaze, clean and free of any artifice.

"She's very pretty," said my sister Nadia, leaning into my ear.

"Maybe you could go down there and find out her name. Please say your brother Shaker would like to say hello."

And I watched Nadia clamber down to the field in her sundress and make her way through a wall of gyrating dancers. Lost in a reverie, the girl still hovered in place. But then, as though mocking my desperation, the crowd converged into itself like a curtain closing over the grass, obliterating my perfect vantage, and I lost sight of her.

Minutes later, Nadia was back all pink-cheeked and breathless. "She said she doesn't know you, Shaker. Nothing I can do. But she was nice."

Hours later, while sitting back on the crowded stairs that centuries of sandals had worn down at the center, I saw her again. Between two chattering friends, she strolled a long path that meandered like a ribbon toward the temple. If only I could know her name, I thought, I would overcome the mute spell that that first sight of her had put me under. Then as the trio strode past, her companion tripped, and as she leaned over to hold out a helping hand her skirt brushed against me. I looked up and she was staring down, sunlight spilling all over her.

"Are you all right?" I said after several heartbeats.

Then she smiled at me, still moving down the steps, and opened a trap door into eternity.

By morning, the field below ours stood vacant and she was gone. All I learned was where she'd come from, like a prophecy— a tiny nameless hamlet, some forty miles from Khanasor, on the south side of the mountain. Sitting like a speck of dust over the desert floor and tucked far from the main roadways, the village was as hard to uncover as a stolen secret. Still, every free day for nine straight months, I got into my car and drove like a man possessed around the base of Shingal in search of her. She was like a ghost. A being from some other world. A narcotic. Block after block, my eyes roved her narrow village lanes, passing cars, peering into the open windows of houses, scouring alleys and crossing fields where people were out harvesting; but it was as though she'd existed only in some lonely chamber built from the ruins of my mind.

Sometimes, I believed I was going mad. Time gave way, weeks collapsed, and the heat of summer beat through the car, but failure could not break me. I must have driven a thousand miles on irrational faith alone. I only wanted to know her name—that's what I told myself. A suffocating man only hopes for a single breath.

It might have been late afternoon in Khanasor, the light low against the plains. I was hurrying through the market, looking for shoes, a dress shirt, or some other trivial garment. Cars moved slowly along the roadways; a recent spell of rain left the ground in a perfumed steam that permeated everything, and I walked alone.

One block, then two, and I passed by a dress shop and glimpsed a neighbor's wife running her hands along the heavy racks of clothes. Catching sight of me wandering by, she raised a palm, called out. And I nodded, thinking nothing—then in a thunderclap that traveled right through me, time came to a halt. Barely a foot away and standing by the counter, the girl was there. I was sure. Moments later, as though sensing my famished eyes, she turned. One look from her was all it took—my world riven in two.

"Shaker, meet my friend," Farida said to me.

"We've met before," I said, my mind fumbling. "Perhaps you don't remember."

"I'm not sure," the girl laughed, coming over. "How do you know me?"

At the first notes of her voice, it seemed the universe came to life. Then she told me her name—Dil-Mir—and made everything new.

ONE PHONE CALL a week turned to three, then five, then twenty. We discovered all the things we shared; our values, love of children and cooking—the want for a home. University degrees. The desire for peace in our time and on our land. Faith in God above all things. After a thousand hours or more, the sound of Dil-Mir's voice in my ear was an elixir, and the darkness that had seemed absolute lifted. Finally she agreed that I could come to see her—it only took half a year.

As we walked the perimeter of her courtyard in the hamlet, eyes on us from every side, she seemed to hover over the ground in her sundress. Every now and again she ran her fingers through her unadorned hair and I'd have to hold my breath a moment.

"I'm from one side of Shingal and you are from the other," she said. "It's a great distance for us. We must take our time."

"I have as much to give as you need to take," I told her.

"Why do you want to keep coming all this way?"

"I like how you talk, how you wear yourself."

Dil-Mir took a seat against the wall in the yard of her plain house, her family all inside, perhaps wondering where all this was going, if anywhere. She tucked her legs under her layered skirt, arms wrapped about her knees, and looked up at me, curious. Her face was as smooth as milk filling a glass.

"Sometimes, your fingers shake a little," she said finally.

"It's from the war."

And I held my hands together as though in prayer to steady them.

"Tell me one of the worst things."

"I don't know that I should."

"I can see from your dark eyes you don't sleep."

"No, not much."

I looked down at my open palms, examining the deep lines etched over the surface. Those hands had carried wounded bodies; the fingers had plugged bullet holes, and lately turned the soft pages in textbooks that I could barely comprehend. Where to start?

"Last night, I saw Migone again," I began. "Riding in the Humvees . . ."

TEAM SPIDER WAS working a section of the desert, hugging the serrated borders of another rat-line village. The steady convoy of Humvees stirred up a dense fog of grit over the derelict streets. On that particular day, I was in the last vehicle right behind Migone's, the IA rigs taking the lead up front. Through the windshield I could see the armada of trucks moving fast and accelerating. The driver pressed down on the gas. Hard to keep up. The wheels screamed as they tore over the ground and I checked the clasp on my belt.

A burst of static crackled over the radio.

"The Iraqis are driving like lunatics again," Migone sputtered.

We were all holding on to our helmets and ourselves as the truck heaved forward. It was like riding in a tin can. I looked out the windshield again and could see the gunners standing in the forward vehicles hugging the turrets. Impossible to tell if they were enjoying the wild ride.

"You ever get a driver's license, Mikey?" Iavecchia said, turning in his seat.

"We don't have those here, sir," I said.

"So what the hell do you do when you want to drive a car?" Migone barked over the headset.

"We just go, sir."

Waves of sand assaulted the glass like thick brown rain. Our truck was hurtling so fast over the road that my teeth rattled and my feet went numb. Seconds later, we heard a loud snap and the underside of the front Humvee flew straight up, spewing an avalanche of dirt.

"Christ, he's flipped it," Migone shouted. "Stop!"

The sun hung the pale red color of a ripening cherry as we rushed on foot through the coarse gloom. Soldiers in fatigues disgorged from the long line of vehicles and rushed soundless to the front through a funnel of smoke and steam. I could see Migone reach the upended truck and I ran to him, breathless.

All anyone could think about was the man who'd been standing in the turret, exposed. No one had to say it.

"Where was he?" Dil-Mir said.

"Trapped under the truck. It landed on him."

"Did he live?"

"How could he?"

From underneath the heap of metal blood kept pouring out. So much of it. It was on our boots. Everywhere. I kept thinking his body must be empty. Migone looked down and put his hands over his head. Hordes of soldiers were screaming in a high-pitched mess of Arabic and English, surrounding the truck and trying against every law of rational physics to lift it. Some of the IA people were howling like children. It was chaos. Finally I ran to get a jack from Migone's truck, but I didn't want to see what was under there—what had happened to him. It was bad.

"But you did. You saw it."

"Yes." I drew out the word like a long needle.

My legs had buckled at the sight of him dragged from that death trap—a young Kurd with a family at home. Wife. Children. Migone knelt way down, feeling around the dead-weight wrist for a pulse—for anything—against all logic. I got in closer to help and saw what I saw: the tectonic force of the impact had sheared off the full back of the gunner's skull, ripping the brain like a big pomegranate seed right out of it. Then, from that visceral mayhem, some irrational instinct compelled me to search for the missing parts of the dead man.

"Bodies are things, Dil-Mir," I said. "That's what I learned out there."

"They can break."

"Yes, into pieces."

"Into pieces," Dil-Mir repeated. "Like your mind—but the mind isn't a thing, is it? You can find its missing pieces and put them back where they belong."

Then she reached out and ran a thumb over my open palm.

"Maybe," I said, feeling her small touch infiltrate my life-blood, and I was back on solid ground in the yard of her small house again.

And the macabre vision she'd had me paint over the curtain of stilled air between us suddenly vanished. I could feel it leave my body like a malevolent cell.

"Some people say there is medicine, Shaker, for what you have. But you can't take too much of it."

"Talking to you," I breathed, wanting to hold her and not let go. "Talking to you is my medicine."

Never too much of anything, my son. And I could hear my father's voice say it—*never too much of anything, but love.*

Chapter Twelve

The Islamic State Comes Home

AT SUNDOWN SEVERAL MEN DISGUISED AS BEDOUIN MOVED over the low-lying dunes along the western reaches of the Jazeera. They got into pickup trucks, battered rifles slung over shoulders, their scrubbed hands still fragrant with gun oil. Strips of cloud spattered the sky like the chevrons of waves and cool winds poured over the shiftless sands; as far as the eye could see there was no sign of civilization. Out there, those forgotten shadows of the war were still free to roam like rogue cancer cells—die-hard Sunni insurgents the foreign occupiers and Shia-laden ISF had neglected to excise. Scores of them would congregate in safe houses nestled along the no-man's-land, mere miles from the border, sip chai, unfurl maps, and hatch their plans.

Abu Bakr al-Baghdadi, also known as al-Shabah, "the Phantom," surviving leader of AQI, had sent small contingents of those leftover fighters into Syria to support the embattled rebels fighting to topple the regime of the "apostate" Shia-Alawite,

Bashar al-Assad. Once there, they joined with several Syrian jihadists to form Jabhat al-Nusra, "the Victory Front," which drew considerable support from the beleaguered Sunni population, who had seen al-Assad's militias "cleanse" their towns and burn down their homes.

Things had gone far better than expected. In the mayhem of Syria's civil war, those rag-tag al-Qaeda jihadists had found themselves a fertile breeding ground. In March 2013, the rebels captured the eastern city of Raqqa and locked their sights on the nearby oil fields. Soon, they were selling crude on the black market, collecting taxes from the terror-stricken civilian population, and increasing their ranks exponentially. By April of that same year, while I was falling in love with Dil-Mir, al-Baghdadi imposed Sharia law over the captured territory, declaring the merger of AQI and al-Nusra into the Islamic State of Iraq and the Levant, ISIL, or ISIS—and resurrected a withering holy war.

BACK HOME IN Khanasor, sitting in the front room before our satellite TV, we watched those events unfold in neighboring Syria with little concern. Most people thought that the risk to our country was still remote—after all, the Americans had left the IA well equipped with tanks, MRAPs, guns, and missiles, and we believed that the foreign powers who lit the powder keg back in 2003 would surely intervene if our nation fell under serious threat. Not to mention, the recent antics of our paranoid Shiite president Nouri al-Maliki were taking up most of the country's attention.

In a doomed effort to protect his power base, our newly unfettered leader had unleashed a campaign to systematically disenfranchise and abuse the Sunni population: arresting its members of parliament, using lethal force to suppress public protests, and incarcerating thousands of civilians, many of them tortured beforehand and held in grim conditions without any formal charges laid. The inclusive democratic government al-Maliki had promised the tribes in exchange for their crucial support in routing out terrorists during the "Sunni Awakening" was now a blatant sham.

In hindsight, we should have connected the dots between what was happening in Syria and what was happening in Iraq—perhaps we simply didn't want to. The fact was, we Yazidis were pacifist villagers eking out an existence in a poor province under a surging nationwide unemployment rate. After years of war, we just wanted to get back to living.

ON A WEEKEND break from school, I stood in Dil-Mir's aromatic kitchen, carving up the fresh meat. Often, we prepared meals together, practicing the domestic bliss we were certain to share after the exigencies of school and finding work were over. Dil-Mir had tied her abundant black hair into a loose braid and wore a simple dress that flowed in a rambling pattern of blossoms all the way down to her ankles. I sat in her perfumed wake, as her hands worked over the cutting board. Rising heat painted the soft arcs of her cheeks to a high pink flush—she needed no other adornment.

"I feel badly that you drive all this way," she said, as soon as her brother left the kitchen. Here and there, when chaperoning family members took breaks, we transformed moments alone into lifetimes.

"Why would you feel badly, when seeing you is a gift?" I got up and stood behind her for a few quiet moments, heat swelling between us, but we never touched. In those days, sharing the same air inside the same four walls was enough.

Dil-Mir turned around and looked at me. "Your face is like a dark moon, Shaker. Those dreams have come back, I can feel them rising from you."

Dil-Mir had a poetic way of speaking that often made me laugh, but not to mock her. She was nothing like anyone, male or female, I'd ever met. In our thoughts and wishes, we were of

140

the same mind. And in her manner of speaking, movement, and dress, I believed Dil-Mir was the epitome of what it meant to be a Yazidi: she respected herself, considered all matters fairly, and never raised her voice against anyone. For the rest of my life, I needed to search no further for fulfillment than her face.

I couldn't share my dreams that day—to say more meant going into the darkness and having a look around. I was in Dil-Mir's kitchen, she was there—it was all that mattered just then. I went back to cutting up the meat.

Dil-Mir moved to the kettle and poured steaming water into a pot and then threw in a fistful of tea leaves. Water hitting the chai went instantly red, and I watched as she closed her kohl-rimmed eyes and inhaled the sweet tendrils of steam. I imagined that we were in a bright kitchen of our own, cooking meals, unwinding the long day like a ribbon while several children napped in their small beds.

"All the news out there. Nothing good can come of watching television and the internet the way you do," she said, always certain everything would be fine.

But it was important to know. To know was to prepare. My friends in the Iraqi army didn't seem too worried. We had tanks and Hellfire missiles—the militants had rusted trucks; ISIS was in Syria—this was Iraq. But then I talked to Brownsword, who was equal parts soldier and scholar—he could take you back in time a thousand years to tell you why things were the way they were. At the sound of his name, Dil-Mir rolled her big obsidian eyes and let out a laugh.

"Oh no," she said. "And what did the professor have to say this time?"

I shrugged and turned to the window. Rain laced the atmosphere though there wasn't a cloud in sight, and I thought of the long drive back around the mountain, alone.

"He said just one word, and it made me think."

"And what word was that, Shaker dear?"

I got up carrying the earthenware bowl and tossed the cleaned off bones into a stockpot. Then I turned around again and put down the empty dish.

"Leave."

ON APRIL 23, 2013, a security team, including members of the ISF, led by the army's 12th Division, all armed to the teeth, converged on a sit-in Sunni protest camp in the northern city of Hawija, in the Kirkuk Province—right next door to Nineveh. In retaliation for a recent attack on a nearby police checkpoint, and to subdue the violent protests that had taken place there, the officers were ordered to dismantle the camp. Without warning, they unleashed their machine guns like rain over the gathering of Sunnis.

By the time the last round tore through its mark, the bodies of over fifty young men in their prime lay strewn in macabre poses over the ensanguined dirt. To this day, many of my fellow Iraqis, whatever their creed, look back on that lethal afternoon as the beginning of the end of our collective hope. From then on, tribal leaders heightened their anti-al-Maliki rhetoric and called for fierce reprisals. In the Middle East it wasn't just an eye for an eye, it was a thousand lives for a life—whoever put more blood on the ground made the lasting impression.

Iraq had finally reached a boiling point: al-Maliki's democratically elected government and its security forces had proven themselves utterly corrupt, dysfunctional, and homicidal. Meanwhile, the Syrian war had emboldened those cells of insurgents, and their malignant hatreds were metastasizing right back over our border. Within a month, over seven hundred Iraqis were slaughtered in a noxious stew of collateral violence: roadside bombs, vehicle-borne IEDs, drive-by shootings, arbitrary murders, and torture sessions gone too far.

Then the real threat hit home.

In the cultivated fields around Rabia, where I'd picked the summer harvests as a young boy, several corpses were found decomposing along the empty furrows. All of them were laborers, each bearing a single bullet dead-center to the nape of the neck. Blindfolded and kicked in the teeth, their hands had been bound behind their backs—one of many ISIS trademarks. By the time their bodies were discovered half-buried in the baked earth, predatory birds had already picked out the eyes from their skulls, just as the insurgents had picked over their bodies for a few crumpled dinars. In the political storm of unbridled revenge tearing up the nation, those simple laborers were insignificant, except for one thing: they were all Yazidis.

Week after week thereafter, similar kidnappings and killings ensued all over the northern region: people hauled out of their cars along the desert roads, girls plucked from the plains, men from buses, even their beds. Sometimes the kidnappers demanded a ransom and it was duly paid without incident; other times the maimed bodies showed up days later, dumped haphazardly into gutters. I'd seen them for myself lying along the road like bags of trash. Dil-Mir was only half right—the nightmares, daymares, and tremors had returned, but now they carried an unstoppable vengeance. My body knew it well before I did—we were all just prey.

LONG DESTINATIONLESS RECONNAISSANCE drives around the province in my dirt-covered white car revealed little more than business as usual. At checkpoints, I watched as officers in loose fatigues strutted down the line of vehicles, new boots sending up puffs of dirt, sunburned lips sucking on cigarettes and sipping sodas from well-stocked coolers. More than a few had hard liquor on their breath, I was sure of it.

Lately, I'd heard stories about hardcore drugs infiltrating the ranks. Heroin. Pharmaceuticals. Hashish from Iran. Those were often the fat-cat divisions, full of well-fed officers earning a good salary, while lazing in the sun counting up cars and sweaty rolls of cash, and taking their sweet time searching trunks. They roughed up suspects, hauled a few in for beatings; weapons were discharged, bones broken, but incidents of unwarranted violence and outright fraud were rarely investigated. For the lower-ranking soldiers, drugs were often the only available antidote to the unrelenting stress of living in a perpetual state of warfare. Meanwhile, the new battlefront churned bare miles away, closing in like a slow-moving hurricane.

Division commanders at the army bases had little time for me other than small talk. Hard to tell if they were even conducting regular training exercises anymore. Still, their good-natured apathy was infectious, and I believed wholeheartedly that the conscience of the world would not neglect us. We fired up hookahs in the yard and talked about the good old days of buffet lines, burgers, and barbecues. We exchanged email addresses, cell phone numbers, and even connected on Facebook.

"Keep in touch, Shaker, and remember that you have the Kurdish armies to protect you."

And I did—they were all I had between faith and outright panic.

Iraqi Kurdistan, also known as the Kurdish Regional Government (KRG), an autonomous region of disgruntled Kurds seeking independence from the rest of Iraq, straddled the eastern rim of Nineveh. It maintained its own government under a Kurdish president, Masoud Barzani, and was home to a legendary force of lethal fighters that had whipped whole empires, starting with the Persians and ending with the British. Just the name of their indomitable unit dripped fear into the veins of seasoned soldiers: Peshmerga—Those Who Confront Death.

During the invasion of 2003, the Peshmerga had been instrumental in finding and capturing Saddam Hussein, and later pinpointed the messenger who led to the detection and killing of Osama bin Laden. The Kurdish warrior tradition of brutal fearlessness ran like venom through their ice-cold DNA. There was nothing they wouldn't do to secure victory—and under Article 114 of the Iraqi Constitution, they were lawfully bound to protect the Yazidi.

HEAT POUNDED DOWN like an iron fist through the violent summer of 2013, and we slipped heedless into fall. When the spells of rain came in, and washed the desert into fleeting greens, I started my last year of high school. Most days, studies occupied all of my time; despite hours interred in textbooks, I'd never quite regained my former academic glory. Those old school ribbons dangled over my mother's bedroom shelves like small frayed flags, there only to taunt me. Bowers was right, years of bomb-dodging in Mosul had left their scars.

On days off when I was not with Dil-Mir, I kept to the roadways of Nineveh, radio tuned in to constant reports from Syria: sharia courts, burned-down churches, the exodus of terrified Christians, and the public crucifixions—headless bodies littered the sidewalks of Raqqa. Once, unable to breathe or listen any longer in the suffocating old car, I got out and just stared a long-time westward, thinking. Even the incoming breeze seemed to smell of carnage.

The television sat sleeping in the corner as I crossed the threshold, but my family all sat around it on floor cushions, grim-faced and silent.

"What are you guys doing?" I said, and put down my bag of books.

"Watching the news," Samir said, and motioned to the vacant screen. Then he let out a strange sound through his nostrils.

"No, we are not," Daki said, and slapped a hand on her thigh.

"That's right," Dapîra said from her corner cushion. "We are not."

I reached for a piece of fruit, and a cloud of small flies swarmed the bowl. The air in the house felt dank; like the return of an outlaw season, times were hard again.

Samir pleaded to turn the TV back on; the timbre of his voice fractured over the room, and the walls themselves seemed to shift. When I turned to look at my red-faced brother, I could see he was holding back a torrent. One finger pointing like a dagger to the empty black screen, he sat there waiting, his eyes right on me.

"What's really going on?" I said, coming in closer.

"The Islamic State just bulldozed right through the Sykes-Picot Line," Naïf told me.

The air in the room pulsed and I took a deep breath.

"They're right here," Samir said pointing out the window. "ISIS is invading." He got up to turn on the news. A sinister black flag covered in white Arabic scrolls emerged across the screen.

"They're not invading," I said, sitting down with my family to watch. "They've come home."

Chapter Thirteen

Blind Mice

THEY RODE IN BATTERED TRUCKS AND ON HORSEBACK FROM AL-Bab, east of Aleppo, and then traversed through the lawless desert into their safe haven of Anbar. Behind their small contingent, the ransacked border checkpoint smoldered, and the butchered bodies of the patrolling officers lay scattered in the ditches. A veil of dust hung low in the pale aurora; the way ahead stood empty for miles in the windless heat. Sunnis residing across the governate, including the chieftains of powerful ancient tribes, welcomed the return of these warriors to their roused battleground, where they'd unite and begin where they'd left off after the infidels brokered the now long abandoned "Awakening."

Embittered men rushed out into the streets with arms held out praising Allah, and opened their war-ravaged homes to the incoming fighters. Meanwhile, Prime Minister Nouri al-Maliki's power-hungry regime continued to slumber under a cataract of hubris, sending in more forces to break the relentless wave of protests and annihilate his rivals, filling prisons with those who railed against him. One month before, government security forces had raided the family residence of Ahmed al-Alwani and arrested the prominent Sunni member of Parliament, who'd spoken out against al-Maliki's parochial administration. The prime minister was now public enemy number one, and tribal militias—who'd once joined General Petraeus's "Sons of Iraq" to root out al-Qaeda—sprung up across the galvanized region. The Islamic State had come to Anbar as their Salafist Sunni brothers and there was no going back.

By January, Iraq's beleaguered military forces retreated from Fallujah, and there was fierce fighting in Ramadi, which fell, as would the rest of the province, not long after. ISIS ranks only increased as they flooded more and more territory like a steadily climbing tide. Their battle-seasoned chiefs understood how to disrupt government systems through a tactical chaos of prison breaks, suicide bombs, and perimeter attacks on critical command centers and checkpoints—and they did so using lightning-fast strategic assaults, which exploited the fear their very name instilled in the weak hearts of incompetent men. Rabid insurgents clad head-to-toe in black cut the heads from the live bodies of their shrieking enemies and displayed them on their vehicles like hood ornaments. I'd seen it all for myself in the propaganda videos and instruction manuals they posted on the dark web to recruit fighters from the four corners of the globe.

IA and Peshmerga officers, from colonels to captains, continued to offer me casual reassurances that the invading horde was nothing more than a mangy unit of homicidal madmen who'd yet to face the full brunt of the nation's modern armies. Prime Minister al-Maliki himself said as much in regular television broadcasts delivered from his office in the Republican Palace in Baghdad.

I kept up with my schoolwork, courted Dil-Mir, and ate dinner by kerosene lamps all through the grim winter, while following the news and checking in with my contacts. I plotted ISIS's steady progression and tracked their trajectory. Anyone could see it clear as day: they were headed straight for the oil-rich capital of empires, chasing after the long-coveted jewel missing from the crowns of so many warring factions—Mosul.

ALL THROUGH THE weeks of skirmishes and enemy advances, I'd kept in regular touch with Brownsword online and through intermittent calls, exchanging intel and analyzing the information we'd gathered.

"How many army divisions are there left in the city?" he asked me.

There were two: the 2nd with five full brigades, and the 6th, also a good size. Moreover, they had a huge arsenal of American equipment and weaponry in the bases: MRAPs, tanks, artillery. Then we talked about my conversations with the officers and commanders, who'd all said the military was ready. Nevertheless, the roads were bloody now, and I gave the details: no more ransoms, militants just pulled people from cars at random and killed them on the spot—including many Yazidis who'd worked for the security forces. Women went missing, too. And there were countless rapes.

I thought the chances of ISIS taking Mosul were too small to worry about, but Brownsword reminded me that no one had even expected them to make it this far. And neither of us could forget Mosul had given the American military a run for her money. Mosul was a nest of sleepers: in the neighborhoods, on the bases, creeping all over the security apparatus. No one knew how many—it could be thousands. This was the chance they had been waiting for.

"Reports are that insurgents are massing on the Syrian border," I said. "Right now."

Brownsword's intel was the same. Something large-scale was going on. Al-Maliki had been warned, but all he could think to do was kill more Sunnis and promote one of his Shiite hench-men, Mahdi al-Gharrawi, as the operational commander of Nineveh.

"This is why I'm telling you to watch Mosul, Mikey—Mosul goes, you get the hell out of Dodge. Fast. We'll send you money, me and Jay, whatever you need."

Still I could not bring myself to leave. I wanted to believe that we would be protected—it was in our Constitution, and I had faith in the laws of man back then. At the same time, black flags were flying from Raqqa, right across the now de-molished border, and all over the former Sunni Triangle. The insurgency was back, but had mutated into an all-out revolu-tion—and it was only getting bigger. I promised Brownsword that I'd prepare.

"Good. You Yazidis are sitting ducks. If I had my way, you'd be out of there already. Get to Kurdistan, then cross into Turkey if you can."

From down below the roofline of our small house, I heard Daki singing to the tambour, soft and melodious. Overhead, a crescent moon sat in the sky like the silvered tip of a giant scythe. I peered into the courtyard at the twinkling lights hang-ing from the gutters, and the barbecue starting to rust in the corner, next to a torn sack of charcoal. An empty bottle of ketchup sat on its side on the table. Brownsword's voice was in my ear, but the man himself was standing on the other side of the world delivering prophecies that were no good to me just now. All I wanted was to keep going to school, get my degree at last, and one day marry my girl. Only then could I leave.

"Mikey, you hearing me?"

"Yes, sir."

"Stop calling me that, brother. We're past all that now. Listen: you remember al-Bilawi?"

Abu Abdulrahman al-Bilawi was from the Dulaim tribe—and hard to forget. Our guys had put him into the prison at

The only surviving photo of my father "Babo" was taken in the mid-1980s during the Iran-Iraq war.

Courtesy of the Jeffrey family

The only photo I still have from my childhood, age six at our family's farm.

Courtesy of the Jeffrey family

Team Shady at Camp Diamondback after a successful mission, 2008.
Courtesy of Ronald Bowers

Working as "Michael the Terp," Hotel Mosul stands behind
me. Years later, this famous hotel would become the backdrop of ISIS's dramatic capture of the city.
Courtesy of Shaker Jeffrey

Sergeant First Class Ronald Bowers and I horsing around on a scorching hot day in Mosul, 2008. *Courtesy of Ronald Bowers*

Team Shady medic attends to the wounded after an IED attack in Mosul, 2008. *Courtesy of Ronald Bowers*

Team Spider in Tal Afar. *Courtesy of Robert Brownsword*

Captain Robert Brownsword kitted up at FOB Sykes. *Courtesy of Robert Brownsword*

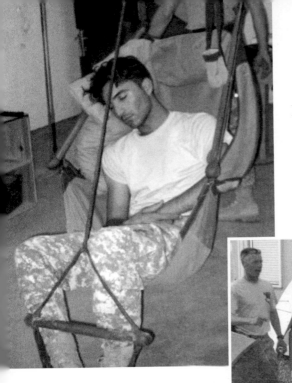

Resting after a mission in the "chair of sleepiness" at COP Destroyer. *Courtesy of Robert Brownsword*

Manning the BBQ at FOB Sykes in 2009 for another post-mission party. *Courtesy of Robert Brownsword*

Captain Robert Brownsword and Lieutenant Colonel Jay Migone. *Courtesy of Robert Brownsword*

Terping for Lieutenant Colonel Jay Migone as we trained Iraqi soldiers out in the Jazeera.
Courtesy of Jay Migone

Taking notes during a brigade meeting with team Spider at FOB Sykes.
Courtesy of Jay Migone

Weapons training in Tal Afar.
Courtesy of Jay Migone

Children at play in Khanasor.
Courtesy of Robert Brownsword

A photo of me taken in the spring before
ISIS invaded Shingal, 2014. *Courtesy of Shaker Jeffrey*

Members of my family fleeing ISIS during the invasion of August 2014. Members of my family fleeing ISIS during the invasion of August 2014. *Courtesy of the Jeffrey family*

Captain Robert Brownsword in Washington, DC, mobilizing the press at the start of the Yazidi genocide, August 2014. *Courtesy of Robert Brownsword*

Refugee camp in Syria with Mount Shingal visible in the distance.
Courtesy of Anne Norona

Helping stranded refugees off the boats on the perilous
shores of Greece, 2016. *Courtesy of Anne Norona*

(Left) With rescued Yazidi children at a refugee camp in Greece. *Courtesy of Shaker Jeffrey*

(Below) Yazidi refugees living in squalor in the camps. *Courtesy of Anne Norona*

(Facing page, top) Volunteering with Yazidi refugee children at a camp in Greece. *Courtesy of Shaker Jeffrey*

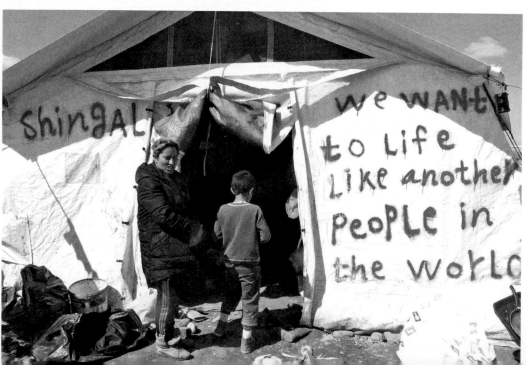

Keeping survivor and
Yazidi spokesperson
Nadia Murad close,
Idomeni Refugee
Camp, Greece, 2016.
Courtesy of Shaker Jeffrey

Anne Norona and Khairi
volunteering together in
northern Iraq.
Courtesy of Anne Norona

Commemorating the anniversary of the genocide with Nadia Murad in Stuttgart, 2018.
Courtesy of Shaker Jeffrey

Standing in front of the Eiffel Tower during a break from a conference in Paris.
Courtesy of Shaker Jeffrey

Addressing German federal parliament in Berlin, as a member of a Yazidi reunification conference, 2017.
Courtesy of Shaker Jeffrey

Meeting
Anne Norona
in Germany for
the first time.
*Courtesy of
Anne Norona*

With rescued Yazidi children at a safe house near the
Black Forest in Germany. *Courtesy of Anne Norona*

Working with *Sunday Times* (London) journalist Christina Lamb in a secret shelter in Baden-Württemberg Germany, summer 2016.
Courtesy of Shaker Jeffrey

Camped out while working the treacherous rescue grid.
Courtesy of Shaker Jeffrey

Team Shaker member Alex
Holstein, California, 2019.
Courtesy of Alex Holstein

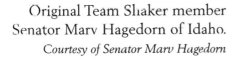

Original Team Shaker member
Senator Marv Hagedorn of Idaho.
Courtesy of Senator Marv Hagedorn

Original Team Shaker member
General Gary Sayler.
*Courtesy of Senator Marv Hagedorn
and General Gary Sayler*

With Khiri at a hospital in Nuremburg after the little boy underwent another surgery to repair extensive damage resulting from torture at the hands of ISIS militants.
Courtesy of Shaker Jeffrey

General David Petraeus, who was instrumental in connecting me with No One Left Behind, an organization that advocates for military interpreters during the immigration process.
Courtesy of General David Petraeus

Camp Bucca in 2005. Every Iraqi knew who he was. A sinister set of brown eyes sawed through my mind, and I recalled a full down-turned mouth set hard in its appetite for wholesale slaughter—which the man himself had a singular ability to orchestrate. His formidable clan was the largest in Iraq, spanning huge swaths of Arabia going back to pre-Islamic times, and its leadership had formed the epicenter of the insurgency during the war. Their cold-blooded members ranked in the millions.

ISIS had freed al-Bilawi from Abu Ghraib prison back in April, part of a campaign directed by al-Baghdadi that left scores of Shia slaughtered right in their cells, while freeing thousands of the terrorists we hadn't managed to cull during the war. Al-Bilawi was now on the ISIS military council, planning some of their biggest operations.

"He's the guy blind mice like Gharrawi and Mosul are up against—you feel me now, brother?"

"Yes. I get it." And a vein of ice-cold air slithered over my skin. "That's not good."

WE STARTED COLLECTING weapons in the spring. Those who did not know how to shoot learned. Often in the afternoons, the ricochets of bullets cracked the great blue dome over Shingal. Most days now, the breeze carried the warm sulfur of a distant battlefield that electrified my senses. Former terps like myself offered lessons out on the plains: hitting makeshift targets and desert rodents that scurried for cover between the mottled rocks. My brothers gathered all of our ready cash and bought whole arsenals directly from the IA, whose grunts sold whatever they had to the highest bidders: Handguns. Machine guns. Rifles. Anything. By May 2014, most every village house had at least one firearm in it.

At the end of the month, seven members of the Islamic State were arrested, and the security forces learned of an imminent attack against Mosul. Lieutenant General al-Gharrawi called on Prime Minister al-Maliki for reinforcements to secure the city, but his request was flat-out refused. Diplomats also traveled to Baghdad with similar warnings gleaned from recent intelligence reports, which also fell on the deaf ears of stubborn denial. The military forces were already stretched thin defending other parts of the country, and al-Maliki's administration believed ISIS had no chance of taking a metropolis of two million, which housed the largest cache of modern weaponry in all of Iraq. Still, every day now, word came in of another enemy advance as ISIS amassed territory with seemingly little resistance. The scales of hope were tipping, and time was not on our side.

During study breaks, I sat alone before my laptop, trolling the forbidden crevasses of the dark web, searching for clues of what was to come. Mosul was surrounded on three sides, and ISIS had choked off the major supply lines, but an ever-paranoid al-Maliki would not accept offers of help from the Peshmerga armies. If ISIS viewed Mosul as part of their burgeoning emirate, the Kurds saw the ancient capital as their historical right, and a paranoid al-Maliki would not dare let the Peshmerga near it.

Christians and Kurds were fleeing Mosul in droves, clogging the main artery into the autonomous region of Iraqi Kurdistan, which took them in without question. Suddenly, the centuries-old demographics of Mosul were shifting in favor of the long-subjugated Sunni population, who remained resolute in the rundown hotbed neighborhoods west of the river. Entrenched in their homes, many sat armed to the hilt and waited for the liberation from al-Maliki's tyrannical regime that ISIS seemed to promise.

LIKE SO MANY Yazidis, Dil-Mir didn't want to believe barren Shingal stood in the crosshairs of the Islamic State, who were still targeting the oil fields to enrich their coffers, while looting banks, ransacking homes of the wealthy, and pilfering priceless artifacts from city museums. All we had were sheep and goats. But this was not a war about profit: it was a battle of ideologies, and to them, we were devil-worshipping infidels. I'd listened to the rhetoric—a cornerstone of their mandate was to rid us from the earth once and for all. Genocide after genocide filled our history like dark ages, yet each time we were caught blind.

Then I told her about what I'd seen: the crucifixions, firing squads, and beheadings. Desecrated bodies of young men, swollen and rotting along the roads, their pants pulled down below the knees.

As soon as the way was clear, why wouldn't ISIS come for us?

"This is insanity, Shaker. You've done what you can to prepare. We all have. Study, go to Dohuk, take your exams—think of university—think of us. Let the armies worry about protecting the country."

The phone close to my ear, I shut my eyes, pretending Dil-Mir was right next to me, wishing I'd taken the hot rambling drive around the mountain. I could hear her sigh and knew she had a strand of hair coiled like an inky vine about a lacquered finger. When she was worried, a single rut cleaved her even, pale brow.

"I would like us to have three children, Shaker," she said. "Two boys and a girl. I see them in my daydreams." Whenever I talked of war, she changed our course, her kind voice leading me well away, talking of the future—hers and mine.

Suddenly, through the wasted miles all my fears began to drift off like the dark remnants of a nightmare. Since the end of the war, a near constant terror stalked me; again, and again, the horrors returned in an all-consuming assault of living memories. Those waking dreams left me unable to envision any fate without full-scale horrors. Only Dil-Mir's voice could tame the beast within; she was my beacon, and in moments like that one, raw instinct was powerless against the quicksand of my perceptions.

"We should name them and make it real," I whispered.

"I have—Maya for our daughter." And she laughed, a little shy.

"A Western name—good. And what about the others?"

"Why don't you choose now?"

As she said those words, I stood up and gazed from the rooftop, across the thirsty plateaus to the long crest of Mount Shingal, dimming to the color of a bruise in the dying light. I imagined Dil-Mir in her small house tucked away on the other side, way past our temples and the deep tombs of kin, and I pictured the breeze that rushed past me now on its way south, buffeting her hair. My wishful eyes roved the faraway horizon, and I blew a kiss to her from my palm.

"We will be together all our lives," I said. "All our lives."

"Yes. Go. Take your exams. And come home to me."

UP AND DOWN the freeway, there was traffic: hatchbacks, delivery trucks, and rusted-out sedans, most of it chugging into the undulating north and then east toward Zakho on the Little Khabur river, which flowed like an arm embracing the full perimeter of the small city burrowed within the safe borders of the KRG, and mere miles from the Turkish frontier. Whole families of Yazidis piled into the beds of pickups were coming back in the other direction, returning to Shingal; faces grim, tanks running low.

"The border police won't let them in. You have your permit?" the driver sputtered.

Security was tighter than ever as I rode in the cab to the school, repeatedly feeling for my student papers. Barzani had closed the border gates, and the police wouldn't let me in without my documents. When I told the driver I thought the

Peshmerga would come to our defense, he spat out the window and glanced at me.

"That what you think?"

I reminded him that under Article 114 of the Constitution, the Kurds were bound by law to protect the Yazidis. I kept my eyes on the green valleys and the sweeping mountains beyond. Soon we'd cross the Tigris, and move south again toward Dohuk, and I'd breathe easier. I had three final exams to complete in the provincial capital: chemistry, math, and physics—and then I was free. University—I was well on my way.

"That constitution is crap," he said back to me as though I'd slapped him. "No one has time to read anything in a war—except maybe the Koran."

Well, I thought—right now, it's all we have. By instinct I fingered the handgun in my waistband and thought of Brownsword, who always did the same with his weapon as we entered dangerous territory. No need to hide my piece, the drums of war were beating loud and clear over Mesopotamia; everyone in the region traveled armed and ready to kill. I had an extra magazine tucked into my vest next to a thin wad of cash. I was wearing my best collared shirt and dress pants, which were already covered in a film of summer dust.

"You students are all the same, full of stupid hope." Then he went on and on that it was good for nothing—people only used that word when they didn't have anything else.

Lately, I was hemorrhaging hope. I'd spoken to another army colonel commanding the brigades farther south in Nineveh—the news wasn't good. Whole divisions were in a state of mounting disarray. Many of the soldiers had abandoned the will to fight before they even encountered the enemy—maybe they never had it in the first place. Meanwhile, ISIS was on the move, barreling in an unstoppable frenzy over towns, filling their war chests while amassing recruits. I ran my eyes over the craggy ridgeline and wondered how many of them were up there, surveying the naked valleys.

CROSSING THE THRESHOLD with my sack that morning, mouth full of naan, my mother had grabbed me by the shoulders just before I went out. Mists of sleep still all over her, in the gloom of daybreak her eyes were as colorless as ice. She was muttering in strange whispers and didn't blink as she stared up at me.

"Go to Dohuk and don't come back," she pleaded. "Don't come back to Shingal."

"Daki, don't talk that way," I said to her. "What's happened to you?" I'd never heard that hollowed-out timbre in her voice; she spoke to me as though she were calling out from a cave. Even now, sitting in the cab on my way to Kurdistan to finally earn my degree, the memory of that voice made me wince. All I saw in her careworn face was abject fear.

Not knowing what else to do, and time running short, I touched her cheek, soft and warm as dough, though her hands were frigid. "Daki, I will come back, and we will be safe. I won't leave you. We have to stay together. There is always hope—you must hold on to it."

Now, sitting in the cab, it pained me to think of what I'd said.

THE LAND I gazed upon from the broken cab window, growing greener as we neared the deep rivers, had carried the weight and scars of thousands of sieges. But ISIS was different—a new breed of soldier, of jihad and of a merciless God. It would take more than modern cannons and Western rhetoric to defeat a dogma that ran thicker than lifeblood through vengeful tribal veins. I'd seen what was out there, decaying in the gutters along the 47, and in the furrows of Rabia; hanging from plank crosses in the city squares of Raqqa; scattered out in the wasteland desert under circling birds of prey; and now in the all-knowing domes of my mother's terrified eyes. Crazed fighters were pouring in from all over the world, selling off their souls and every worldly possession to fight for Abu al-Baghdadi's medieval Allah. And I'd witnessed the capriciousness of war—this one born from the womb of hell.

The sun at its zenith beat down and my tongue was so dry it stuck to the roof my mouth. I sucked down the last tepid drops from my canteen. Flocks of blackbirds rushed in from the valley and swept over the freeway in a great arch like flak, wings beating shadows over the car. I held my breath a moment and then felt a rising thunder gallop through my chest as the ground beneath the wheels suddenly rattled and groaned.

"Look," the driver shouted, jutting out his chin. He squeezed the steering wheel in his fists and hollered. "Look!"

They crossed the border into Shingal at midday, thousands of them: Peshmerga troops crowded into big transport trucks. Whole brigades, five to six battalions in each, passing by one after the other like a long freight train. Thousands of soldiers armed and ready to fight. Each one had an assault rifle strapped tight to his broad shoulders and was grinning ear to ear. They waved as cars stopped along the roadways and people got out and cheered. Behind those huge personnel carriers, an endless convoy snaked for miles all the way past the ridge like a mighty river. After the troops, even more armor flowed forth from the KRG: tanks and artillery, barreling down the freeway, gathering wind and pushing past us in a great gale of indomitable military power. Yazidis stood watching from the ditches, arms outstretched, some openly weeping—hope reborn.

We were nestled under the wing of one of the great armies of the ages. Whatever came, we would survive.

"The Peshmerga," I shouted. "We are safe." For the first time in weeks, I took a long clean breath.

And I pulled out my phone to call my mother.

Chapter Fourteen

The Invasion

THE CITY OF MOSUL SLUMBERED UNDER A THIN MANTLE OF low-lying cloud, still far too early for the muezzin call. Silent and dark, minarets rose like daggers into the carbon night, citadels luring the contingent of jihadists rattling fast across the desert from strongholds in Anbar. Some of the militants had come all the way from Europe to join the crusade for a new caliphate; but most were die-hard tribal warriors and old Saddam loyalists, who'd sharpened their knives on the necks of unbelievers during the foreign occupation. They were headed for the sympathetic western reaches of the city they didn't intend to capture—not yet. The plan was to take over several strategic Sunni neighborhoods—in which scores of sleeper cells waited—free the inmates from Badush Prison ten miles up the Tigris, and then take the nearby oil reserves.

Bearded militants standing in the trucks shouted like madmen to the starry heavens, some doped up for a wild fight, each one prepared to die a martyr. When the phosphorescent limits came into view, glowing like faceted gemstones set into the wide river valley, the fighters went quiet and stared out in hungry awe. Then they hunkered down, uttering prayers to Allah, lowered the *shamags* covering their faces, and checked their weapons.

Closing in on the perimeter checkpoints, commanders gave the signal and set off a swift riot of suicide bombs and bullets. Immediately, the Iraqi guards who hadn't already abandoned their posts threw down their rifles and ran. Those who survived the initial onslaught were summarily shot or beheaded, and the convoy moved on, bloodied and galvanized.

Four days later, towering columns of choking black soot rose from the smoldering city blocks, and over half a million inhabitants, one quarter of the population, had fled north into the KRG. Corrupt IA commanders and officers either never gave the order to fight the ISIS invaders, or else simply bolted into the dense urban grid, donning civilian clothes, never to be seen again. A few mortar shells and heavy bursts of machine-gun fire directed into tactical locations were all it took for those indigent fighters to provoke the terrified retreat of whole armed divisions, who left the largest arsenal of modern weaponry in the Middle East, aside from Israel's, behind for the taking.

When Lieutenant General al-Gharrawi requested immediate reinforcements, the prime minister again refused, forcing the general to pull back in a chaotic retreat, his units racing east over the bridges and fleeing to safety on the other side of the river. Ensconced in Baghdad, government officials watched in a stupor of disbelief as those frenzied scenes of defeat unfolded, and Prime Minister al-Maliki tried to reassure the country that the great fight was not yet over. But it was far too late—the capital of the Assyrians, and throne of the Ottomans, was lost. The black flags of the Islamic State were already flying high over every civic building in Mosul.

Sitting together in the crowded front room, we watched news coverage of Iraqi army soldiers tearing off their uniforms and running scared into the wild miasma.

"Mosul fell like a plane without an engine," one man said into the camera.

"This is insanity," I hollered at the screen. "They have to fight them."

Behind me Daki made breathless sounds as she paced the back walls and then shuffled from the room. Covering her face with her blue shawl, my grandmother went after her. Outside the open window, all of Khanasor stood in an eerie afternoon stillness. A lamb bayed once from a nearby courtyard, but there was no other sound except for the same cataclysmic chatter coming in from neighboring TVs and radios.

"You should have stayed in Dohuk, *brako*," Naïf said to me, puffing at the hookah. "At least Haji and Samir are safe. They won't come back from Kurdistan now."

"We still have the Peshmerga," I said, thinking of the metal armada I'd seen cross the sea of desert into Shingal. "It's going to take a crazy battle to get control of this thing."

"If it even comes to that," he said. "Let's wait and see. Wait and see." And he filled his lungs with sweet shisha smoke.

"Look at a map," I told him. "ISIS is just about to trample into Tal Afar. After that, it's just one short ride along the highway into our little villages—that's all."

"It's the oil and the banks they want. Not our empty dirt." Naïf shook his head and blew out a fog of smoke. "Don't panic just yet."

BY NIGHTFALL ON the tenth of June, gleeful jihadists commanding captured MRAPs and tanks paraded down the city freeways of Mosul, horns blaring and men shouting; others roamed the cleared-out streets on foot, welcomed on all sides as liberators by the al-Maliki-weary residents. Charming and articulate, smiling commanders of the Islamic State subdued the few guarded denizens with promises to maintain all civil services, and encouraged people to go back to work—business as usual. At first, life for the long disenfranchised Sunnis living there seemed far better under ISIS command than it had been under the murderous scrutiny of al-Gharrawi's disciples.

The same day, another ISIS unit drove north along the Tigris to release hundreds of Sunni prisoners from Badush; they transported six hundred Shiite inmates three and a half miles out into the desert, forced each one to kneel over a ravine, and then mowed them down with machine guns. Soon after, they trampled Tikrit and kept going mile after easy mile, until the Islamic State had its boot on the throat of more than thirty-nine thousand square miles of territory in Iraq and Syria. The speed of the enemy's conquest was spellbinding and sent shockwaves around the bewildered globe. The largest and most forbidding terrorist network in history now controlled vast expanses of two oil-rich nations, and was suddenly proficiently armed. Every Yazidi in Shingal sat dumbstruck in their concrete homes, eyes blinking at television screens, and held their collective breath. Overnight, latent fear mutated into raw all-consuming terror—you didn't need a prophet to tell you that we were next.

MERE DAYS AFTER the siege in Mosul, uniformed agents of the Assayish, the KRG's secret police, entered the villages of Shingal. Going door to door, they were on a mission handed down from their headquarters to uncover and confiscate all personally held armaments. Crouched on our rooftop, I watched them approach Khanasor in their official fleet of dark cars and vans, racing along the single cement road into town like a cruel omen. Not long after, echoes of commotion boiled up from the adjacent streets: gloved fists pounding on doors, shouts, revving engines, and the incessant barking of dogs. Tensions among the Yazidis had reached a fevered pitch, and voices exploded from the blocks just outside our house. A few random shots were fired, children bawled, and then the streets went silent for a time. I ventured out alone, my handgun wrapped up in an old cloth and left behind in the rain gutter.

The agent who met me at the end of our block stroked his dark goatee and smiled thinly as he spoke.

"We're conducting a search for illegal weapons," he said.

It didn't seem to matter that the Constitution allowed registered residents of Shingal to defend themselves—every family was permitted one firearm. Regardless, up and down the lane, officers pushed into homes and hauled out old rifles, AK-47s, and handguns; the armaments were piled like kindling into crates. Residents looked on stone-faced from their thresholds.

The officer watched and nodded. "Right," he said, and then gave me his sweat-stained back. "We've been getting reports of illegal weapons caches."

"ISIS is just down the road," I said, trying to keep my voice steady. "They could come here any day. You know this. You can't leave us here helpless. We have the right to defend our own lives and our community."

"You have the Peshmerga to defend you. It's your right to exist under their protection. They are trained for what's coming—if anything is coming at all."

By sundown, and just before we sat around the floor cloth to eat meager bowls of couscous and plates of stale naan, most all the weapons in Shingal were gone, dumped into vans and carted away. The Peshmerga soldiers smoking cigarettes and holding sentry along the rim of town remained mute, allaying our uncertainties with casual smiles and pointing out their own heavy arsenal. The Iraqi army is full of chickens, we were told.

Naïf still had an AK in the back of the car, and I still had my Glock. For some reason, they never searched our house. They had lists of who had what—I guess we weren't on it.

"What the hell is going on, Shaker?" Naïf said.

"I don't know. I'll make more calls."

IN THE HIGH heat of late morning, a great horde of bedraggled Shiite refugees came drifting in a smog of stirred up dust down the long road from Tal Afar. Some rode on horses or donkeys, but many were crammed tight into slowly moving cars, small children sitting way back, legs hanging from the open trunks. Each face stared out vacant and covered in a thick film of grime, the full whites of their eyes showing the horrors they'd just escaped by a hair. Hours later, more stragglers arrived on foot, their dragging feet bleeding and covered in a dry paste of red mud. They'd fled fifty miles west over the open desert, leaving all they owned behind, as ISIS contingents trampled through their neighborhoods, some firing machine guns into homes, others grabbing occupants and beating them one at a time in the streets. After two days of bloodshed and havoc, the Turkoman city known as the home of the children of Eden fell hard on the sword of the Islamic State.

Immediately, Yazidis in every village opened their houses, and we set up receiving centers in the schools and public buildings. Anyone who had anything to give—blankets, mattresses, and food—brought it fast. We fed and clothed whole terror-stricken families, and listened stunned to the breathless tales they had to tell.

"They are not human," an old man told me, his bony hands shaking as he clasped a tin cup. "Get out if you want to live."

"Where can we go from here?" I asked him and pointed out the open double doors and into the sea of night.

"South," he said. "All the Shia must go south. Tomorrow, at first light if we can."

"We aren't Shia," I said, carefully dressing the open wounds on his old callused feet.

"Ah, Yazidi, Yazidi," he said, and took in a tired breath. "They will come this way, believe me."

"We have the Peshmerga here now. Didn't you see them out there?"

When he said nothing, I looked up to see his gaze gust over me, pupils staring out dark and sober.

I went on: "There are thousands of them, patrolling all over Shingal."

"Ha," was all he said, and looked down into his cup. Then his shoulders rose once and fell back again as he sipped the last of his drink. "Good luck to you, boy."

ALL ACROSS SHINGAL, families gathered at street corners, in courtyards and kitchens, under awnings in the market districts, and outside the doors of our temples while waiting their turn to pray. Casual conversations no longer existed in Khanasor; the exchange of malignant rumors had replaced every former pleasantry. Under the spindly mulberry trees in the foothills, our elders sat on grass mats slowly sipping chai, boiling the water in small kettles over the dug-out fire pits. Fanning the embers, they spoke in hushed warnings, citing the more than seventy genocides that had plagued Yazidis over centuries.

Higher up along the serrated slopes, past our burial grounds, thin reefs of war smog slid westward. Some people told themselves all the talk was merely paranoia and went about their business, herding sheep and hoeing the furrows. Others packed up cars and tried to get to the KRG, only to see the Peshmerga round them up and turn them back time and time again. A handful of people sneaked through the lines on foot under the cover of night, met up, and hid themselves away among relatives already living there.

I watched neighbors load hauls of cucumbers, tomatoes, and bread into cars and ferry them in large baskets to the network of caves cut like ancient secrets into the slopes of our holy mountain. My own family simply waited, watching the news, as I checked in with the Peshmerga units. There wasn't much more we could do. Living out in the great open plains of Shingal, hundreds of thousands of Yazidis were cornered; closed borders and enemy territory surrounded us on all sides like impenetrable walls.

At night I got into my car, lights off, and made covert excursions out into the foothills to look over the south-facing terrain, past which the enemy lay in wait. Always I thought of Dil-Mir in her house across the dry valley, and often called her from up there on my solitary shelf in the sky. She'd go out and we'd gaze at the moon awhile together, whispering sweet nothings into the wind, and wish each other a good night.

Near the end of July and from a perch of rock, I pulled out a set of binoculars and methodically scanned the slopes. Past the main road and out over the distant southern badlands, I spied unfamiliar convoys of vehicles and tracked their paths. Coming and going in tight formation from the direction of Anbar, they crawled steadily over the sands. From miles away, you could see the taillights from their vehicles dance over the ground. Occasionally, I'd lose sight of the caravans as they snaked into the low buttes and I'd have to wait, sometimes over an hour, before they came back down, and disappeared again into the pitch.

"You get any numbers?" Brownsword asked me.

I could hear his fingers tapping fast against a keyboard.

"They ride in groups of half a dozen or more," I said. "All around, and always south of the mountain. And there's steady traffic moving in from Syria, all the time now."

Migone was in on the call; I could hear the slow hiss of his breath, and every so often the clanking of ice as he brought a drink to his lips. There was no border anymore, he explained— just big open territory. When ISIS had Mosul in its teeth, their commanders had called for reinforcements from Syria to help finish the job. Now my people were right in their way—we had to be ready to run.

Brownsword and Migone were getting a contingent together to beat down doors in DC and to lobby for support. For now, we just planned: Iraqi Kurdistan was out—Assayish were everywhere, crawling all over the line. The only safe haven left was the mountain. I was to stay in tight with Yazidi contacts in the Peshmerga; keep reporting traffic patterns; acquire extra batteries for my cell; check in daily.

"How about morning, noon, and night," Migone added. Then he said to keep the phone and the Glock on me at all times.

SKY AND LAND stood so calm as time carried us into August. The air redolent, wheat cut on the rolling farmland, crops all harvested, tilled fields bare under a clear blue sky. In town, laundry hung from lines and cooking smoke drifted as lambs and goats stood lined up along laneways and we prepared for the summer slaughter. Looking out over Khanasor, you could almost imagine that an everlasting peace cloaked our part of the world, keeping us well away from any danger. And yet, tension reverberated everywhere; in those dog days we lived strapped to a huge pyre, drenched in petrol, waiting for someone to strike a match.

It was the early morning of our seasonal feast, when the holy men ended their forty days of solitary prayer and fasting. Daughters and sons and extended kin from every corner of Nineveh and beyond journeyed where they could, from the nearby cities where they worked the construction sites or went to school, and gathered to celebrate in the villages tucked all around the sacred mountain.

People dressed in traditional clean white garb handed out colorful sweets and cool drinks, as neighbors strolled up and down the thoroughfares greeting one another. All of us were trying hard to set aside thoughts of what was really happening in villages just forty miles to the east that had become the edge of the earth, where homes burned and men in black balaclavas ripped their rivals limb from limb. Only the oblivious children played carefree in the shock of midday sunshine, sugar coating their glistening lips and fingers, no notion yet that their whole world teetered on a blade.

Everywhere I went, people spoke only of ISIS and what they might do to us. We were the placid children of Adam; they were fanatics from a fallen world. So we crowded into hot kitchens and under sweltering tents, ate and drank, and feasted some more until our bellies stretched like the skins over drums. As soon as I could, I found a quiet place and called my Dil-Mir to tell her I loved her.

"For how long?" she whispered and laughed.

"Until the end of the world, and ever after."

Past midnight, the tambours still strumming, I languished on the roof. I heard the low whine of one man singing several houses away; his wife hushed him fast and he went silent. Under the blanket of warm air my body felt heavy, and I stared up into the pitch of night, a single star shining in the east. Wine and moonlight soaking my mind, I traveled lazy and only half-aware through a lull of waking dreams. Thoughts of Dil-Mir's hair the first time I touched it, reaching out like a starving man as she passed by. Wind moved across me, and I drifted out of my own skin, lids heavy as silver coins over my eyes. I smelled warm shisha; heard Brownsword cackle and Migone call out my name:

Mikey, Mikey, sing us a song.

And I answered: *I have to sleep now, sir, we ate so well.*

By now, the whole village was slumbering in their small gray houses—it was the dead hour just before dawn. Sky and ground merging, we might have all been lying at the bottom of an ocean. Within that deep soporific quiet, the air around me began to vibrate. I sat up on my mat, stared out into nothing, and listened.

Moments later, I was in the far beyond outside of Khanasor, wandering the empty plains at night. Sounds were closing in fast—heavy and hell-bent. The grind of armored metal rumbled through my chest. Then, out of nowhere, the earth buckled under me as I stood staring into the horizon. Before the just-rising sun, a dark band of trucks appeared, hurtling across the ground and sending up a tidal wave of exploding dirt.

From somewhere far behind me, people started jabbering, and I heard my father call out: *Tell the others to come.*

The man in the first vehicle looked over as they closed in, his shawl falling to one side. I knew those eyes set in a dough of pockmarked skin—RPG just laughed and pointed as his shrieking brethren of the apocalypse pulled out their machine guns and assaulted the heavens.

They were coming straight for us, and I hollered back at the shadowed village. *Run, run, run!* —but my limbs stood frozen.

Then I snapped up, eyes bulging, my cold hands shook. I got to my feet on the roof, still in a heart-stopping stupor, and stared way out. Heat lightning flashed along the hills and a distant roll of mountain thunder rumbled over Shingal. On the ground, my cell phone was stirring, and I grabbed it fast.

No voices—just the *thud-thud* of artillery fire and then dead air.

"Hello. Who is this?" I said again and again, but the signal cut out.

I raced down into the house, where the others were already gathering. All the children were fast asleep in beds and on floor mats, crowded in the rooms around the courtyard. When Daki saw me, she grabbed my hand and didn't let go.

"Did you hear all the trucks? There's trouble," she whispered. "On the south side. Most of the people there are still asleep, and we can't get through on the phones."

"I know," was all I could say, hearing my own strained voice as though from the other side of the room.

I went to get Naïf's hookah from the shelf, put in a ball of tobacco, and sucked down a hot drag. For the next two hours all I would do was smoke and make calls, hundreds of them, to units hunkered down all over the region. It could all be a mistake, easily enough—someone heard a gunshot and started firing, setting off a violent chain reaction. Such things often happened in the fog of war. I had my laptop open and cell phone ready, scrolling down my contact list. I tried Dil-Mir first and several times, but there was no answer.

Meanwhile, the others were packing up the car, loading in food, water, and blankets. We already had things ready and had rehearsed our exodus down to the minute. First sign of trouble, we were gone. Naïf brought out his rifle and checked the magazine. In other rooms, and from the adjacent houses, I could hear drawers and cupboard doors opening and shutting.

"Just take the pictures, forget the rest," I heard my sister-in-law say.

"We will drive the car through Rabia," Naïf said. "If there's an invasion, they have to let us in. I don't care what they do, we are crossing the border."

"All right, take your car with your family and Daki as planned," I said. "Where is Dapîra?" My grandmother had gone to a cousin's house to celebrate and hadn't returned.

"We told her to stay where she was, and that you would come get her if they haven't got room for everyone."

"OK, I will. The others have their vehicles, and anyone left over can go in the next-door neighbor's delivery truck. You can fit fifty people in there if you have to. He's in Dohuk and left the keys in the glove compartment just in case. I already talked to him."

"What about you, Shaker—you have your car all gassed up? The plan was to leave together."

"I'll come later. The Peshmerga are out there, I have to drive to the checkpoints, find out what's happening."

"Daki won't leave without you."

"She has to. You tell her I'll go find Dapîra and bring her with me if I can."

"But you're not going all the way to your girlfriend. You can't."

"No, I'm going to tell her to get out, but I think they're still sleeping over there."

Children wrapped in blankets paraded through the front door in a daze of half sleep. No one spoke, not a word as they filed out, blinking. I watched them go, the cell phone next to my ear. Military reflexes returned to me as though doors were opening in another hemisphere of my brain. Suddenly, I was back out on the bases, in the MRAP just leaving the wire.

Soon, several Peshmerga officers were giving me the rundown—there were enemy forces approaching. Several times the air went dead, and I could barely hear a thing over the torrents of static.

"ISIS is using an electronic signal-jamming system to scramble the lines, probably lifted it off the IA," I told Naïf. "It's hopeless right now. Just hurry and go. There's no doubt—this is it."

AFTER THE OTHERS left, I got my handgun and went back up onto the roof. I could see the shadow of the mountain stretched over the desert like a slumbering beast. Something was happening on the other side, but that was over sixty miles away. The atmosphere over Khanasor was as still as a snapshot. Then my cell phone chimed.

"Dil-Mir?" I said.

"No, it's Alyas, Shaker. You must send for help."

The voice of my old schoolmate was hollow and made of air. It was hard to hear him; he might as well have been a ghost calling out from another world.

"Where are you, what's happening?"

"In my parents' house in Sabaye. We can't get out right now. Just listen to me. Hold on . . ."

Then I heard a shot crack over the line like a streak of lighting. Seconds later, the deep hiss and thud of falling mortar shells. In the background, a woman howled like a gale of wind and I heard him tell her to stop.

"Alyas, talk to me," I said.

Every cell in my body quickened to a gallop and the atmosphere seemed to thin. I crouched low, holding a hand over my other ear. Guns boomed again over the line and I heard my friend gulp down air. Part of me knew I might be speaking to a dead man giving his last living testament.

"Okay, I'm here," he whispered.

"What's happening?"

"They came for us before daybreak," he began. "From the road to Tal Afar, in a long line of beat-up trucks, dark scarves shrouding their faces. They had guns hidden in the two hills behind the village."

"You must get out."

"Not yet, we have to wait."

"What kind of arsenal do they have?"

"Not much. I don't know. A few mortars. It didn't take much more than that. We knew right away who they were and what they wanted. People hid in their homes, under tables, inside empty grain bins, anywhere. We did everything we could to keep the children quiet."

Another explosion, and the line cut out for a moment.

All over Khanasor, others were waking to their phones and getting out of beds. I could see their panicked forms moving to windows and staring out.

"What are the Peshmerga doing? They need to hold the lines and evacuate the village."

"They left us, Shaker. Before it even started."

"What—all of them?"

"Not the Yazidi officers, but all the rest. Every last one of them. Didn't even fire a single shot. It's not good."

"It can't be. It can't be. What about their arsenal, what have they left you with?"

"Nothing. They took it all and left. Listen to me, Shaker—this will happen to you next. Today, tomorrow. In an hour from now. I don't know. First they will take the south side, and then come around and attack the north. The desert is swarming with them. There is no one to protect us. It's a bloodbath."

"My God. You must get out, now—"

Then I lost him to vacant air.

And I ran.

Fast.

Chapter Fifteen

Shadow on the Mountain

FULL MORNING, ALREADY BAKING HOT. OUT IN THE ERUPTING streets, a live wire of unbridled fear surged, and the raw scent of animal panic engulfed every corner. People poured from their homes and charged into the melee, mouths slack and hanging open. Some climbed onto bicycles two or three at a time; the infirm were loaded into rusted wheelbarrows. There was no time for conversation—even the smallest children moved in stunned silence. Many would not speak again for weeks.

Every nerve electrified, I slid into the car, mind tallying the number of people that could cram inside it—five at least, and maybe three more lined up in the open trunk. I gripped the wheel to steady myself. In a satchel, I'd stuffed batteries for my cell phone and an extra magazine of bullets. The handgun and a hunting knife were tucked into my belt; I checked them now. Then I shoved the key into the ignition. My hands were shaking.

Click-click-click-click-click.

I tested the switch for the headlights—nothing. The battery was dead, and I knew it was over. Those who had vehicles were all long gone.

A full tide of dazed figures pushed past the open window of my useless car; their open palms hitting the metal roof sounded like falling hail. White eyes staring straight ahead; hands dragged gaping children, or hauled livestock from tattered ropes. The aged hobbled along, bewildered in the wake. From what we knew, ISIS was surrounding Mount Shingal like a lasso; our chances of a clean escape grew more tenuous by the millisecond.

Stepping out of the car, I moved forward and the horde swept me up and into itself. Blazing over the end of my street, I could see the banner of open desert sky and everyone pressing toward it. There were so many, an avalanche of human beings, the same loud animal instinct compelling us—*get to the mountain*. The scene was multiplying many times over, playing out in every nearby Yazidi village that ISIS hadn't yet taken.

Then my cell phone went off in my pocket and I grabbed it, legs in a gallop.

"Mikey, it's Rob. I got Jay on the line, too. What's going on over there? We've been getting crazy reports."

"ISIS has the south side of the Shingal," I shouted over the static. "The Peshmerga abandoned their positions. We are next." I was panting and it was hard to hear. "I don't know any more yet."

"So it's as bad as we thought."

"Worse. We have nothing. No one here to protect us."

"You on the run now, brother?"

"Yes—to the mountain." And I knew my voice was cracking. "Pray for us." I could say no more.

"Go, Michael—just go."

THE THRONG HEAVED forward, discharging into the searing gulf of desert. Bodies streamed over the flatland as though the heart of Khanasor had detonated, sending out a wild rush of human shrapnel. Soon, there were more than twenty thousand of us on the run, unleashing a tempest of sand that billowed up several stories. We all just dove into the violent haze, momentarily blinded. Inside the swirling dust, forms pushed past me: coughing children, a woman cloaked in sheets pushing a cart full of photographs. Four boys teetered by on a bike. Whole families coated head to toe hung together as they hurried along like pale figures made of clay. Wailing babies belched grime and then went quiet.

Soon, I sensed concrete under my feet and realized I'd forgotten to put on my shoes. I stopped by the road, pulled down the checkered scarf I'd coiled around my head, and spat out a glob of grit. Just then, I felt the thunder of armored trucks rising like a storm from the west, moving straight for us. Instinctively, we all gasped and broke out as a single entity, rushing across the open plain.

At first, the withdrawing units of Peshmerga didn't slow, consuming both lanes of the freeway as they sped east on their way to Iraqi Kurdistan. As the convoy gusted through, I saw great oiled barrels of artillery rising from flatbeds and turrets; and the noses of machine guns jutted from the laps of fighters crammed into the personnel vehicles. Stock-still, the soldiers sat as silent and impotent as wax statues.

Hollering now, I raced toward the traffic, limbs pumping, fists clenched. I'd sucked in so much dirt; it coated the insides of my cheeks. My scoured gums had started bleeding. Arms raised, I stood in the road, not caring if they crushed my body—our last hope was hurtling past me in a hurricane of false promises.

"Stop—stop now!" I shouted against the wind.

One of the last trucks in the line slowed.

"What are you doing?" I hollered into the open window. "You can't just leave us. You have to fight."

"Orders," the driver yelled over the din, shrugging. "Nothing we can do. Nothing."

Gnawing at a chapped upper lip, the soldier in the passenger seat rammed his chin into his chest and sighed. Hard to tell what he was thinking.

"Orders from who?" I brandished the phone in my hand as though it contained the truth.

The driver signaled to the sky. "Higher up," he said. "I can't help you."

The wheels began to turn faster, and I grabbed at the open rim of the window.

"They are shooting people in the villages," I screamed. "Who gave the orders? How high up? Please—leave us weapons. Anything."

Then the other soldier slowly shifted his downward gaze to me—eyes so clear, you could see the shuddering of a conscience like a second self within him. A moment later, he looked away.

"The top," he said. "The orders came from the top. We can do nothing."

The engine revved and the truck sped off.

THE RIVER OF evacuees split into a delta; one thin line stayed by the road, shuffling toward the Kurdish autonomous region; the other streamed wide, heading south into the deep embrace of the alluvial steppe plains that rose toward the foothills. I was on the rutted path for the mountain when we heard the low metallic groan of more trucks approaching. People stopped in their tracks in the coarse fog trying to figure out which direction the sounds were coming from, and what they meant—salvation or slaughter. Peering back through the murk, I saw a battered pair of pickups zigzagging toward us. Headlights beamed a dull yellow through the dinge. You could see men in black *shamags* standing like dark silhouettes in the flatbeds.

Then I heard the unmistakable snap of the first bullet buzz past my ear, and I threw myself into the dirt. For a moment, it was like being back in the helter-skelter of Anbar, the insurgency in full swing. I rolled over the ground and waited, hand on my weapon. Instantly, the energy of the mob shifted; a rogue wave of hysteria pushed them forward into a frenzy of thrashing limbs. As the *rat-rat-rat* of gunfire diced the air, a man standing next to me went down. Then others collapsed like felled trees. People wrapped their small children into their chests and tore ahead. A woman in dusty robes just stood in the lethal fracas, arms held out like wings, as she keened in Kurmanji to the sky.

I scrambled to my feet. We were running directionless now; every child baying in an eerie chorus. I could feel my shirt and pants stick to my skin as though they'd been glued on, and the naked heels of my feet burned raw. Forbidding miles away in the high heat, the ark of the mountain stood mottled and shimmering like an apparition. My mind beseeched it to come closer—we were still hours away on foot.

"What's happening?" a young boy said, staring up and grabbing my hand; the vibrant blue of his lit-up eyes was shocking to see through the tenebrous dust.

"Just keep running," I told him.

"I can't find my family."

"We're all going to the same place. Don't stop. No matter what happens."

Behind us we could hear the high-pitched war cries of the masked men as their trucks crashed into the teeming throng, resolute in their jihad.

"Allahu akbar!"

"Takbir!"

"Allahu akbar!"

"Takbir!"

Cyclones of bullets raised the ground to a raging boil and the masses reared up all around me. Chaos swallowed the boy; I felt his fingers slide away into time. I kept going with the pack, the shrieks of girls and women erupting from every direction.

Voices cried out to God in heaven; the sun flared like a blood-shot eye through the gloom.

Then the sound simply ceased—the earth at war fell silent—and I kept running through the preternatural hush. Suddenly, I no longer knew or felt anything. Time had collapsed, stretching formless into a bleak void. There was only the shared blood of our long-hounded ancestors, beating through our hearts and roaring through our veins. We had all been here before, many times: Yazidis reduced to hunted animals caught in a biblical stampede, fleeing for our lives—for who we were, as one.

Maybe the random killing was all part of the sport, or maybe they were just employing a guerrilla tactic used to great effect in the run-up to the invasion: after a targeted rush of carnage, the soldiers of the Islamic State simply moved on.

Minutes later, as the pickups sped away toward the road, we could hear the bloodbath start up again—across the barren miles, the muted cries of the slaughtered were unmistakable. When the last desperate echoes reached me, I ran harder.

HOURS LATER, BESIEGED villages burned. Mulberry trees smoldered and flocks of birds shot out of the smoke like eruptions of onyx beads. In the distance that we didn't dare breech, squalid white flags drooped over houses, the occupants no doubt begging for the promised mercy that ISIS would never grant.

By now, the passing multitude had spread way out over miles, and we pressed onward under the open broil, parched and limping. Every so often, ISIS snipers took potshots at us and we'd all drop to the ground. Sometimes, dilapidated cars and tractors full of families rumbled by. Then, as though tearing out of a dream, a horse mad with fear galloped past me, kicking a path through the exodus. I stopped in the sand and watched the beast disappear as it thundered into a cor-rugated stretch of furrows that had once made up the lands of my father. I knew those undulating fields better than the creases over my own palm, and could only stare out in a near stupor of longing. Then I glimpsed a white shirt billowing along the tilled fields.

Suddenly a young boy again, before anything had ever happened to us, I ran out to him. Dressed in my sandals and cap, I dashed across the soft watered ground straight for my father, my king, calling, "*Babo, Babo,*" until my voice gave out. Standing there under his crown of silvery hair, he turned to me at last, kissed his hand, and held it out. Then the world went full white, and I closed my eyes.

When I opened them again, the desiccated field was empty.

THE CELL PHONE started up, and somehow I knew it was her.

"Dil-Mir—thank God. Talk to me fast. I don't know how long this signal will work."

"Shaker. We are surrounded. On all sides."

Her voice was like wind. I could hear people in the background jabbering.

"Where are you now?"

"In the house with the others."

"You can't stay there, Dil-Mir. You have to run—now."

I was staring out at the formidable wall of mountain standing between us.

"No, no. It's OK. They stopped shooting. Everything is quiet."

"Dil-Mir, listen to me. You must get out of there. Don't think, just leave for the mountain."

"We put up a white sheet over the house like a flag. Those who do this will be spared."

"No, no—that's a lie, Dil-Mir."

"It can't be—they stopped shooting. Only the few who didn't listen or tried to escape were killed. They told us to put up the sheet, and we are still all right."

I was on my knees in the dirt. "The white flag is a lie. It's a lie."

"I have to go. There are trucks."

"Dil-Mir—get out. Forget the flag. Forget everything."

But she was gone.

And I could not move from the ground.

Still naked miles from the foothills, a hatchback raced past my pathetic form kneeling there, and stopped. Then a man got out, hoisted me up by the armpits, and helped me into the back seat, squeezing my body in next to three other men. Two women shared the seat up front.

Someone slipped a pair of sandals onto my ruined feet.

I heard a baby gurgle and the car started up.

A stream of tepid water poured into my mouth.

I gulped it down, gasping.

"Where are you from?" said the old man pressed against me. "Keep your head down in case they shoot at us."

"Khanasor." I was wiping the paste from my eyes. "*Yaho, yaho . . .*"

"We came from Kocho for the feast, and went to Khanasor to find our cousins. There's hardly anyone left over there."

"Do you know anything about the hamlets on the south side?" I asked.

"Those tiny villages are full of ghosts," a woman muttered from the front seat.

I could see the back of her head; her wild conflagration of ruddy hair quavered as the car bumped over the ground.

"What do you mean?"

"They just want the girls. Everyone else but the young boys are shot. It's the same in every village."

Two miles later, the car engine sputtered and wheezed across its final yard. We all got out, left the vehicle behind like a picked-over carcass, and started walking again.

WE WERE UP on the higher plateaus now, where groupings of dead lay scattered like mannequins. Flies were already buzzing; and the steady hum in the unforgiving swelter made the skin creep over my bones. Some of us stopped to bury the shot-up children, using flattened rocks to cut though the dirt until the pads on our fingers scraped away and we could no longer dig. All the passersby moving up the slope whispered out prayers and kept going. Under the pummeling sun, we piled stones in small mounds over the shallow graves. I thought I heard more wounded cry out from behind rocks, but when I looked, I could not find them.

"Is that all?" said an old man who'd helped.

"What else is there?" another one muttered.

"Those are someone's kids."

"Not any longer."

"They belong to God," I said. "And the mountain."

Then I turned to face the rising cliffs.

Whatever energy remained in my limbs went into gaining a solid purchase on the steady climb up the first craggy slope.

NOW SHOTS WERE ricocheting right along the incline, as ISIS trucks full of shouting men marauded across the surrounding terrain. I came across the bullet-riddled body of a boy showing a wet chasm where his chest had been. I closed my eyes and crawled over him and kept going for the ridgeline.

As more ordnance hit the mountain, loosened mounds of rubble slid down the slope, pushing back climbing forms. At any moment, it could all be over, and I waited for the end to come. But thoughts of my Daki and Dil-Mir kept me climbing; nails broke off past the quick. Here and there the elderly who'd abandoned the arduous climb just sat dust-covered on the rocks.

"You must try," I hollered to one woman.

"No," she said. "My body says it's enough. None of this is worth surviving."

MOUNT SHINGAL, A long shoulder of desolate rock fixed to a sixty-two-mile range, rises from the prehistoric floodplains to a height of more than 4,700 feet. Over one hundred thousand of us made it to the summit, though no one would ever make an official record. Thousands perished in the cruel climb, including countless children. Prowling ISIS fighters shot many; others were simply too small or weak to withstand the diabolical elements. No water, food, or shade—it was over 110 degrees Fahrenheit. Up there, huddled on a parched ledge in the vacant sky, scores of families were trapped and people were dying by the hour. While the base of the mountain had become an ISIS slaughterhouse, the top was a merciless inferno.

I climbed way up to the crest of Shingal, now the rim of hell on earth, and stared across the unfolding scene. Standing there alone without any kin, without anything whatsoever, I bore witness to the forsaken horde of my people spread way out below for as far as the eye could see, all of them moaning and pressed together on the rocks into a single quivering shadow. Right then, I didn't know how any of us were ever going to survive.

Chapter Sixteen

Taken

NIGHT FELL SLOWLY OVER SHINGAL, AND ALONG ITS DIMMING ether the baleful smog of war slid by, passing beyond the ridge like a callous afterthought. Far below, along the bleak moonscape of pulverized villages and ransacked squats, the black flags of the Islamic State were going up on water towers and electrical posts, unfurling over the sides of crumbling buildings. Gunfire flared across the blue twilight, and flames licked out the cores of whole villages, some of which were too insignificant to be found on a map. Many would never be inhabited again.

Those Yazidis who hadn't managed to flee in time huddled in the burgeoning darkness, hoping Arab neighbors hadn't lied during the days before the invasion, when they'd offered reassurances that ISIS would spare them. By now, I'd heard that story over and over again as countless numbers lay executed all over Shingal—another three hundred thousand of us were on the run.

My own family was hurtling along the setting eastern borders, trying to find a clean way into the KRG—at least, that's what I hoped. From a prow of rock, I stared out over the panorama of Nineveh like a man trapped on a condemned ship, every square mile a death trap that had been laid months in advance, but prophesied and decreed for centuries.

Behind me and from their cruel beds of rubble, over which they'd placed pieces of cardboard or cloth like derelict rafts, people were sending up desperate prayers like smoke signals to God. Women clutched small wedding photographs of murdered husbands; others had nothing left to hold but themselves. Stunned children sat in a collective daze, leaning against each other, or sagging over their exhausted mothers, not even blinking and never daring to ask when they could go home. For hours into the eventide, fathers wandered the miles of cliffs and caves like shepherds, calling out the names of their lost daughters: *Nasreen, Adeeba, Nadia, Kamila, Sabeen* . . . Through the long night I heard those haunting echoes, and I can hear them now, as though their voices still circle the earth.

I laid my beat-up bag of bones down over the gravel and thought of the small bodies we'd lowered into that hard, hallowed ground. Some still had their eyes wide open like tiny mirrors to the sky, lids already too stiff to close. The souls within were long gone, and we scraped the dirt so gently over them. I held a rock in my hand now and squeezed it hard, my whole body releasing a silent primordial scream.

There was no voice for what I'd witnessed. Twenty-four hours before, I'd been in our family kitchen, music filtering in through the open door, sipping red wine. And one hour ago, I gave my last scrap of bread to a young boy with a soiled eyepatch, only to have many other children flock behind him, sitting together like wingless birds among the stones, their faces bloodied and heads all wrapped haphazardly in bandages.

"What happened to you all?" I asked a girl among them, motioning. It looked as though someone had taken a serrated knife and scored her kneecaps and shins.

"We fell down the mountain when the men in trucks started shooting at us," a redheaded girl said, her face flush with freckles. "I gave the badly hurt ones most of my portion and now I'm so hungry."

"Where is your mother?"

"I don't know anymore. Please," she said. "A little bread?"

"I'm sorry," was all I could say and held out my bare and filthy hand. "I have nothing."

How I hated myself then.

AT FIRST LIGHT, we formed contingents and gathered in a narrow cave where we'd collected all the weapons we could find. A few men went to search for stragglers or to bury the spoiling dead, who littered the dirt in mounds of colorful clothes. I moved along the peaks to speak with the families, and they told me, in their turn, both what they needed most and what had happened.

It was always the same—water, food, medicine. Then long gruesome tales of ISIS. I remembered the strengthening power of talking, and let each person go on until their speech gave out: the cars and trucks hauling their kinsmen away, how quietly the men all went—their eyes already halfway to where they were going. Soon after, the outbreak of gunfire, bodies piled in ditches. The pretty girls who slit their own throats before the militants could touch them. And I heard the voice of my beloved—

Let the armies worry about protecting us.

When my group reconvened again in the afternoon, I told them what I knew for a certainty: we had no choice—no one was prepared for those conditions. The sheer number of sick and injured—broken bones, bullet wounds, infections. We would have to go down into the farms at night and collect whatever we could.

"Cucumbers and tomatoes are full of water," I told them.

"Insanity," another man said. "ISIS is waiting for us to do just that. They have their guns pointed at us from every direction, shoot at anything that moves and laugh about it."

"There are wells at the temples if we can get all the people to them," someone offered.

"The wells are tiny and the lines are so long."

"How long?" I asked.

"Two days—that's what I calculated."

"Two days for what?" I asked. "For each person to take a turn at the water?"

"That's right—that's how long it will take for so many to get there."

Not believing him, I ascended to a higher ridge for a better vantage, and glimpsed down along the incline to the thirsting corporeal stream that snaked so slowly toward the first temple, along interminable corridors of rock. All those forms shivered in the broil, wilting over boulders as they waited to gain a single pace.

"This mountain is a graveyard of the living," I said, descending again, covered in a thick sheen of sweat. "We have to go down."

A few of the men nodded. Someone handed me a half-filled canteen, but I was too ashamed to take a full drink from it. The heat was as consummate as a sledgehammer; we might as well have climbed into the mouth of a volcano.

"How long can a human survive without water?" a boy called out, his spindly limbs webbed among the naked branches of a barren tree.

No one gave him the answer.

186

ON THE CUSP of sunset, we made our way along the daggered rim toward the north side of the mountain, and then went our separate ways silently toward the outlying farmlands. The south side was still too dangerous, but I could see clashes lighting up the northerly hamlets like carnivals, and I knew from the others there were skirmishes in Khanasor.

Sometimes, a cooling breeze wafted over and I had to stop and feel it cover me like a salve; then I'd sense the stink of death sneaking through and gag. Nothing in my gut, all I could do was spit up mouthfuls of bile and try to be quiet about it. There were too many dead to hope to bury, and it shamed our people to leave them without any dignity, but we had so few ways now to remain human—let alone Yazidi.

There was no one way down, and I had to feel a path along the crooked spines of the gradient, always keeping low, sometimes crawling on my hands and knees as I'd been trained to do in the military. ISIS was no doubt equipped with night and thermal vision, and I did all I knew to avoid detection: hiding behind rocks or confused backgrounds, and keeping my skin concealed as I slipped from cover to cover. In the thermal crossover as the day transmuted into night, the changing temperature would make it easier to mask my roasting body, but I knew already the way back under a full night would be far more precarious.

When I stopped to relieve myself, voices chattering in Arabic passed through me like a chill. One hundred feet below, I could see the spectral outlines of their forms. I held the AK out over a rock, scoping the two fighters who were passing a jug of water between them. The man who'd given me the weapon was a former Yazidi Peshmerga soldier—he'd shot five ISIS fighters with it as his own Kurdish unit fled, and wished me good luck. I told him I didn't want to kill anyone, and I meant it.

Now I slithered in, going from one boulder to another as the militants stood there chatting, gulping the water as though they hadn't a care in the world. The paste in my mouth grew extreme and I swallowed it down like gravel, almost choking. Not far from a makeshift mountain road, when a car full of ISIS soldiers tore past, I cleared my throat and sprinted closer. Then I slid sideways to a projection of slate twenty feet above them, and listened.

"Forget what anyone tells you, the ones in Kocho are the most beautiful. So many blue eyes there, you can make an ocean."

I heard the wet sounds of the other one parting his lips. So close, I could smell their rancid sweat.

The other one explained they would not get those girls, because the sheikhs would want them for a prize. Still, their contingent would soon have the whole town to themselves, and they decided it didn't hurt to go have a look before the captives were shipped off to Mosul—

"Maybe take a little taste."

"Some of them rub shit on their faces. Send them to Syria with the used ones. Leave us the virgins."

And they both started laughing; their taunting sounds echoed up through the quiet night and thrashed me.

My ruined hands grew hot, and I felt the AK's metal slide down my palms. It took everything in me not to mow those men down right then, but I looked up at the crescent moon, the watchful eye of our God's highest angel, and held it. I clutched my imperiled faith like the edge of a precipice over which I was dangling. When the pair moved off and disappeared, they'd tossed the jug to the ground, and I took what was left of their water.

TWO HOURS LATER I was on my knees between tall vines, filling my sacks with cucumbers, careful not to make a sound. In the distance, silver beams of searchlights brushed over the fields and I thought of the others out there picking. Every few minutes, I got up from the row and searched the terrain. Lamps flickered in outlying buildings, and I could see the shadows of doomed families inside. White flags were draped from so many rooftops. The warm smell of naan wandered by and I felt a fist clench inside my gut.

ISIS soldiers patrolled the roads, sometimes going into homes and abusing the occupants. Ten yards from me, two militants dragged out an old man and made him kneel over a gutter, where he vomited, the barrel of a pistol held fast against his neck. I could see the creased outline of the man's face and believed his old eyes were looking right at me—but I could not save him. They didn't shoot him then, just kicked the back of his head and left him there whimpering. As I backed into the undergrowth, I heard a single gunshot and bit into the heel of my hand.

At the far end of a crop of tomatoes, I came across live men I recognized from the mountain; and just past them, several teenage girls cowering among the creeping vines. Trembling like leaves, they spoke using wild hand gestures, pointing to the village.

"There's a man out there with a hatchet," one of them breathed out. "He's cutting the heads off the small children who try to run."

No one wanted to believe her, but we could see the truth seep in the full whites of her eyes. I placed two fingers softly against her lips and then just held her.

We found more people hiding in the fields, tended to their wounds and terror, and then took them back up with us.

ON THE MORNING of the second day, I ascended to the highest peak of Mount Shingal to hunt down a clear cellular signal. From their cavernous eye sockets and craggy perches, children watched me go, a few rambling in a strange delirium. They appeared snow-covered as they drooped there like fallen things under layers of dust.

"Wait till the rains come," a boy cried out. "Did you hear the thunder?"

"Quiet," another one said. "They'll hear us."

The phone hummed in my hand as I powered it up, my pulse taking long pauses as I searched for more bars—so far, nothing. It was getting hard to think straight. I got up and clambered a few yards along the peak, so high now that the atmosphere stretched way out and simmered. Finally I heard the ping of an alert, and then another and another—suddenly a chorus of cyber-voices found mine like a multitude of hands reaching out into the dark. And I fell over the unforgiving dirt, eyes straining for tears.

In minutes, I discovered that many of my family had made it just inside the safe zone of Syria, where a camp for Yazidi refugees had been set up. Many others had found the same open route. Heavily armed units of PKK (Partiya Karkerên Kurdistanê), or the Kurdistan Worker's Party, a controversial guerrilla organization from Turkey, had given them full protection and were guarding the camp.

Then, huddled over my screen, I tried over and over again to reach Dil-Mir. Each time I met dead air, but would not abandon the hope I'd pledged to keep for her; by now many girls had made it into the foothills and were hiding along inclines and in caves, where there was no cellular reception. It could take weeks to find her, but I would.

All around me, others were scrambling along the crest, their frantic voices rising up like flares. People wept dry tears into their palms as they listened to the first sounds of the lost, and several times I saw men fall to their knees as I had done.

Somehow, Brownsword managed to reach me, and hearing him speak into my ear, the sky all around seemed to spin.

"You're alive," he said, and I heard him swallow the air. "Some of the guys were sure you didn't get out. But Jay and I told them—not Michael, not the Archangel of Shingal." Then I heard him holler out to the others who were with him.

The timbre of that voice on the line was so strong and clear and I grabbed hold of it like a rope at the bottom of an abyss. "Brother, we can't go on up here. We need help."

"We know, brother. It's just hitting the news. How many of you are up there? They're saying a few thousand."

"No," I hollered, and jumped to my feet, pointing wildly as though he could see me. From where I was standing, I could look straight down along vast rivers and pockets of people all massed over every open space. "Fifty thousand just here on this side, maybe a hundred. If I throw sand in the air, it will hit a thousand people when it comes down. We are dying every minute that goes by. And there are men with hatchets cutting off the heads of children—shooting the rest. It's hell on earth, brother, I'm telling you. So many dead to bury, the air stinks of meat." And I could say no more, I was wailing.

"Christ . . ." And I heard Brownsword passing my information on to another person. "Brother, listen to me—Jay and I are on our way to DC. We want to arrange for air drops. The Obama administration needs to hear all this."

"You tell him we need help. Water, food, medical supplies," I said. "Now. Right now."

"I got it."

"Immediately. We won't make it out of here alive, I'm telling you." I could not think of how to convey to a man in California the diabolical dungeon I was standing in with what was left of my people.

"You don't have to tell me how bad it is—I know. But we're going to need your location and any enemy positions. Can you get that?"

"OK, I believe you. Just the water even."

"Listen, is there any way you can get that info? On enemy locations, arsenal, you know the drill. If you can't, you can't."

"ISIS is everywhere, in every village, all over the desert. They're surrounding the mountain. More of them are coming in from Syria."

"Have you been down the mountain, Mikey?"

For several seconds, I struggled to breathe and nodded my head. Then my heart settled into a steady beat. "Yes. I've been down the mountain. And I'm going again tonight, and every night, to get food and smuggle people out. They're taking the women as sex slaves and butchering the men. There are ditches full of rotting bodies."

"This is a genocide, Mikey. That's what you're in right now."

"Genocide," I whispered.

It was the first time I'd heard the word in English, and I felt it scrape down my throat as I said it.

"I'm so sorry, brother."

"It's not the first time," I said. "But after this one, that's it for us."

A murky beige sea seemed to surround the mountain on all sides, and I looked around at the forms crouched over the rocks, phones pressed to their ears, hoping for proof of life from their families. And I could talk no longer.

Then girls started calling—one after the other and without end. They had smuggled out phones, or stolen them from their captors, and were begging for rescue. ISIS was sending them on buses to other towns, like Tal Afar, where they holed them up in schools and warehouses. Once there, they were examined like livestock and their names, ages, and sexual status registered; virgins were separated from the married women.

Others languished in homes all over Shingal. Those who re-sisted were beaten; the mothers who refused to convert saw their children tortured. Some had already been raped, others were considered too pretty to despoil right away—especially those with green or blue eyes and light hair. Those ones were saved as stolen treasure in remote locations for ISIS commanders.

Already I was taking down lists of those we could reach, charting locations on Google Maps. For the rest, I sent out alerts on Facebook—right away an avalanche of the taken descended. Then those among the free Yazidis in the KRG and elsewhere in Iraq began to mobilize online, exchanging information.

All around the mountain, fathers, uncles, and brothers cleaned the sand from the barrels of rifles, and I stared down from our perch at the scattering of towns below, galvanized. There were still Yazidi souls to save down there, and we would have to fight to free them.

Meanwhile, Brownsword and Migone were on their way to Washington, to corral the Capitol and lobby for aid drops. Bowers was also calling on his contacts, some in the intelligence community—all of my brothers-in-arms were back with me now.

Then, in my energized state, a number I didn't recognize called and I held my phone close, hoping—knowing.

"Shaker?"

"Dil-Mir!" I shouted. "My God . . ." At last, the torturous heat left my body like a cloak of flames going out, and I could breathe again, as I hadn't for days. "I love you."

There was a pause. Static on the line.

"Dil-Mir?"

Then I heard her voice.

"Yes, it's me," she said. "I've been taken."

And everything in me broke into pieces.

Chapter Seventeen

The Situation Rock

IN THE EARLY MORNING HOURS, A CARAVAN OF MODERN PASSENGER buses rumbled along the desert turnpike toward Shingal, sweeping into ISIS-occupied villages—and the dreaded thing began. From a sheltered berm folded into the foothills, I watched the scene play out, damned to stand alone and bear full witness. A couple of guns and a hunting knife held up against a large contingent of fanatical soldiers of the Islamic State, all of them carting Kalashnikovs—I was as powerless as a limbless man.

Kneeling on the hot ground, I faced the sterile immensity of the badlands—no angel of mercy or savior in sight—and would not allow myself the reprieve of looking away. Then, from the dark mouths of dreary mud huts, women and girls as young as eight stumbled out into crooked rows, militants shoving them along like cattle. Most of the girls cowered, heads hanging low in their chadors; some fell to the ground again and again. The children looked about, blinking into the sunshine, and tore at the shawls of their young mothers, who staggered forward as though they were made of stone, arms wound about their petrified bodies.

I was close enough to see the gapped teeth of the leering ISIS ringleader, who stalked the wavering line of the seized, slipping his hands under fabric to grope at flesh, tongue probing his cheek—and I pressed a thumb over the blade of my knife until it sliced the skin. How I wanted to carve that wet thing right from the gash of his curled-up mouth. And yet I was trapped inside my own blistered skin, unable to move or else be discovered, and the raw truth forever lost.

Over one hundred women were driven out before me that day—I watched them go. Soldiers had already dragged many more screaming from the isolated region on the south side of the mountain, my Dil-Mir among them; thousands more would soon join transports from other towns, where ISIS would sell them while passing many out to fighters as *sabaya*—sex slaves.

When the women stepped onto the buses to a group of men already waiting inside, the sudden eruption of their high-pitched wails sheared the heavens. Through the tall windows as the engines roared to life, I glimpsed frantic movements. Bare shoulders and legs. Hands pressed against the glass. And I just knelt there in the shallow refuge of the berm as those moving dungeons slowly departed. In the coming days, it was a scene I would have to watch play out again and again. Arms held way up, I let out a muted cry.

Right there in the dirt, I understood what I should have always known: we were just grains of sand, scattered over a great map of pipelines and oil fields. First, we'd watch our women stripped of their final dignity; and in another blink we'd be long gone.

"IT'S A QUESTION of logistics," Migone said.

Leaning over a wall of rock, I cradled the cell phone, lifeline to the free and able hemisphere, against the sunken hollow of my cheek. Below, a flood of people were slowly filling the narrow berth of a ravine, staying low to keep out of sight of the marksmen while making their way to try another temple. One of the wells had already run dry. Scores had died in the wasted effort, either from sniper bullets or the ravaging elements. Before they collapsed themselves, a number of mothers had dropped the corpses of their babies along the scabrous pass—nothing more to be done.

I listened to the surreal sounds of modern America in the background: honking horns and blaring sirens. Two pallid Yazidi boys in threadbare army pants shuffled by, sharing a single pair of boots between them. I watched them pass, my fingers traveling over the rough skin of the face that had become a stranger to me. Making the monumental effort to focus on the task at hand and chisel a way out—all the calls and messages coming in and going out—seemed pointless.

Migone was holed up in a hotel room in Washington, DC, within view of the White House. He and Brownsword and a crew of veterans had spent several days straight knocking on every door in the Capitol. Congress was in summer recess, but the Senate committees—Intelligence and Armed Services—asked for reports and made recommendations up the linked chains of command. Right now, Migone was waiting to hear back from "Leanne" at the Department of State.

"We need enough assets to move that many people off the mountain," Migone went on. "We're talking about inserting security teams by air, but then you need troops to hold the terrain."

"Get a corridor open," Brownsword said. "And install some kind of ground element to secure it."

The talk was of arranging convoys of trucks. Trapped on the mountain for so long, it was unlikely that my people could even stand, let alone walk. Convoys needed fuel, and a destination capable of supporting so many; the evacuation would need to be done in stages: the terrain posed many challenges, as did obvious requirements for basic medical care, rehydration. The operation could take days, or maybe even weeks. Time we didn't have.

Brownsword and Migone's strategy to speed things up relied on the media, and I was crucial to that plan. They had waited right outside the White House, stopping every single camera crew. I had to be ready for calls from all of the major news outlets—never use my real name, keep my batteries charged, practice every word I would say, keeping it as concise as possible. ISIS would be tracking cell phones; I'd have to keep moving and scatter my signals.

"It's not hard to explain," I said. "We're dying up here."

I don't remember which one of them told me that I wasn't going to die on Shingal, but I was sure it was the kind of lie I'd heard combat medics tell stunned soldiers, whose shredded arteries were hemorrhaging over the sand.

"What's the latest in the villages?" Migone asked, steering us away from the abyss we were falling into, but hurling me inadvertently toward another.

"I told you they are moving the women. Who knows where. I sent the details on numbers and locations I have so far."

"Right," Brownsword said. "Tal Afar for one. Some of them. We have unconfirmed reports."

"Yes, I heard that too," I said. "But it doesn't make sense. Raqqa, Mosul, I get—that's where ISIS's commanders are."

"FOB Sykes in Tal Afar has that big airfield," Brownsword said. "They can keep the women in the bunkers and sell them off to the Saudis. Private planes. As I said, unconfirmed—but that's what we're hearing, anyway."

A part of me wanted to pack it in, like the old women languishing in the gullies, waiting for the end to find them. Then Dil-Mir slipped into my mind—and with her, lurid images of what the grimy hands of ISIS were doing came at me like the cracks of a whip. If I couldn't rescue her, I didn't think any of this would be worth surviving.

"We need weapons," I said finally, clearing my throat. I turned away and spat out a glob of blood-streaked phlegm. "A lot more. It's the only way to get things done right."

"Yeah. We can't do that right now. Believe me, we've been looking into it," Brownsword said. "Listen, there are teams getting dropped, but you won't see them. More of them are going into Erbil."

"Then I can get what we need from here," I said and offered no more.

"All right," Migone said, and paused. "You know what you're doing. I know you do."

"I do, brother."

And we closed the long bridge between our worlds once more.

AT DUSK, THREE of us maneuvered like shadows down the ragged slopes and fanned out into the plains—myself, Hassan, and Imad. Hassan and I were former terps; the last one would have started university in the fall, if ISIS hadn't splayed our very existence under a guillotine. Hassan was also a friend from Khanasor, and we'd played games of tag and football together over that very ground. All of us had lost women to ISIS— mother, sister, sweetheart—and were as resolute as would-be martyrs in our mission.

A hot steady wind cut in from the west, and we could hear the thudding sounds of artillery fire. In the east, the air looked like it had ignited. The curvature of the moon going full rose slowly against the blackening ridge behind us, and the coming night was as clear as glass when we stepped into it.

Three hours of trudging over the sands that swallowed every weary step, we followed Imad's compass over the boundless desert. Finally, we lay flat against the dunes and waited until we spotted the signal: patterned clicks from a narrow beam of light. We returned our flashes and then snaked our way toward the grouping of several dingy vehicles.

Part of me feared a setup, and I checked the chamber of my handgun before traversing the hollow pitch. Connections in the Kurdish militia groups operating out of Turkey and Syria had made contact on the mountain, and the meeting in the desert was choreographed down to the minute. The men inside had already provided their bona fides—fighting in Syria, some had already killed large numbers of militants. Exhausted, I shambled headlong into the truck behind the others and offered a breathless Kurdish greeting.

It had been two days since I had had anything to eat or drink. A Yazidi wearing a gold necklace of the Peacock Angel handed me a bottle and just stared, taking in my wrecked body as I chugged the water; the gulping sounds I made were savage. Watching through the rearview, the driver warned me to slow down, just before I lunged forward and belched out a waterfall. Then I crumpled against the seat, feeling hands wipe down my face as voices told me to just sleep awhile—though we didn't have a long way to go. Then, in the blue light of the moon, we tore fast and all-dark toward the border.

OVER THIRTY MILLION Kurds still live spread out over the vast territory of ancient Kurdistan, a region spanning parts of Syria, Armenia, western Iran, southeastern Turkey, and northern Iraq— making it the largest stateless ethnic group in the Middle East. After the defeat of the Ottoman Empire in World War I, short-sighted European civil servants carved the realm into pieces according to their narrow national interests, and sowed the seeds of hatreds that flourish to this day.

Washington, DC, has long considered the PKK militia group—now operating against ISIS while protecting Yazidi refugees—to be a full-blown terrorist organization. During the

1980s, in a quest for their own Kurdish state within Turkey, the PKK was responsible for a violent series of guerrilla attacks against diplomatic offices, kidnappings, and suicide bombings throughout the country. After the Turkish government cracked down hard on their factions and arrested their leader, the PKK retreated into northern Iraq, eschewing ferocity in an effort to gain some semblance of political autonomy. While I dozed in the caravan crossing into the Syrian safe zone under the protection of hardboiled PKK fighters, their decades-old history and current agenda mattered little to me, a half-starved Yazidi who'd just crawled out of the quarry of hell.

While the Peshmerga had fled into the sanctuary of their own borders, the PKK and their protection units, known as the YPG, had stepped in to fill the lethal breech. They escorted fleeing masses into the harbor of organized camps, where there was plentiful food, medical care, and shelter. And now they were about to give us the weapons we needed to fight off the militants and free our women, while also organizing heavily armed units to go up against the Islamic State in Shingal and rescue Yazidis trapped on the mountain. In August 2014, the PKK and YPG were our only bridge from certain extermination to survival. There is no doubt that without them, whole generations of Yazidis, including me, would all be dead.

By the next night, I was back in the same truck with Imad and Hassan, this time wide-eyed, well fed—and reenergized. A stack of oiled AK-47s, boxes of ammunition, and loaded magazines sat in the trunk; and we had full canteens of water and as many rations as our group could carry.

In a remote corner, tucked along an empty edge of Shingal, the truck came to a halt. Several Yazidi men had been waiting—we shook hands as brothers, and then watched as the fleet sneaked back into the night toward the foothills, where they'd meet up with rogue Kurdish units already embedded along the cliffs and caves. The night before, when I asked a militia commander why they would bother wasting resources to help my people, he said something I will never forget:

"Since the ancients, we have shared this land as brethren. In all that time, what have the Yazidi ever done to us—or anyone?"

Across the fields, I could see the silhouettes of houses rise like shadows of themselves, and heard Hassan's stomach moan. We scanned the open dirt roads before moving forward in tight formation. Several families, including young girls destined for the slave market, were holed up within rooms of farmhouses, and we could see the dull flicker of kerosene lamps turned to low in the target dwellings—as planned.

Then a pair of militants limped out of one of the houses, holding their protruding bellies and belching. They crossed the yard and clambered into a vehicle, started the engine, and then just sat there idling. Moments later, the headlights flicked on and beamed right at us over the length of grass. Pressed flat against the terrain, I could feel my chest heave against the coarse earth as I labored to breathe; and I thought of the petrified animals that we'd hunted with slingshots when I was a boy—their black, unblinking eyes. I felt like one of them now—insignificant and ensnared. Minutes passed, not one of us moving a muscle, and then at last we heard the wheels churn gravel, and the car sped off.

When I stood up, a female face as pale as a moon slid into the frame of a glassless window. Her spectral sockets showed like caverns, and I stopped in my tracks. Then her right hand went up, and she slowly made a signal, indicating there was no one else inside. We moved forward in unison, crouched low, eyes roving.

Before the night was over, and for several afterward, we plucked dozens of girls the same way from their oblivious captors. For those holed up in numbers far too large to effect immediate rescues, I retrieved the coordinates and passed them along to the armed groups working the terrain. Once in the embrace of the mountain, I shone a light into each pristine face, looking for the one that was mine—though I knew full well she was miles away by now, in Mosul.

ISIS didn't have enough manpower to watch every nook and cranny of Shingal, and the girls kept in constant contact, concealing phones and risking instant execution. They waited for us to come find them in the fields and elsewhere. Some had small children in tow, none of whom had to be told to stay quiet. You could tell from those glazed eyes that they'd already seen far too much.

The Islamic State had decreed that *sabaya* and their prepubescent children could not be separated, but in the occupied cities that rule was routinely broken. They removed the youngsters to indoctrination camps, forced them to watch live beheadings, and pummeled their minds so they would forget the basic human decencies that existed before the Islamic State.

Over a period of days, armed groups like ours continued their perilous missions with no casualties on my end at first; but once, on our way back, a sudden blast of machine-gun fire tore right across the field we were traversing. Returning fire, we broke apart and fled. Bullets shaved the heads off stalks, tailing our retreat like a detonating line as we ran the switchback passes. In the wild scattering of our live souls, Hassan called out once into the starless firmament and was never seen again.

WEAVING ALONG THE summit, I sidestepped boulders, stumbling to chase and hold down a solid signal. I was waiting for Bowers. We'd been exchanging messages and he'd relayed my constantly incoming material to his state senator, Marv Hagedorn of Idaho, while working to mobilize other connections. The bars on my screen fluctuated, and I felt the rise of that abysmal hunger stir all over again. My body had had the benefit of two full meals from the PKK, while those left to waste away on the mountain chewed on dead leaves and dug around for insects.

For a moment, I thought of simple rain: its soft perfume and the gentle pattering sounds it made against our roof back home. The yearning for the simple luxuries of a vanished past came at me in pounding waves that overtook all else. When the phone started to buzz against my thigh, at first I thought it was just the pulsing of the atmosphere and didn't answer. Traveling the deep of my mind, I'm sure I was floating in Haji's well listening to water lap at the sides and then gush over the rim.

". . . CNN, is this Mikey Hassan?" a male voice said on the line. "Did you hear me? We have a crew embedded with the Peshmerga."

Suddenly, I was on my feet, a roaring sound flooding my ears, and I had to take a full breath to steady myself and draw out the words I was supposed to say.

"Yes. Hello. This is Mikey—I am a former combat interpreter and a Yazidi. We need help now. Tens of thousands of us are trapped and waiting to die up on Mount Shingal. The decomposing bodies of our children are scattered all over the slope—"

And then I fell apart for a moment.

"OK, Mikey—apparently there's a plan in motion for helicopter aid drops. Water. Food. We heard you've been sending out possible positions—are you still on the mountain?"

"Yes," I said. "Stay away from the south side. It's crawling with ISIS." Later in the week, I would send safe coordinates to Senator Hagedorn, who would direct CNN to move to a more protected location in Sinjar City. The senator became a steady and able lifeline, mobilizing in real time as I provided critical intel. While the crisis unfolded, it was well known to the senator that President Obama was following reports on CNN, and he was using that to our advantage. "How many can you fit in the choppers?"

The man on the line went quiet for a moment, and I could hear him breathing for an eternity.

When he spoke again, his voice was monotone: no one knew any details about evacuations yet—they were just tag-alongs and didn't have any say over those kinds of logistics. And then he said what others would say after that: just hang in there; they needed to hear what was happening and tell the world—so I kept on talking.

I wanted to tell him the world could find out later, after they rescued every last Yazidi—but even in my deteriorating state, I knew better.

I spoke to journalists several times that day; and soon after, other members of the international media reached out like an army of beacons. Most of them had never heard of Yazidis before, and used the same list of buzzwords—"devil worshippers," "Zoroastrianism," or mistook us for full-blooded Kurds. When my parched mouth opened, it let out all I knew in a methodical rush of harrowing details, and each listener grew dead quiet.

More and more calls came in: journalists from the *Daily Mail*, the *Washington Times*, the *Times of London*; BBC, ABC, NBC, *Headline News*, and the Associated Press; and so many others from across the globe. A few remarked on my good English and took recordings—I caught myself wondering if those testaments, lasting a minute or two each, would be the last my family would know of me.

And I was up there roasting—people all around me moaning in their sleep, wasting away half-comatose into the earth—when Bowers sent out another message. In his last dispatch, he let me know that he and Hagedorn had a two-star general working to connect the dots on my intel, and that they were running my identification through the system.

"The minute you got plugged in, Mikey," Bowers said, "Turkish intelligence lit you right up."

Ankara must have gotten wind of my foray into Syria with the PKK, but I didn't say a word about it—not when so many were counting on me to find a way out.

"You know me, brother," I said. "Tell them you know me."

"Doesn't matter," Bowers said. "They think this could be some kind of ISIS trap."

"Did you tell them I was a terp? I worked for those guys. I got shot!"

"I know Mikey, don't worry—they are going to tether your cell signal directly to CENTCOM."

"What's that mean?"

"US Central Command—they have positions all over Iraq. So, every time you use your cell for anything, it will ping at the Pentagon and they will track you. Hagedorn and General Gary Sayler are setting things up for you to keep in communication."

Right then, I knew I'd have to prove my bona fides and go back down many more times alone, to send out intel in real time. By now, I'd been lying under the full broil without end and my scorched limbs ached as though I had lived a thousand years. But I said I would do it, and I would—or we were all dead anyway.

At the first falls of twilight, I changed batteries in my phone, crawled out of my own wrecked skin, and slid down the gradient.

Out on a mission as Mikey the terp.

All over again.

GUNFIRE WANED IN the villages, and the farmlands seemed to slumber, their harvests over for all time. No sound issued from the narrow roads, but I could see the enemy traffic coming in and going out in steady lines. My screen set to Google Earth, I zeroed on Shingal and set to work, methodically marking the precise locations of armed units—those on the move and others stationed along the perimeters of the occupied villages. The procedure was simple: pinpoint the spot on the satellite image, call up the coordinates, and send each one up past the clouds, where they would pivot down into the waiting arms of US Central Command. For the next three weeks I would follow the procedure many times over, and retrieve more information from the "friendly" fighting groups maneuvering on the ground. Senator Hagedorn became a steady hand, keeping track of my activities while directing me to several of these contingents, which would provide protection and support when and if I needed it.

Running through the dead gorse along the rim, I flew over the terrain, my feet and legs freed from their cocoon of pain, as though a second being inside me had come to life. I scaled and crisscrossed Mount Shingal; several times hunkering PKK units guided me to various locations in their trucks until I had counted every Islamic State contingent within sight, getting in close enough to smell their sweat and count up their guns.

When I heard from Bowers again, he had another man on the line he referred to as "the Congressman," though I never caught his name.

"You're all good, Mikey," Bowers said through crackling static. "Patching you through."

And I collapsed, all the rushing blood dispersing from my veins as though it had turned to air.

"It's great to talk to you, Mikey. I just want to tell you how much we appreciate your service to our country. We have some other people on the line who are very interested in hearing what you have to say." Those others, all assembled into what was referred to as a "situation room," included General Gary Sayler and several military and intelligence officials, who would come to my aid many times again. The Congressman said, "Mikey, we're with you now and we're listening, so you just go ahead and tell us everything you can. We're going to be having a lot of calls from here on out."

And so from my hallowed rock, I did.

Chapter Eighteen

Exodus

THE SKY RIGHT OVER ME TORE OPEN FROM END TO END AND rattled the stones—but when I looked up, there was nothing to see but the fullness of night. And yet the roaring wake continued, far past us now and dissipating as it pushed a deep trench of sound that seemed to rip the lid right off the earth. When it was gone, we were all left in an eerie void of silent wonder, and sat around gawking. It was Thursday, August 7, 2014, our fourth night on the mountain. Above, the half moon shone a dirty yellow, and the besieged wilderness of *beyaban*, the desert below, stood as still as time.

A few of the stronger ones, roused from their fitful slumber, started climbing up even higher, scrambling over the boulders. Then the boy next to me jumped in his bedraggled clothes and pointed to the murky east.

"What are those?" he hollered. "Angels?"

I sat up and squinted as he took my hand and pulled.

Crossing like a figment over the great dimmed vault, a floating cluster of huge white canopies drifted along, lazily spreading out by degrees as they shed altitude and descended toward our sacred perch. I was on my feet and moving forward carefully among the others. Our link to reality so tenuous now, we didn't so much as trust our own eyes.

"Balloons!" I heard a girl cry out.

It was as though we were no longer where we were in the dead of night.

"Should we hide?" a woman shouted.

"Where—where can we go?" another one lamented.

I ascended the black ridge carefully with the others, and watched from another vantage. Still miles away, I could barely make out the long cables suspending massive crates to billowed parachutes—and knew at once that it hadn't been a lie.

"Expect drops," Brownsword had told me hours before. "Expect them soon, brother."

And for the love of God, I had not believed him.

Up and down the mountain, those who could run ran fast, tumbling over uneven ground they could barely see—this way and that, zigzagging like startled sheep. Others, who could not withstand the exertion, hung back in the obscurity, muttering that it was just an ISIS trap. From where we were, I knew we could not get to a landing spot in time to avoid the certain mayhem; already you could hear the rising din of the awakened masses, on the move like a gathering wind. Then, out of nowhere, a great white hope sailed like a deflating moon through the air right over me, and I felt its soft shadow sweep by like a calming hand. It went down a hundred yards away or more, into the blunt jaws of a deep gully.

Now I was clamoring like the others, famished and desperate to get there, but in short order it was impossible to move—there were so many of us.

"Let the children in first," a mother screamed to no avail.

Cascades of people stumbled half-blind into the ravine and tore into the crate, pulling off the cords and yanking out the contents of stacked boxes marked HALAL—and that's when I heard the shrieking.

Farther down the gorge, where another parachute had dropped its load, people were swarming a crate, heaving at the sides and trying to lift it.

"It's too heavy!" a man barked.

When I got there, a small girl next to them was on her knees, and I saw then what she was holding. She had a bare foot cradled in her lap, attached to a long twitching leg, and past it a male body lay pinned and moaning under the full weight of the container.

We shoved until the load shifted off the man, and someone dragged him out from under—alive, but badly injured. Several times, I called out for a doctor; my echoes traveled the gorges and came back with nothing. There were few medical professionals on the mountain, and they were hard to find as there was no shortage of those needing help; and as stranded as we were, their bare knowledge was often no more useful than a hose without water.

We gathered around the injured man, who flailed there wide-eyed like a hooked fish, and someone shone a light slowly along his trampled limbs. His bladder had let go, soaking his pants. The stench of fetid urine was as pungent as vinegar, and a few of the others gagged.

"I think something in me snapped," he rasped. "I heard it."

We all knew that his back was surely broken.

By now, a crowd was forming, and people with lanterns were going at the boxes and tearing them open like a hungry pack of dogs.

"Don't move," I told him. "When morning comes, we will get help."

It was all I knew to say.

Then I made my way over to the ransacked boxes to see what was left to eat or drink.

THE SAME NIGHT, nearly 150 miles to the east, US fighter jets cut across the atmosphere miles over Nineveh, tracking two ISIS armored personnel carriers on the road to Erbil, the capital of Iraqi Kurdistan. One of the planes released a five-hundred-pound bomb that took a precision nosedive to the earth, reducing the target to a heap of burning metal. Soon after, air strikes demolished ISIS vehicles and artillery that were being used to support the enemy forces advancing on the KRG.

President Barack Obama had ordered the attacks to protect American civilians working in the US consulate in Erbil, as well as the more than two dozen military advisers stationed in the city. At the same time, he authorized immediate humanitarian aid drops over Mount Shingal. For many war-weary Americans listening to his televised announcement, it was the first time they'd even heard of the Yazidi.

The moment President Obama looked into the camera, described our dying plight, and said, "Today, help is here"—I was sitting in the dark on a mile-high shelf over burning Shingal, a brutal fate closing in on all sides. Every one of us up there who heard the president that night, on radios or huddled around phones, felt his resolute American voice infiltrate their withered skin. At last, it seemed the world was seeing us, and we were so grateful.

"Expect more," Brownsword told me. "This is just the beginning."

SOON THE SKY was howling again and flashes went up like struck matches stitching across the outlying plains. We knew those sounds for what they were—bombs crashed into the ground past the mountain, the earth beneath us shifted, and plumes of smoke went up over the leas. Many cried out in fear and held their children close. I stood on the cliffs scanning the beleaguered landscape below, as ISIS antiaircraft guns spat out streams of impotent shells.

Way down the gradient, a few ISIS contingents clustered in the folds of the lower slopes unleashed their machine guns, calling to Allah for strength, and then to their commanders for swift reinforcements. Meanwhile, PKK and YPG units had carved a foothold across the western side of the mountain. ISIS now faced unrelenting hostility from both above and within, and hunkered down.

Night after night, American fighters sliced through the skies, their ordnance smashing into targets as ISIS fought tooth and nail to hold their ground. I already knew what they were up against: probably F/A-18 Hornets from the Gulf, off the USS *George H. W. Bush*, and Reaper drones out of Kuwait and the UAE, remotely piloted from tiny climate-controlled tin huts thousands of miles away in the Nevada desert. By now, US Central Command had acquired enough intelligence on enemy positions to annihilate dozens of ISIS targets scattered all over Shingal.

By the second week of August, with so many still trapped on the mountain, I was sending steady streams of intel out through Senator Marv Hagedorn and General Gary Sayler. As "friendly connections" on the ground scouted exodus routes, I went deep into ISIS positions to pinpoint the precise locations of large groups of captives, before special armed groups embedded all over Shingal executed swift rescue missions. It would be years before I would learn that just one of those operations saved more than five hundred women from a warehouse in Shingal.

Still, there was a price to be paid. ISIS commanders had finally zeroed in on me and were actively calling for my capture. I knew from contacts that my name and picture were already circulating across the Islamic State's vast network; Brownsword had long warned me that I would find myself at the top of their kill list. It didn't matter much: if a jihadist didn't kill me first, the desert sun certainly would. We waited out the battles and hoped for more crates to fall from the sky.

DAYS LATER AND still trapped on Shingal, so many of us would have perished were it not for those air drops. There were just enough provisions to eke out a feeble survival, but no way to know when and if we would ever get off the mountain. Finally, from the western edge of the range, PKK fighters started arriving in caravans of empty tractors and trucks that tore up the slopes. Convoys came for us over several days, straight from the pocket of Kurdish-controlled Syria, while ground fighters guarded rendezvous points. I determined to stay on that holy ground until the last Yazidi had been saved, and kept in close contact with the rescue groups. The infirm and the elderly went first, their heads held way down—ISIS militants scattered throughout the hills shot anything they saw to pieces.

From my position along the highest eastern peaks, messages about routes to safety came in continuously, and we set about mobilizing rescue teams. Once again, I plotted out safe paths all over Mount Shingal and was told that sooner or later the friendly forces would open a track. Meanwhile, I scanned ravines for the most vulnerable Yazidis. After so long up there, many were too frail to move, so we formed a human chain, carrying them down fast on our backs.

"Is this a good idea?" an old man said, lolling in my arms. A bullet had already grazed his hand, and the makeshift bandages were soiled and soaking through.

"It's the only one we have," I said, passing him like a bundled infant down into the tractor well, as YPG guerrillas roamed the perimeter. Then I rushed to collect groups of small children, who stood trembling and forlorn like rats along cave walls. We ferried them into another truck, between sniper bullets pinning us to the ground.

Day in and day out, we carried on under the hammering broil, until thousands were on their way to safe zones. Those of us who oversaw the evacuation had been the strongest ones; but all through the day, backbreaking work and heat pounded us down, and the aid drops became more precarious to reach. By then, I was long prepared to die—most of us had already forgotten what it meant to be alive. I couldn't even tell you what day it was, or what time. Still, we continued, not knowing if our turn would ever come. Hope was becoming too heavy a thing for us to carry much longer.

MY BODY SEEMED weightless on the boulders; sleeping forms as still and lifeless as piles of bones scattered all around; empty cartons lay strewn like shoe boxes among us, not a scrap left to eat nor a drop to drink. And so I lingered awhile in a dream with Dil-Mir, walking the banks of the inky Tigris at night.

"I have to go back, now," she said, and squeezed my hand.

"Just one more minute," I said, but when I looked over she was already miles up the river, rafts of trash floating by on the current.

Somehow, when I sat up in the gunmetal light, I could still feel the pressure of her hand over my palm, and the air smelled of sewage. It took me a long time to get my bearings. A few children had started stirring; all of us had grown too tired to move in more than small increments. Wasting days had come and gone, and nothing more had happened. Then, out of the quiet, the windless air seemed to ripple like a sheet, and the sky thrummed. I stared out into the listless void, nothing more than the brown sea all around.

"Look at the bird," a girl whispered.

And I was sure she was in a state of delirium.

Then, as a shadow emerged from the horizon, heads all around me pivoted like weathervanes—it was moving straight for us. Dry layers of soil lifted and began to seethe and simmer. In a moment, I was on my feet, beating blades overtaking the last gallops of my heart.

The rest of them were already running as luminous shapes dropped from the sky.

"Water!" the horde cried out, as plastic bottles crashed and broke open over rocks.

Suddenly, across the plateau, it was all-out pandemonium, and I darted forward to join the pack. I saw toddlers sitting dumbstruck in the melee lick up what they could from the ground, before someone hoisted them onto their shoulders.

As the Iraqi chopper descended, I saw a man hanging out from the hatch with a camera poised on his shoulder; next to him, another figure in body armor and a collared shirt stared out and pointed. You could see his full-blown horror, and I wondered then if we'd spoken to one another in one of the dozens of calls I'd taken from the media.

Immediately, the swarming crowd rushed the open hatch, tossing in their flailing children—I saw an infant pitched like a sack right into the hold. In a panic, the journalist grabbed a few arms and hauled them up, but the flying machine banked sideways and tilted; a woman in a pink chador dangled off a landing skid, until she fell into a trough of dirt.

Left behind for nearly three weeks after the invasion, we just stood there staring into the gritty sunshine, our bony arms reaching out like crooked sticks to the sky. It had been my choice to stay among my own, and now there was no way out. In the distance, water was falling again, but we could not get to it in time. In that jungle of withered Yazidis, I looked around me as though seeing us all for the first time—not even human anymore—our last hope now a speck on the horizon. And then my mind floated, way up over Nineveh, far away from that shelf holding up the doomed. It was all over, I thought; we were never getting out of there—and I was ready.

And we might have all believed that was the end, if it hadn't been for the echoes of gunfire and then the groan of trucks riding the ledge far below us. Not long after, a full contingent of PKK were rushing up the slope and out of the underbrush.

"We have little time," was all they said, herding us as one down a serpentine path.

Soon, I crammed into the back of a flatbed with fifteen others, machine guns pointed out the back and firing haphazardly.

"Just keep shooting," the fighter next to me hollered.

And so I steadied the barrel and fired, the metal in my hands growing hot, until we were near the bottom of Mount Shingal. Then, as the truck veered into the open desert, the sounds of war gave way and we headed west, racing borrowed time into the blazing sun.

Chapter Nineteen

The Smuggler's Route

UNDER AN APOCALYPTIC SUN, THOUSANDS MARCHED ACROSS blinding sands toward the protected sector of Kurdish Syria one hundred miles away, forty hours or more on foot—and I was among them. The fighters had let us off just past the conflict zone, before racing back to ferry another load. My eyes strained against the searing light reflecting off ice-white ground, as I dovetailed into an endless crawl of the beleaguered in their stinking clothes. And yet, I did not feel forsaken out there among my people in this, our third cataclysm of August 2014— we'd all made it out of the villages and then off the mountain. If I've ever clung to our endangered faith, it was during that long journey of the living dead.

Members of my family waited at the end of the line, holding a place for me inside their tent at the makeshift refugee camp— our God and angels were all we had between us now.

216

Listless, I drifted the cruel hours away, vacant under my sagging skin.

What's the word in Kurmanji for hot? I heard Sergeant White call out.

White had been dead as long as my boyhood, but I saw him clear as day, lounging in a beach chair way out over the sand, dark leg propped over one knee, huge grin widening under his Ray-Bans.

"*Sekir*," I whispered. "Sort of like sugar."

Well, it is damn sekir out here, Shaker—run and get us a couple of cold sodas. You look like you could use one.

"Yes, sir—OK."

What about me? Dil-Mir said into my ear, and I felt her hair brush past.

"I'm coming for you," I told her, holding out a hand into the fathomless shine.

THE SOUNDS OF wind filling canvas sails like huge lungs came to me; I breathed in heavy air that no longer reeked of death. Though I'd never been to the sea, I thought I smelled an ocean. An IV line dripped into my vein, and I tugged at it.

"Shaker? They found you outside the gates," a woman said, palms cradling my face. How soft her hands still were, and I didn't need to open my eyes, or hear that birdsong voice to know the healing touch of my mother. How to find a word for a gratitude so immense that it tore away the seams of my heart—I let out a feeble sob.

"Where are the others?" I rasped, my open eyes seeing only a great blur as though we were floating underwater.

"We are here in Syria, in the camp," Naïf said, touching my leg. "Not all of us. We haven't located Dapîra yet. Some cousins are missing—and others. Khairi and most of his family made

217

it to the KRG. Everyone is scattered. It's a miracle we have all found each other. You're all bones, *brako*—dried up as leather."

"But alive, alive, alive," Daki laughed, and kissed my forehead. "Soon we'll go to a camp in the KRG and then another one in Turkey—and from there you'll go to Germany."

"Germany," I said, still coming to terms with where I was—among more than one of my own, and living. "How?"

I squinted at the smudged forms of other people gathered all around my cot.

"Smugglers," Samir said. "We put all the family money together. We have enough to pay for one person—you don't have a wife and kids. We need you to go where it's safe, Shaker, they're still assassinating terps. From what I've heard, you've moved way up on their list."

I only nodded, the sensation of my mother's fingers dancing in my hair, lulling me. The others were all jabbering away. I heard the word *miracle* again—and fell deep down into the longest sleep of my life.

Have you spent your packet yet, boy? Babo breathed into my slumber.

No, Babo, not yet. Not yet.

When I woke up, we joined the long transport caravans that ferried survivors under the full protection of Syrian Kurdish forces into the KRG. More evacuation routes were opening up along Shingal. Together with what was left of my people, we stayed there in a refugee camp many months until we would move on into Turkey. Our country and our homes were lost to us.

ON MARCH 26, 2015, in a river valley of soft blowing grass tucked between Turkey and Bulgaria, where poppies flourished and families took weekend picnics, I was with a group of ten other Yazidi men and women when I met "Rasho," the first of many smugglers I would come to know.

"We go in through the wilderness at night," he said, licking his finger as he thumbed through our cash. A weeping crust sat over his face like a fungus and his nails were grooved and yellow. Right away, I could tell he was doped up.

"First rule: don't talk, and never tell me your name. Any of you make trouble, I leave you behind for the border police. They aren't your friends, believe me."

THROUGH REEFS OF fog, we could see the glow of lights spread along the frontier. There was a lot of traffic still on the roads: delivery trucks, farm vehicles, other refugees betting their lives on luck. Seven hours straight through forests of oak and beech, over streams, under bridges, and no one spoke a word. The plan was to meet up with vans that would take us into Sofia, the Bulgarian capital. This was just the first leg of a long trip, straight through the Balkans.

We were on a wooded path straddling the winding tongue of road when a figure grabbed me from behind and shined a light into my eyes—ISIS fighters, I thought, and went numb. They shoved the women into cars and lined up the men in gutters, before leading us one at a time into the bowels of the forest.

When my turn came, I stood head down, hoping it would be a single bullet, fast, and I waited for it. Nothing. And then I fell right into frantic English, only to feel the smack of brass knuckles against my mouth, loosening a tooth. It was the first of many blows I would take. A man tore off my clothes and strapped me to a tree.

"Why are you doing this?" I said, but it didn't matter.

"We have to check your body for contraband," a silhouette muttered, as he took a swig from a bottle.

All the men in my group were beaten in their turn—our phones and wallets stolen, our dignity vandalized. I thought they were a gang of criminals marauding the border until they put us into their cars to shuttle us back to where we came from, and turned on their sirens.

It took three attempts to get out of Turkey. By the time we made it into Sofia, we'd been beaten twice more. Days passed and we continued, mostly on foot and without much to eat, but hunger had become a postscript to all the pains that plagued me. At prearranged points along the migrant route, we encountered several smugglers—all of them addicts, one just like the other.

Once in the capital, we were afforded the reprieve of a cold shower and some bread in the squalid flat of another runner. This one with arms and legs like clubs, he snorted pinches of cocaine off his wrists, in between pounding energy drinks that littered the footwells.

"I'm sorry for my temper," he kept saying in between bursts of rage, as we sped toward Serbia in the back of his dilapidated van. "I have troubles."

Left to wait for the arrival of the next runner in an abandoned house, we sat against the crumbling walls, staring at one another, still afraid to speak.

"I don't know about you all," I said finally. "But if I don't have some water soon, I won't be able to go on."

"What do we do?" An old man said, releasing a steady fog of cigarette smoke. "It's been eight hours in here pissing in a bucket. He's not coming, I tell you."

"We don't even know where we are," a young woman whispered from the depths of her chador.

WHEN THE POLICE showed up, I tried out my English again, and this time it seemed to subdue them.

"You have language—that's good," the Serbian officer said, nodding as he took down our names. None of us gave our true identities.

"I worked for the Americans," I offered. "During the war."

"Then why don't you go there?"

FOR THE NEXT three days in the pouring rain, we all stayed locked inside a razor-wired and overcrowded detention camp that was nothing more than an elaborate garbage dump. Everything in there existed in a foul state of decay: the mildew-covered tarps set up over islands of mud; the moldy bread and gray stews they gave us to eat; even the refugees, scurrying between the derelict tents with battered tin bowls held to their hollowed-out bodies, fleas sucking away at their scalps.

"This is still better than ISIS," a woman said to me as we stood in the registration line, waiting our turn to get out.

And I nodded—it was true.

The Serbians registered my details, put me into a police car, and then transferred me to a jailhouse up the road.

"You got any weed—or some coke?" one of my cell mates asked, jutting out his chin. His sweat stank of rot, or maybe it was just the cell. There were more than two dozen different versions of the same scuffed-up hooligan in there.

"I got nothing," I said, and I held out my hands.

"What the fuck are you good for then?" another one said, and threw a hard shove into my shoulder, testing things out.

By now, I'd sat in rooms facing rabid militants who would have grabbed any chance to slit my throat. I'd climbed out of a mile-high purgatory in the sky, down into a nest of terror-ists—these thugs were nothing to me. Maybe they could see it in the way I took over one darkened corner, and just sat there, staring out.

A few days later, an officer slid back the bars.

"OK, you're done," he said. "We have to make space." He handed me a train pass and pointed to the doors. "Go to the station and get on the train to Budapest."

Outside the jailhouse, I wandered across the street into a public park, where I encountered my fellow Yazidi travelers lying around on the benches.

"You guys get train passes?" I said.

"Yes, to Budapest. There's another camp. I've heard it's the worst one."

"No, I'm not doing that. Let's go to Munich instead," I said. "That's where our people are waiting for us."

Start to finish, the journey took thirty-three days.

THE ARRIVAL CENTER for asylum seekers was in a large pristine building, in which legions of the weary and war-torn from around the world waited. I sat in a brown leather chair holding my ticket—number 634. I'd borrowed the dress shirt and pants from another Yazidi. To look at me you'd never have guessed the horrors that lurked behind my eyelids—and I was so grateful. On that cool spring day of April 15, 2015, Germany gave me and every frayed soul in that place the chance to be a human being again.

"I have evidence," I told the man at the wicket. "And I can get much more."

"Of what?" he asked, looking up from the screen on which my pertinent details appeared, gleaming over his round spectacles.

"A genocide," I said. "I need to know where to go—to document what happened."

Then he sat back, took off his glasses, and rubbed his face. When he looked at me again, I saw myself in his eyes, and he held me there a long time before speaking.

"Look behind you, Mr. Jeffrey," he said. "That room is full of evidence of many terrible things people have done to each other. All we can do here is help you be free."

So I did look behind me at all of them, and then back to him again and nodded. *All right*, I thought—*free, that's a good start*.

Chapter Twenty

Nadia and the Warehouse of Souls

RAIN POLISHED THE COBBLESTONES AND I STOOD IN THE hypnotic downpour—head tilted, mouth wide open— transported back to the mountain, among the scores diminishing from thirst. A passerby glanced once and disappeared into the lit-up city, but I just stayed on the sidewalk until I was soaked to the bone.

Those first weeks in Germany, so much as turning on a tap meant weeping for hours. The comfort of a mattress shamed me to the floor. I was wedged between worlds that were impossible to reconcile: the smell of coffee in the cafés; the scent of decay on the hillsides. Laughter in the markets; shrieks of terror across the sands. Children playing in a park; children bleeding over stones.

Even Facebook was a pilgrimage into a hollow of losses— husbands, sons, wives, daughters. Cousins, neighbors, friends.

Dil-Mir.
No end in sight.

"EVERY MASS GRAVE has to be documented," Brownsword told
me. Soon after I entered Germany, we reconnected and got right
back to it. "Numbers. Identities. Precise locations. Eventually,
elements destroy evidence."

I soon found out that Interpol, the UN, and the Red Cross
were already aware of the mass killings and graves. Germany
was crowded with people like me, and they'd heard our stories
a thousand times. I didn't know how much more I could do. My
people were scattered: in rubber boats over the Aegean Sea, on
foot crossing the Balkans, huddled in train stations under tarps,
sleeping in forests and public parks. Lost. Captured. Enslaved.
No one knew how many of us were left, or was even bothering to try and tally the numbers. Brownsword told me I was a
member of an endangered species, and I felt those words bore
into me like rusty nails.

"You've got to mobilize," he said. "Concentrate on the living
for now—the taken. Survivors. All those you can get to."

THE RESCUE GROUP started out virtual and nameless, consisting
of fourteen close Yazidis and me. I set up our main page and
sent out an appeal like a searchlight into the void. By the end of
the first day, it had already illuminated a multitude—that cheap
Android phone transformed into an army in my palm:

First, Yazidis looking for other Yazidis.

Then people from everywhere who could put them together.

Soon, legions in peril found us:

*My daughter Almas escaped on a boat to Lesvos and
vanished.*

**My sister has a friend in the camp there and has found
her. Here is the number.**

We are lost in the woods of Hungary with no food. Our smuggler has left us.
I know a police officer in Budapest, he will come get you.

My neighbor is holding Yazidis in his home outside Mosul.
Tell us when he leaves the house.

I'm pregnant and in labor under a bridge outside of Sofia.
My brother's friend is a doctor at a hospital in the city. We will send him.

I'm a twelve-year-old girl named Sibi, from Kocho. I got away from my captor.
Stay where you are, we will try to trace your signal.

At first, our rules were simple: to join the group you had to have a connection to a core member, most always a Yazidi. Core members had proven their intent—saved a life.

The Android became as all-consuming as heroin. I was tethered to it seventeen hours a day, coordinating the constant stream of rescues—I could not let it go. Entreaties from the taken, orphans, and the adrift were coming in constantly. And with every plea, I released a prayer for the one girl whose lost voice haunted me. At first, we got people out using crowdfunding to pay smuggling fees, which ran into the thousands.

Soon our web of volunteers from all over the Middle East and Europe mobilized into an extensive underground railroad, made up of a series of safe houses and runners linked like stations. Some girls were shuttled back to their parents in Iraq. Many came to Germany, where they cloistered in shelters designed to treat the devastating traumas particular to survivors of slavery.

As often as I could I escorted them, returning frequently to check on their progress. Other times, especially when speed was of the essence, I'd have to go find a captive myself. When a Yazidi mother reached out about her fourteen-year-old daughter, who'd been abducted in a camp near Ioannina, in northwestern Greece, I crammed into the back of a runner's van by nightfall.

A THOUSAND EYES watched me as I crossed a purgatory of cold mud and raw sewage to a sea of rundown army tents. Five miles from a picturesque lakeside mountain village, the camp sprawled like a giant pustule. Right away, the group of Yazidis I'd made contact with broke from the lingering masses and approached me clutching torn-up plastic bags full of old clothes.

"Nisreen is way over there," a woman said, pointing from her cocoon of rags. "In the very last tents before the hills."

"Where is the security?" I said, my shoes sinking into the slop.

"They're just volunteers and come when they can—which is hardly at all."

"How will I know which tent she's in?"

I looked out through the bank of fog.

"You just will."

A MOB OF men clustered outside a large tent that served as an improvised mosque, smoking rolled cigarettes and warming scabrous hands over a small fire pit. On a makeshift table outside the door sat a bowl of water and bars of soap. The sounds of an imam droned through the canvas.

"You here for the girl?" One of the men said, giving me a once-over.

"I'm her brother," I said. "Our family has not given permission."

"You're a pig with no rights. She will convert and belong to Allah."

"I thought you weren't allowed to smoke," I said, pulling back the canvas flap.

"I thought we cut off all your heads," another one laughed, and spat at my shoes.

Inside, over a patchwork of threadbare rugs, stood the imam, caressing his beard like a pelt. Concealed in a burqa, a frail figure stood before him, hands fidgeting.

"Take off your shoes," the imam barked. "She's about to give the Shahada."

"Shut up," I said, and went straight for him. Without another word, I jacked a balled fist into his open mouth. I felt the bones in my hand snap, and the stunned holy man fell back, stumbling over crates of bread and soda cans.

Immediately, the men from outside came into the tent. Then others, who'd come from the village as a ragtag security detail, filed in after them and an all-out brawl erupted.

The girl cowered in a flimsy corner. She fixed her blue eyes on me, wide and unblinking as I fought my way through the scrimmage. Someone smashed the back of my head with something, but I kept moving forward. Finally, one of the Greeks fired a handgun into the roof and the lecherous crew disbanded.

"I knew you were one of mine, as soon as I saw you," Nisreen said, tearing off her dark shawl and breathing hard as we rushed along the muddy paths out of the camp.

Back in the van, I gave Nisreen my phone—her mother in Germany was on the line.

"You do this a lot?" the driver said, over the girl's elated sobs.

"Lately," I said, cradling my wrecked fingers, and told him I had one more that day.

"Good for you," the driver said after a moment. Then he nodded many times and grabbed my shoulder. "Let's go."

THE BOY WAS sixteen years old and I'd been warned that he'd lost his mind. We drove to a safe house in the mountains, where my contacts were keeping him. They'd smuggled the emaciated teen there to avoid the local refugee centers that would surely have detained him. The child would not have survived the camps, most of them harboring criminal detainees who loathed Yazidis. The group had already alerted a hospital in Athens, where a specialist team waited on standby. It was my job to get him there safe and sound. Later, we would try to find his family, and take him to them.

He looked straight ahead, saying nothing—the innocence that should have come with that last layer of baby fat, all but obliterated. I caught the driver stealing glimpses in the rearview.

"What's wrong with him?"

"They made him do things," I said. "ISIS has training camps. Pump them full of drugs. Children are forced to do and see terrible things."

The driver nodded and glanced again at the boy in the rearview as though trying to decipher what existed behind that vacant stare; there were screams lurking just beneath the silence. You could feel it—those boys were all the same.

When we reached the hospital, the driver held the door open as I guided my charge out of the back of the car. I thanked the man and we said our good-byes.

Then the driver took my hand and squeezed it hard. He told me to keep doing what I was doing. Every person working on those rescue routes always said the same thing:

"Save as many as you can."

OVER THE NEXT six months and into the New Year of 2016, I traveled in and out of refugee camps hunting down Yazidis, working in the filth so many lived in while trying to carve out a new life. When I volunteered as a UN translator, they offered lodging in nearby hotels; but I refused, staying instead among my own—eating what they ate, and sleeping where they slept.

Many of the camps were no more than neglected ghettos where extremists coming in from Iraq and Syria were carving out their own turf. Yazidis were regularly abused; women and girls who'd escaped captivity found themselves face-to-face in the bread lines with their former rapists.

In the camps along the coastline, I helped drag in the daily arrivals of migrant-crowded dinghies, constantly searching faces for one of my own. Those rubber boats were death traps: no life vests, and none of the refugees knew how to swim. Every day up to a half-dozen boats came in holding over one hundred desperate souls. And every day people perished, either out at sea or trampled in the inevitable panic as we struggled to haul the vessels in through a relentless onslaught of pounding waves. At sunrise, the tides delivered the bodies, so often of small children and infants, who lay as limp as discarded rags on the beach.

But the day I found maggots creeping in my bowl of rice, something in me broke.

"Please, please, send Nadia," I said, calling up YAZDA, a Yazidi rights organization that had recently found international fame for its soft-spoken figurehead, Nadia Murad. "Our people are living like stray dogs. Something has to be done."

A survivor from Kocho, Nadia had been chosen as the global face of our people, her mission to convince the world what it should have already known—ISIS had committed genocide against us. And it wasn't over.

"Hello, dear *brako*"—*my brother*, Nadia said, when we met outside Idomeni Camp, her mournful eyes resting on mine. In them, I saw our shared and infinite sorrows as she held out her small hand.

"Hello, dear *xweşko*"—*my sister*, I said, entwining her fingers in mine, and our friendship began. We'd meet and speak again many times in the coming months.

Kocho was a village in Shingal, now famous as the site of the most brutal massacre of the invasion of August 2014. In a single day, ISIS militants slaughtered over six hundred men from Nadia's village, beheading most of them, shooting or burning the others alive, including her six brothers. The young women and girls, including Nadia, were all taken into sex slavery. Nadia Murad had escaped what my Dil-Mir was living—in a word, she gave me and so many of us hope.

For two weeks in April 2016, Nadia and I toured a succession of camps together; the media and mesmerized Yazidi refugees followed her every move as she pointed out the abysmal living conditions. What the press did not know was that dozens of brazen militants were nestled like barbs among the dense crowds—looking on, and seething.

Nadia had addressed the United Nations, met with dignitaries and heads of state, made speeches all over the world—and ISIS sent her death threats on a daily basis. As we walked the camps through the hordes, I kept her close, scanning the faces among the crowd. Sometimes, the enemies were easy to pick out: lone wolves hanging back, stalking the periphery, or watching intently while murmuring into their phones. Most of the time, I knew they were blending right in—as they would when they received their asylum and moved freely across Europe with their benefits packages and travel papers.

In the evening, when Nadia went back to her hotel exhausted and demoralized with a few other members of YAZDA, we all sat together as what we were—one Yazidi family.

"Are we helping, dear *brako*?" she asked finally. "Do you think?"

"I don't know," was all I could say. "It was so brave of you to come. We are all so grateful."

"They still haven't investigated the mass graves all over Shingal. All of my brothers are there."

"So many," I said, thinking of my own missing—grandmother, cousins, uncles, and aunts. Neighbors and friends from school. "We have to keep working and not just for the living."

As was inevitable, one after the other, we fell into the survival stories that bound us. While we were together, Nadia lost yet another friend from Kocho—that one to an IED. When the bad news came in, we all sat on the floor and wept together. Then we were quiet for a long time.

"I met the prime minister of Greece, Alexis Tsipras," Nadia said at last. "And do you know what he called the refugee camp?"

"No."

"I will never forget it. He called it a warehouse," she said. "A warehouse of souls."

"Yes," I said. "And all of them are broken."

Chapter Twenty-One

Infiltrating ISIS

IN THE DAYS AFTER NADIA LEFT, I WORE OUT THE HOURS thinking. Long spells of howling rain cut the electricity, dimming the camps. Our border runs went to rivers of mud. The tents leaked like sweating skins and we huddled inside them, shivering in our sodden clothes. All the while, I imagined our dead left in silent heaps under the open sky back in Shingal, waiting for someone to deliver those souls to God—and the names to their families.

At night, restless spirits stirred across the living realm that had abandoned their bodies to the naked dirt; hollow calls penetrated my dreams. In the morning, my limbs were leaden, and I wasn't sure how long I could go on buried under the shame of doing nothing to redeem our dead. Then Brownsword called again and yanked my mind free.

"I'm gonna be passing through the KRG on a contract," he told me. "I have a satellite camera that can geotag—you know what that is?"

"Sounds better than my Android," I said, sitting straight up.

"Damn right. This thing will upload every picture you take with precise coordinates, including compass bearings and elevation. If I leave it with someone, can you get it and use it?"

"Yes, brother," I said. "I can—and I will."

By now, I knew the migrant routes like the back of my hand; no one bothered anyone going back into the mouth of danger, while multitudes were pouring out.

I CROSSED THE border from Turkey into Iraq and made contact with the man with the camera. I'd left all my identification behind and would be known by yet another alias, "Hader." By the time dawn flared, several connections had provided safe passage into the liberated area of Shingal. Bearded and dressed like a simple shepherd, I traversed the rolling steppe plains toward home.

In that late spring of 2016, many factions were still fighting all over the region, vying for terrain, with the front line between the Peshmerga and ISIS standing along the southeast. Survivors had provided the approximate sites of mass exterminations, and I'd already plotted out a track to document what was left of the evidence. Though a few villages had been freed, those graves stood all but ignored.

Distant buildings still exhaled the smoke of war, likely from the IEDs left all over the liberated towns. Sporadic gunfire and distant shelling pounded away like thunder, hard to tell from where. As the vacant and crumbling forms of Yazidi villages finally came into view, I had to fight off an awakening of my memory that started up a vicious assault. Several times, I stopped to wipe down my eyes, which watered without abatement, and then I simply sat down in the sand awhile to still a raging pulse—telling myself again and again not to feel, not there, not until it was over.

The first town I went to was my own, Khanasor—it would be the hardest by far to face. Several friends, neighbors, cousins, and extended family members remained unaccounted for, and they sustained my resolve: I was there to find out what had happened to them. A handful of defiant Yazidis were returning to the freed areas of Shingal, but Khanasor was still considered unsafe. The shelled-up ground appeared silent and deserted for miles. Still, I stayed low; if a roving militant or even the Assayish caught me there, I'd be shot on sight. Pictures of me with Nadia Murad in Greece had circulated, and ISIS commanders finally put two and two together. Moreover, the ruthless KRG secret police knew I had been vocal to international journalists about the Peshmerga withdrawal and President Barzani's marginalization of my people, even as their public relations campaign actively worked to disprove that absolute truth. People like me stood in the way of rewriting history.

Lying flat against the ground, I watched my forsaken village from a gully. No bright clothes flapping on the lines. Not a single note of tambour music riding the oblivious wind. Buildings in ruins; walls reduced to piles of rubble. Surveying the terrain, I remembered sitting high up with Haji in our onion field and looking down on our town that sat like a giant nickel over the golden plain—strange to see it now, reduced to a concrete skeleton.

I came upon the shallow ditch over which I'd been told militants had made the captured kneel to rest their foreheads—each would have known what was coming. I climbed the low lip. Not a soul around for miles. I stared into the beating sun of the Angel's eye, asking him to carry me through what I was about to witness. Finally, I offered my gaze to those who'd been waiting so long for me.

Instantly, my legs gave way, and I slid down to the bottom. For a long time, I stayed on my knees, not moving, hands flat against the hard earth. Then I crawled the ground like an infant, weeping quietly so as not to be discovered, and all alone in that shallow pit of horrors. Right away, I knew I was too late to be of much use—forensics teams with DNA kits were needed there now. Not a refugee with a camera.

What was left of those Yazidis lay scattered: Tibias and femurs. Rib cages. Portions of jaws. Cracked skulls piled up like broken bowls in a corner. Wasted pairs of jeans, so many of them. Eyeglasses. Shoes. A plastic doll. Clumps of hair. Relics of real people; remnants of my living home. And then, I glimpsed the washed-out blue shawl I knew so well, and my hands went right to it. I held the faded fabric to my chest, where it tore to pieces that fell through my shaking fingers. The rest of my Dapîra lay strewn like shattered crockery in the ditch. And I looked at her a long, long time—whispering so many things I don't wish to remember just now.

But my mother's mother was more than a fractured shell, and I fought to see past that blinding desecration. At last, I found her smiling face—in the morning before school, when she reached up laughing to tousle my hair. Then her singing voice traveled out of my boyhood—we were kneading dough for our bread. Her floured hands so soft over mine. Finally, I forced myself against every impulse to turn away and let her go. Leaving my grandma, my Dapîra there—like that—was the hardest thing I'd ever done.

And if that wasn't enough, farther along the dugout I came upon the red Arsenal football club jersey I'd seen every long-ago school day. Images flashed: Saïd running wild down the street to school, his tattered satchel spilling its contents. Those wayward shoes and big brown eyes. He was always the first to offer up a joke, or one of his patchwork socks for our soccer ball.

"Saïd," I said. "I have found you."

I took a picture of his remains, bowed, and kept going, the sun arching across the sky. I saved that long sharp grief like a blade that would cut me to pieces later. I had to hurry now—there were so many time-devoured bones, thin and white as alabaster, thousands of Yazidis waiting to be counted.

I went to as many mass graves as I could reach. Forty-five locations were on the list, scattered all over the foothills and near the crest, but there was no reaching each one. Farther south along a series of berms, I could see distant black shapes of militants and took what pictures I could.

Shelling from the front lines intensified as ISIS fighters attacked, using heavy guns mounted to trucks. I took note on positions and activities, then doubled way back to a plateau, getting rides there from Yazidi contacts hunkered down in the foothills. Diehard fighters still protecting the mountain told me ISIS had suffered many losses and had been pushed out of Shingal; but rogue militants still roamed the hills, killing off any of my people they could. In the shadow of Shingal, I photographed the bones left along the slopes. Then I gathered intel from rebels and witnesses still left on the terraced farms farther down.

On the way back, I slipped and dropped the camera into a crevasse. The lens smashed to pieces over the rocks. And I looked at it, all of me just as shattered—mind finally splintering. I'd done all I could.

For now.

BACK IN GERMANY again, I spent time at an isolated safe house in Stuttgart, helping freed women and children reach treatment centers. At night, I continued to work with a group called United Rescue Aid, tracking refugee boats crossing the perilous sea to Greece using a GPS monitoring system. Sometimes, I'd sit there checking on the journeys of several vessels at a time all night long, the dinghies sending out coordinates every ten minutes, until they reached safe harbor. If the rafts ran into trouble, it was my job to contact the nearest ships whose captains had joined the network, and mobilize a swift rescue at sea. Those pathetic overcrowded crafts held my people, and once ashore,

I would help marshal teams to meet them. When you're the member of a vanishing species, every life saved is the future entire—and I could not rest from that purpose.

Then, while drinking a cold cup of coffee, watching the boats, I finally received the one message that I'd been frantic for.

"This is Dil-Mir," she began. "Have I found you?"

Every nerve ending electrified—I filled and refilled my lungs with air like a man who'd just been pulled out from under the ice.

"Yes. It's me, Dil-Mir. I love you. Thank God you're alive. I knew you would find your way here. Now, I will find my way to you. Tell me all you can." How many times had I imagined that moment? It almost didn't seem real.

"I only have one minute. Must be careful."

"OK. I need your location. We are getting girls out all the time."

"Two brothers have me and another girl. They make us cook and dance."

"Where—do you know? We can get your GPS from your device."

"Syria. But they move us. We are being sold again, at a slave market outside of Aleppo."

"When?"

"Soon. Come find me. We can't live this way. The things they do to us."

"I will come. I promise you."

"I'll be back again to tell more."

Then, like a gust of wind, she was gone.

In that relentless season of cold rain and impenetrable fog, I thought the worst was almost over—my Dil-Mir was alive. I would not think about what they'd done to her—the time would come to deal with that. Between the loaded ships coming in, and the women and children pulled from under bridges, abandoned houses, carried across borders and out of fields, we'd saved hundreds so far. She was only one.

Only one, but my everything.

WHEN A FRIEND who'd been fighting in a Yazidi unit with the Kurds reached out, a brand-new plan fell into place. Three ISIS fighters had been killed. As he stood over the warm bodies on the outskirts of the Syrian desert, he called on WhatsApp to ask me what to do.

"Did you check for identification? ISIS issues ID cards—I need those," I said.

"Yes, got it," the Yazidi answered. I could hear him rummaging, the sounds of a zipper opening, as he ranted under his breath at the corpse.

I instructed him to take whatever he found. One of the militants had a Motorola cell phone and I knew that ISIS issued them to their soldiers; like many terrorist groups, they had their own communications channel. More treasure than I'd expected was coming off the first body and I warned him not to mess around and just bag it.

"Now take pictures of the ID cards," I said. "Front and back. The fighters, too—their faces. Every angle."

The cards were basic, laminated. No photo—easy.

"There should be a slave certificate," I said. "Maybe it's attached to the ID card."

He found it right away—good for one *sabaya*. A gift from the Islamic State.

"Sick bastards," he muttered, still rummaging. "They're organized."

"Well, I'm angry and organized."

"This guy is fat. Why are they all so fat?" And I could hear him roughing up the body.

Then I told him what I told everyone: "They are fat because they are pigs." And then I added that I would have to chug

German beer and eat bratwurst to get into shape for what I was about to do.

"What are you talking about?" Behind him the scraping of a shovel digging in the sand. Another voice in the background was muttering.

"Who's with you? I hear noises."

"Just one other—a Yazidi. You know him, don't worry." He sounded breathless; they had to get rid of the bodies fast.

It turned out, both men wanted in on the mission I had just begun to formulate—ISIS had the man's sister; the other needed to rescue his young daughter. They were both held captive in Syria—like my girl.

"If you're with me," I said, "we have to plan this thing down to the minute."

"Plan what, exactly?" The other man was asking now from the background, but he was already committed.

"We are going to infiltrate," I said. "Infiltrate and extract."

And I heard Brownsword's voice in my ear: *Concentrate on the living—the taken. Survivors. All those you can get to.*

I was going to get Dil-Mir.

Chapter Twenty-Two

The Slave Market

THE GREEK FORGER WORE A STAINED BUTCHER'S APRON, AND glazed rolls of fat hunkered under his chin like a stack of donuts. When I slid back the corroded van door, he had his hand buried in a can of smoked sausages. As the Middle East hemorrhaged refugees and terrorists, an illicit web of runners and counterfeiters burgeoned across Europe. If you knew one, you found the other—and I knew plenty.

"How long will it take?" I asked the Greek, who sat on a crate in the back. "I need three cards for now." The requisite ISIS beard was just sprouting along my jawline.

"Three, four weeks, maybe. Busy time of year. Passports mostly. But we like you—you're some kind of crazy vigilante."

"Perfect. Half the cash now, as agreed."

I held out a wad of euros raised through my cohorts in Iraq and a few generous associates.

"Put it there," he said, motioning to a tin box at his feet. "You want a ride back? I'm dropping off some merchandise."

"Sure," I said. "It looks like it's going to rain, hard." Sheets of blackened clouds raced over the sky. It would be another long, wet night.

And he told me that business always picked up after a storm. "A few will die on the sea before morning," he added. Crossing himself, he kissed his briny fingers.

Then he called out to the driver. I crawled inside, kicking aside beer cans as I took a seat over newspapers piled up in the corner.

BECOMING A JIHADIST took manic study into the collective psyche of men for whom mass killing, torture, and rape were homages to God. Penetration of the Islamic State's communications toolbox was simple. I roamed their encrypted messaging sites, scrutinizing traffic—militants talking to would-be militants about the glories of jihad—and absorbed the crazed pontifical lingo that I would practice out loud on long solitary walks.

May Allah reward you with a thousand virgins for your goodness, Brother. Inshallah—God willing—I will have many as a martyr in His kingdom.

I took in hours of propaganda videos: child training camps, hangings of gay men, heretics burned alive; drownings, crucifixions, and the beheadings of journalists and "spies"; jubilant fighters waiting for the distribution of Yazidi sex slaves—all set against the Islamic *nasheed*, a rhythmic a cappella chant.

Then I crawled still further down the gullet of the Islamic State, whose minions must have no doubt that I was one of them. Inevitably, I made it through the multiple relays of an overlapping network accessed through "The Onion Router," or TOR, an illicit browser that ferried users anonymously straight into the dark web. Within that infamous corner of cyberspace, cretins, criminal gangs, and international terror networks prowled. Inside it, I learned to think just like them—discovering, in the end, how little it took. After Allah and the establishment of a fruitful caliphate, their most effective weapon was a young jihadist's primal weakness—the promise of wanton sex.

How many can we get and what if I want a new one?

You will be satisfied, brother. Allah has given us his blessing.

The older ones understand too much. The young girls don't know a thing and you can do what you want. I've had dozens of each and know what I'm talking about.

Make sure she has breasts. If she doesn't, wait for them to start growing a little. We can share our sabayas. You will show me what a man you are.

These were the savages who had my Dil-Mir. Over and over again, I had to restrain the inescapable onslaughts of rage. Out of that shattering torment, Brownsword's battlefield creed rose like a mantra:

Thinking and feeling are two different animals, Shaker, that belong in separate pens. The first one keeps you alive, gets the job done—the second gets everyone killed.

And then, always, Dil-Mir's last desperate text:

Come find me, Shaker. Hurry.

THE STATIC OVER our headsets fused into a mayhem of Arabic voices; in the background the dissonance of battle raged on. I was crouched in a dune with one of my partners, listening. It was the summer of 2016, and we'd spent the last two months studying the enemy, growing beards and layers of fat, memorizing the Koran, and refining our plan. Now we were just inside the ISIS radio transmission zone, eavesdropping on the enemy's private channels, as I'd done many times with the American military. My eyes strained against the darkness toward Aleppo, past which Dil-Mir was alive and waiting—so close.

"The slave market is in two days, listen," Ismail said.

Every fighter will get his share. Come, brothers, and partake.

"We're on," I said. "Tell Hezni to get the vehicle ready."

"Do we tell the women this is it?"

"Only hours before—in case there's a hitch. Can't get their hopes up, but they must also play their own parts—no sign of recognition whatsoever."

I'd crossed the line from Turkey carrying forged IDs, water, and nothing else in my satchel. Then I met my contacts and donned an ISIS uniform: fatigues, black *shamag*, careworn jacket. Hezni had also brought an elaborate makeup kit and would practice on us several times.

"Your skin is too light, Shaker."

We were in a safe house miles from the target point.

"It has to look completely real, Hezni," I said. "They will have my picture up at every checkpoint. A lot of people would like the chance to take off my head."

"Don't worry," Ismail said. "He's done this a few times."

"That right?" I said as a sponge moved over my face.

Hezni nodded, saying nothing, as was his way, and studied his handiwork.

I held up a cracked mirror. "It's good," I said. "I look like a lazy Arab terrorist."

"You look fat," Ismail laughed. "It suits you."

"I've been eating lard for weeks."

In the predawn hours, Dil-Mir came online.

"At noon we will be sold," she whispered. "They don't know I speak Arabic, so they talk freely. There are many fighters and sheikhs coming."

"We will be there. You will not recognize me. I have a beard and have put on weight."

Her breath wavered. "I'm afraid, Shaker."

"I am not. Love for you is my strength."

Hezni had acquired a Syrian ambulance complete with paperwork. The drive to the small settlement on the fringes of Aleppo took less than an hour, and we parked off to the side of an abandoned farm road. From a distance, I made out swarms of black-clad men in the streets. Hezni waved to the ISIS fighters walking past and gave the standard greeting.

"And peace unto you," they offered back, without a second glance.

"Smile, Mohammed, it's distribution day," Ismail said to me, and patted my arm.

"Yes, brother Waleed. I am grateful." And I grinned like a madman.

Behind us, the caravan of buses full of slaves approached. From the ditch, I watched each one slide by on the fractured road, tamping down a cyclone of emotions as we stood in the blinding trails of dust. It took a titanic focus and control not to race forward shouting her name. Through tinted windows, I caught only frantic shadows, but I could hear the muted baying of the women. Somewhere inside that demonic caravan, Dil-Mir awaited her rescue—that thought and nothing else centered my mind. As the procession turned into the lot, I joined the rest of the men and raised my arms, cheering to praise Allah.

SKIRTING THE EDGE of the market, we moved along the glut of feral men. A loudspeaker announced the arrival of more concubines against beats of music and wild bursts of male laughter. The smell of sweet cakes and cooking smoke wafted past—just like a summer carnival. Walking through, I had to swallow down my own bile. Girls in black niqabs filed through the jeering crowd, whose raw scent intensified like heat. Hezni nudged my arm and we spread out, each one on his own now.

Stalking the bazaar, I swapped greetings with the other men as my eyes roved. Wearing a famished look was not out of place there, and I felt a rivulet of sweat snake down my back. Over one hundred women were grouped according to age, origin, and sexual status: virgin or used. Lashings of garish eye makeup showed through the slits of their quivering veils. Smiling brokers called out figures, and some of the women held white placards listing their prices. Many cheaper than a carton of cigarettes—those were the older hand-me-downs.

"Come get what your right hand possesses," a broker hollered. Behind him girls stood chained in a row.

A man stepped up and pulled back a veil, revealing a pale young girl, a gash of rouge smearing her lips. "Open your mouth," he barked, hooking her jaw. "She's perfect," the broker said. "Untouched and ready. You can enjoy her first. And she has already submitted to Allah."

The girl glanced at me, glassy-eyed as a lamb before the knife.

"Ah, don't you look hungry, brother," a man said, coming up to me. "Can I help you get your *milk al-yameen*?"

"Well, there is one I want," I said, pulling out a cracked Nokia phone taken off one of the dead fighters. "Found her online." I showed him the picture of a bewildered Dil-Mir that I discovered on the sex-slave marketplace.

"Let me see. A Yazidi. Used—but very, very pretty. Go see the man in the back."

"May Allah reward you for your goodness, brother," I said.

Resolute in my stride, I walked toward a small constellation of girls cowering behind a red rope. Here more affluent buyers skulked in their extravagant robes, tugging veils and lifting skirts. Big hairy hands slapped thighs, squeezed breasts.

"This one has good flesh, but I want lighter hair," a sheikh said.

All I could see were slivers of Yazidi eyes, almond-shaped and blinking through the fabric. Slowly I hunted—so sure of the mission now. Each draped gaze looked down as I passed, but one—and I locked my stare to her. Hard to tell.

"*Assalamu alaikum*," I said to the man in charge.

"And peace be upon you, too," he replied through a wilderness of gray beard.

"A brother sent me to you for this one." I held out my screen.

"She costs more," he said, waving a hand. "These ones all do."

Then a sheikh with a long cane walked by, hitting each woman hard on the back. "Get ready to walk to the buses."

"Brother, we just got here," I said—easy smile like swallowing a razor blade.

"Orders," he said, and shrugged. "They need you to go fight. I'll mark her down for you."

"Brother, I've killed plenty of *murtadin*. I'm here to take one of their women as my prize this day." Then I handed over my card. "*This* day."

"Ah." He chuckled and patted my cheek. "So this is your first *sabaya*. May Allah reward you for your bravery, but the rules have changed. You must buy now."

"How much?" I said, my throat squeezing out the words. "For her?"

"I will consider," he said, studying me closely. "A fitting price for a very hungry man." Right then, I thought he could see everything through the sweat on my brow.

In a moment, the loud speakers crackled to life and the market rippled into silence.

"Go fight with your brothers for our glory. And I will arrange a sale."

Nodding, I gave him a WhatsApp contact. "Today."

"Soon enough, you'll have your price."

Then the women filed out, roped together like livestock, and I just stood there watching them go. Her form was a noose about my neck, and with every step she took away from me, it tightened. Then her head tilted slightly, a pale hand coming free from that dark cocoon like the wing of a bird—and I was sure.

"Dil-Mir," I whispered. "I'm here." But the shape had already vanished.

No choice now, I dovetailed into a black river of the depraved on their way to the mosque, where I'd take off my shoes and bow among them.

Chapter Twenty-Three

Saved by Mosquitos

AFTERNOON, SEVERAL DAYS LATER, AND MY PHONE SAT SILENT. Between heartbeats, I waited and tried for rest. I'd been back to the market two times, but could not find Dil-Mir, or uncover her whereabouts. Outside the abandoned shed, leagues of seared ground stood as raw to the sun as my mind to the long, flaying hours. While ISIS contingents prowled the cauldron, my partners packed up and went back to wherever. All three of us empty-handed, for now.

At long last, an alert rose in the dead space like a buoy light, and I lunged:

10,000 euros. Non-negotiable—the standard smuggling fee, not a sale.

Suddenly, the game had changed and I was dealing with a brand new player. Without a doubt, the man at the other end was a runner brought in for a private job. The broker must have finally sniffed out my heretic blood—another desperate soul to plunder. Come nightfall, my new plan was in motion: clamber back across the frontier; set the network to raising flash funds; race to Greece and then Germany to solicit help from every quarter. Sell off my possessions: watch, old laptop, clothes, all for a pittance. It didn't matter—each scrounged euro was another strand in the lifeline. If I could strip the skin from my flesh and trade it, I would.

It will take time—I wrote back.

One week—was the answer.

Not enough.

It's all you have.

CROSSING A SPOONED-OUT valley in Turkey, I was on my way to another pick-up point, when Dil-Mir called again.

"Why didn't you get me out?" Each word was made of wind.

Alone, I went down into the swaying grasses, forehead against my knees, cradling her voice in the dark well of my lap. Along the branches of nearby trees, singing birds congregated; all over the ground insects pulsed; through my veins, the raging blood roared—and Dil-Mir's sobs were so feeble against the chorus of the unbothered world, I had to strain to hear her.

"Listen to me," I said. "I will come back. They want money—I'm going to get it."

"Please, don't leave me here. I can't live as a *sabaya*. They rape me. Every day. Three, four times. Many men. My body is broken."

"I will get you out and we will put you back together, one piece at a time."

"And then what? People will look at me—you will look at me, and see it."

"Dil-Mir, the ones who get out are *survivors*—you are all our treasure, not our shame. I love you more today than any other day." How I meant it.

"I wish I was dead, Shaker. I thought it was finally over, and now I'm still here."

"Only a little longer. We will keep talking. And I will come back."

"How could you leave me, Shaker? You were just here."

And then she wasn't.

MY WORLD GONE to wishes: to get the money in time, to meet her at the checkpoint, to carry us both way back to where we once were. To walk the cobblestones of Berlin, arms entwined, learn German together. *Liebe:* love. *Für immer:* forever. To be at home with Dil-Mir, and nothing else—make us one with rings.

To never have answered the call when it came in, and simply lived my whole life oblivious, searching the boundless continent of false hope.

Anything but this.

"I am Farida. Are you Shaker? I was sold with Dil-Mir."

"Yes, Farida. Where is she?"

"She's gone."

"Gone where?"

"Gone, Shaker. Hanged herself with a veil."

I SAW DIL-MIR again strolling the serpentine path to the temple, her long abundant hair worn *por vekeri*, free. A faint smile told me to follow her into the enveloping mists—right to the edge of all things.

I'm back now, Shaker. Let's walk.

Where can we go?

We can't go anywhere. Just here.

This little white room—that's all we get?

Suddenly, a man shone a light like a tiny sun into one eye, and then the other, but I was far less than half-aware.

"What's wrong with him?" said a female from the other side of me.

Then a studied voice listed off my ailments: Stomach infection. Malnutrition. Sounded pretty bad. He knew I'd been in Greece working in the camps, eating bugs, maggots. Someone else said strange people were looking for me. Apparently, I'd had death threats—that's why no visitors.

"Came in trying to sell his kidney and collapsed," I heard them say.

And that's when I remembered the moment: hauling my body through the emergency room doors, hollering and holding up my shirt, begging for a surgeon to take the organ.

"His kidney? That's crazy."

"The man's had a crisis. Been incoherent for over a week. Keeps getting up and crawling the walls. We can't stop him."

"What kind of crisis—drugs?"

"No—" He listened to my heart for a while. Slow and steady, because I was already on my way back to elsewhere with my girl. "He's just a Yazidi."

"Oh," the woman said, clucking her tongue, and I'll never forget that sound and the thing she said next—so full of pity and yet so far removed. "Poor thing."

Across the urban hive, church bells struck the hour and I counted the chimes from one to the end. Through those watery echoes, sirens blared, and the dull machinery of mankind hummed. Slowly, I rose from the deep, making my way up toward an opening window of consciousness. All the while, I heard Brownsword and Migone talking away in my ear.

What's going on with him? Brownsword said. *This is not good. Maybe it's the pictures—no one wants to know.*

Don't tell him that, damn it. Get up, Mikey, Migone barked. *What are you doing sleeping like a princess when there's a war going on?*

I don't think I'm well enough, sir, I said. *I've had a crisis.* Somehow, my mind and limbs had gone their separate ways again. And I wanted to stay and linger with Dil-Mir.

Crisis? Migone said. *Look at you, still got half your baby fat— time to move.*

Yes, sir. It is. I know it.

Stirs of cool air whispered over my skin; bands of crimson shot through my lids, and I heard someone sigh. Slowly and still blind, I started hunting down parts: arms, hands, digits. Then eyes wide open—deep inside another sugar cube. Reborn from the shadows, I took in a huge gulp of air that tore open my lungs. Then I heaved, coughing up streaks of blood that spattered the sheets like cherry syrup.

"Don't worry about that, Mr. Jeffrey, you're fine," said a female nurse in soft German. "Glad to see you so awake. How do you feel?"

"*Tot*," I rasped. Dead. Then I asked her where the colonel was, where all of them were.

"No one else here," the nurse said. "But your phone kept buzzing. I had to shut it off." Then she floated over, all honey-colored curls, offering the Android like treasure from her open palm. "So many calls from everywhere came in. Journalists. People in England. Lots of Americans. One English woman—now she was just relentless. We gave no information."

"That will be Anne," I said. "They don't like when I disappear."

"If I might ask—what is it you do?"

Then I looked over at the nurse; antiseptic soap coming off her hands filled the bright space between us. She had a beatific smile that blended right into the walls; every perfect part of her seemed to effervesce a sure and carefree youth. My empty guts churned over themselves—God help me, I didn't want anything to do with her.

"Survive," was all I could think of to say, and looked down at my phone.

The first person I heard from was Anne Norona, an English nurse living in Cornwall, whom I'd met online through the rescue grid while working the camps in Greece. Increasingly, Anne and I were joining our efforts, conducting countless virtual missions to help the most vulnerable Yazidis—but never once meeting in person. Anne was what techies refer to as a meta-administrator, a user who has been granted certain technical freedoms in order to safeguard their platform, of one of the largest Facebook communities in the online grassroots universe. Not to mention that she secured funds, medical personnel, and collaborators for the most severe cases, all at spellbinding speeds.

When a group of fourteen Yazidis, including children under five, were stranded with thirty-two armed smugglers on the attack in the woods of Gevgelija, in Macedonia, it was Anne who'd coordinated over a thousand messages and mobilized a swift rescue. If there was a child needing a life-saving operation, a torture case requiring specialized treatment, or a last-minute nail-biting rescue to execute, we often called her first.

During my time in Greece, our groups worked together seamlessly as a boy and his debilitated sister were making the treacherous crossing from Turkey to the Greek island of Lesvos. I made contact with the siblings right on the shore, while the network set to work acquiring the terrified girl a visa from the German embassy, and a surgeon willing to operate on her fast. Nineteen-year-old Najwa, who was in end-stage glaucoma, had only 15 percent vision in one eye and 5 percent in the other. Time was now the main enemy; if Najwa did not have surgery within a few weeks she would go completely blind. In the end, every facet came together: Najwa's sight restored, she was reunited with her family.

"Shaker, where are you?" Anne said.

"Berlin—busy."

Then she asked me to meet her the next week in Stuttgart.

"Christina Lamb from the *Sunday Times of London* is coming to the shelters. Everyone has been trying to find you."

FROM THE STATION at Stuttgart in the high heat of August 2016, I made my way into the deep forests of Baden-Württemberg, where survivors and their children lived secreted in a series of quiet and isolated sanctuaries. All through the cities, triggers lay in wait like land mines: trucks, dark-haired men, the prying eyes of passersby, and sheer multitudes of refugees. For some girls, the very men who'd raped them now roamed the cobblestones, free among the displaced. Many of the survivors received death threats and lived in a constant state of terror. Reports to the police accomplished little—lately there were too many such incidents to keep track of. The sanctuary's location was a well-guarded secret, and to prevent reprisals, the use of social media was not permitted.

On foot, I walked up to the sterile medical compound as a warm breeze pushed past the soaring trees; shards of sunshine cut through the moving canopy and danced all over me. In that hidden place, the government and Yazidi elders ran the Special Quota Project, and so far, over a thousand survivors of sexual slavery had come through the program to heal through art, yoga classes, and intensive therapy sessions. So far, not one patient had taken her own life—a landmark among those for whom suicide was often the only escape from their eviscerating pain. How many times I'd imagined shepherding my Dil-Mir to that very haven.

Meeting Anne Norona there was like discovering a long-lost, blue-eyed sister in the woods. Inside a swell of warm light, she was waiting. At first, we just took one another in—merging so many frantic words typed on a screen each day into an actual person. Immediately, a multitude of missions came to mind: like the night the Turkish coast guard sank a boat full of Yazidis, and people trapped on the doomed ship screamed over the lines as our rescue chat coolly organized aid from nearby vessels. Most of the time, in the great hub of thousands, you never encountered your cohorts in the flesh, and it was a privilege to meet this way. Together, Anne and I and all the others were waging a war against an abomination—and I struggled now not to betray recent events. The truth was, less than half of me stood there, breathing.

Dark-haired Anne Norona was an uncommon woman. A single mother who ran a sideline Botox clinic to fund her brazen humanitarian efforts, she'd spent two years in Haiti, and had worked as the main medical recruiter in the squalid camps in Lesvos, where over two thousand refugees a day poured in—soaking wet, some with hypothermia, and all of them traumatized. It was there that Anne witnessed the profound plight of my people, who were persecuted and bullied even in the camps. Already, she had plans for a clandestine aid trip into Shingal and was raising funds to provide the most basic needs of Yazidis still hunkered inside the dark folds of the mountain, afraid to ever come down—rogue ISIS fighters still stalked the terrain.

By now, Anne had developed a sixth sense for every form of human suffering. Even in my pressed suit and through my smiling banter, she saw me for what I was—a shattered man.

"The girls are cooking for us in there," she said at last, taking my arm. "Come eat, Shaker. You need their Yazidi food, and they need you."

And we went inside.

EVERY TIME IRAQ or the Yazidis were in the news, journalists called on me, and I had grown accustomed to their indifferent successions of questions. Christina Lamb's cool English poise betrayed very little, and neither did I. As we shook hands in the corridor, I knew I was looking at a woman who'd seen things—up close. She'd ventured right into the battle zones she wrote about, and it showed as clearly to me as the flaxen color of her hair. And so, I entrusted our fragile survivors to her mighty pen. Yazidis had to trust someone, or our stories would all be lost. So many of our people already were.

"You didn't answer our calls for a while," Christina said. "The doctor who put us in touch mentioned a crisis. Tell only if you can. We know not to take your picture."

At first, I gave up only a few raw facts: Dil-Mir, an escape attempt, suicide—and no more. Somehow, I wanted her to hear the spoken name of my beloved, who belonged in that very place with us, but would never make it—never, no matter how I wished against the truth.

"May I see a picture of her?" Christina said, looking right into me.

Turning away, I held up a shot of my smiling Dil-Mir.

"Ah," Christina breathed, and her hand rose gently.

Then we moved into the room.

Tobacco smoke swirled and women sat around blank-faced; some rocked back and forth, others kept turning their hands over in their laps—I'd seen all of it, many times before. Every now and again, from some other part of the building, we could hear Yazidi children at play, voices high and sounding so carefree. Hard to imagine the horrors they knew: mothers raped, fathers slaughtered. ISIS had tortured many: cigarette burns and beatings—and yet the children giggled, tossed balls, drew pictures of flowers. The doctors there said it had taken some of the rescued a full year to speak again.

In the large room, the group sat together over the floor. All the food eaten: the spiced perfume of home wandered like a ghost. I was against the wall, legs out; Christina next to me, pen in hand. For a moment, I thought of my family stuck back in the camp, waiting to get to Europe. They all thought I was going to the government-mandated German classes, charting a whole new life for us.

As soon as we were all settled, one after the other, female voices rose in the warm room like currents of ice-cold air. From the first word uttered, we were all transported back to Shingal—August 3, 2014.

ISIS took everyone to a school and put women and children on the ground floor. They took some men in cars and drove away, we heard gunshots. . . .

They said: If you don't convert, we will kill you. They wanted the most beautiful ones, so we started rubbing dirt in our hair to make us look nasty. . . .

They took the virgins to Mosul. . . .

I was sold for 350 American dollars. . . .

He grabbed me by my hair, cuffed my arms to the bed, then forced himself on me. . . .

Men came back to rape me every day, three or four times. . . .

The day Mosul falls, I fear ISIS men will just shave off their beards and escape to the West. . . .

And I thought: *So many already have.*

Each time we took a break, I went to the washroom and vomited.

"You all right, Shaker?" Anne asked. "Your translation is perfect."

I'd ventured outside to release a prayer for strength. Just then I had so little left, and it shamed me.

"It's hard," I said. "We keep telling the world, and it closes its doors."

"We can do more," Anne said. Money was the biggest obstacle—each soul cost, and there were so many of them reaching out.

"What we do is all that keeps me going," I told her. Between us, thousands of Yazidis and other terrorized refugees had found safety: on boats, in vans, the trunks of cars; on foot, or carried out on backs; into hospitals, safe houses, camps, and shelters like the one we were standing in.

"What do you think of the name Mosquitos?" Anne said.

Anne Norona had a proud reputation for always buzzing in ears: asking, cajoling, doing, saving lives; healing the sick, traumatized, and maimed; bringing torn families together. So did her two Yazidi cohorts. All of us were one and the same—never giving up. It was the perfect moniker.

"I love it." And I laughed for a fleeting easy moment, not recognizing the sound of my own unbound voice.

Back in Greece, we'd merged networks, but Anne realized that the most severe Yazidi cases needed a specialized organism within the massive system. A secret Facebook group, the Mosquitos, would preserve those precious lives. Anne handled cases stemming in Iraq, while I continued to look after the German side.

Standing in the Black Forest of Germany, we shook hands, forming a bridge between east and west, and the moment was not lost on me. At my end: legions of security personnel, police, border agents, coast guards, military and government officials; activists and volunteers in the Turkish, Syrian, and KRG camps. Journalists, ordinary Iraqis, Turks, and Syrians, smugglers, do-gooders, military vets, mercenaries, and private contractors. At Anne's: medics, doctors, surgeons, nurses, members of parliament, benefactors, professors, bakers, blue-bloods, bankers, heads of NGOs, aid workers, masses of international volunteers, and all those she'd hounded for help or a bank draft. We connected galaxies of laptops and cell phones into a single universe, like a modern-day resistance movement from the Second World War.

"Right," Anne said. "We just carry on."

"And keep getting bigger—stronger," I said. Warm blood transfused through my veins, every sinew in me awakened. "*Yaho*, Anne. It's good." Right then I felt there was nothing we could not accomplish together—all of us. And I was not alone; I was a Mosquito.

"*Yaho*, Shaker. It really is—just be careful."

BACK IN BERLIN, I held the key to my small asylum flat and went up the iron staircase. Walking the narrow corridor over a stained patterned carpet, I stopped: the door was hanging open, right off one hinge. The soldier in me instantly roused, I checked for the folding knife I kept tucked in my pocket, and crept along. My small room stood ransacked: mattress slit down the middle. Drawers pulled out. Clothes and papers in heaps. Then I backed away from the wrecked threshold, checked the hall—and ran.

Chapter Twenty-Four

Hunted

ON A DARK DECEMBER AFTERNOON IN 2016, ANIS AMRI, A failed asylum seeker, surveyed the black tractor trailer parked at the ThyssenKrupp warehouse just outside of Berlin. Having made his scheduled delivery of steel, the Polish driver, Lukasz Urban, was at a nearby kebab shop, eating what would become his very last meal. Sometime later, the thirty-seven-year-old father of one called his wife and then returned to the truck, where Anis shot him in the head at point-blank range. As Lukasz slowly bled out over the passenger seat, his hijacked vehicle lumbered away from the lot.

At 8:00 P.M., Anis drove the massive trailer at high speed down the center of the bustling Breitscheidplatz Christmas market. Before the crushing wheels, a multitude of merry-makers heaved forward in a wild rush. Some were sucked under the carriage—twelve people were killed on impact; fifty-six left with multiple fractures and severe internal injuries. The market was two blocks from my new room in the heart of Old

Berlin, and I opened a window to a mortal uproar of screams and sirens.

This had already been a year of terror across Europe: coordinated suicide bombings in Brussels; another truck massacre in Nice, on Bastille Day; a Syrian extremist who blew himself up at a music festival in Ansbach; people stabbed on a train near Würzburg; a priest murdered and parishioners attacked in a church in Normandy; more explosives found at a Christmas market in Ludwigshafen. Continued rapes and kidnappings in the camps.

By the October 2016 publication of Christina Lamb's article in the *Sunday Times of London* and *The Australian*, I'd been changing locations every few weeks, or even days. Inevitably, I had blown my own alias; social media accounts hacked. Undeterred and borderline irrational, I would only expand my efforts in earnest into and throughout 2017: joining Nadia Murad at conferences; organizing rallies and protests; speaking out against the Assayish and Muslim extremists on Sirius Radio and NPR, and at symposiums in Berlin, Brussels, and Paris—while continuing the daily life-saving missions with Anne, the Mosquitos, and the full network universe. The battle to get the better of my enemies consumed full days and nights like an overpowering amphetamine—no sleep, scrounging for scraps.

In between, I somehow found my way, on and off, to the compulsory German classes required of all refugees. The trouble was time: every consumed minute could mean a life—another Dil-Mir—my whole existence. Without a word, the young female teacher took a look at my haggard face and seemed to understand that I was part of some underworld that was much larger than myself. Often, I sat in the back of the classroom working out missions on my Android, and counting on my natural aptitude for language to get me a passing grade. When I finally explained to the instructor that I was part of a Yazidi rescue group, she nodded, looked down, and quietly excused my absences. In gratitude, I did learn German and only took on more and more cases with Anne at my virtual side from her Botox clinic in Cornwall; my American brothers regularly checked in from their hemisphere.

"Keep your work confined to German soil from now on, brother," Brownsword told me. "Just the humanitarian missions—got it?"

In short order, he advised that I stop saying negative things about Barzani and his government on social media. Sometimes, caught in a vortex of fury, I railed against them on message boards, about how the Peshmerga were ordered away from Shingal, leaving us to certain slaughter. "Sooner or later, the Assayish will decide to join the party and come after your ass, Mikey, believe me."

It was too late. Their agents had eyes all over Europe and could hack their way right into Facebook. Every now and again they sent a thug to my flat, or a crew would follow me like a pack of dogs onto a commuter train or rough me up in an alley, utter threats. If President Barzani wanted me to shut up, he could start by letting my people out of the filthy camps and back onto their own land. Most Yazidis agreed that he wanted our people gone from Shingal—ISIS was a convenient way for him to acquire his own country. And I told as much to Brownsword.

"OK, it's high time to get you out of there. You need to get that visa to the United States right now. We filled out the paperwork while you were still a terp, for God's sake. Two factions have targets on your back."

"They'll have to catch me—that's the thing."

"Brother, hearing you talk, it sounds to me like they caught you a long time ago."

But I would not listen. The war I was waging was in my blood and there was always one last mission that I thought would get me closer to winning—to beating ISIS by taking back all those they'd taken. Exposing Barzani. Justice—it was all I lived for.

Within six months, I was popping anti-anxiety medication and unable to sleep more than an hour at a time before another nightmare yanked me out of my skin. I'd grab the Android, check the boards, and get back to work.

Since the dawn of 2017, I'd been living in various small inconspicuous towns around the North Rhine–Westphalia region, two hundred miles west of Berlin. From there, I made daily visits to newly arrived Yazidi families to help them navigate the German sanctuary system. Other times, I shepherded the newly liberated through the rescue network off trains and airplanes and out of smugglers' vans into hospitals, rehabilitation centers, and safe havens.

Daily messages coming in one after the other at all hours kept me busy with the relentless stream of new cases coming into Germany. Sometimes several a day needed tending to; so many maimed Yazidi orphans with nowhere to turn. Still, I kept my promise to Brownsword to stay on safe soil—most of the time.

Many of the rescued Yazidis remained shell-shocked for months, unable to reconcile that new world of cobblestones and cathedral spires against their collective lifetimes of mud huts, bullets, blood, and sand. I filled out forms and, through the Mosquitos medical teams, arranged urgent care and acted as interpreter between them and the labyrinthine German bureaucracy. Oftentimes, I just sat drinking sweet chai in their cramped rooms that reeked of rancid cooking oil and soiled diapers, listening to heart-rending stories: loved ones lost, butchered, or taken. Most incoming families were clustered around the Westphalia region, and though establishing a predictable travel routine could prove lethal, I had no choice; for so many Yazidis, I was the only lifeline. Every single time I grabbed a moment to rest, eat, or even shower, I hated myself for taking the luxury.

Meanwhile, as more and more ISIS operatives slithered into Europe, associates in Iraq had passed along the message that I'd been marked for immediate killing—days of on-the-run safety in Germany were over. Now, I was living in a covert war zone, and receiving regular reports of ISIS fighters spotted roaming the picturesque streets with devil-may-care audacity, often coming right up to their former Yazidi captives and calling them out by name.

Then, I had stumbled at last right into what I thought would be my most lethal mission against ISIS. Salman was a young Yazidi attorney operating out of Iraq with a wide but covert network of his own, spread along the frontiers of the Middle East and right into Europe. Our common purpose as Yazidis brought us together in the online void, and we kept our sensitive communications distinct from the wider network. From a safe house by the frontier, he'd been tracking ISIS fighters and their slaves as they shuttled into Turkey, and was compiling the constantly evolving data: aliases and precise locations; the identities of the Yazidis shackled to them. Established in comfortable homes with a steady current of funds, ISIS militants became so brazen in their freedom that they held slave auctions inside Turkish towns—many of the sales were listed on the dark web. Between just the two of us, we kept careful track of the auctions and followed the movements of each slave; in secret we raised funds and organized individual extractions and infiltrated sales as best we could; but with few effective contacts in the country, our eager agents faced an army of obstacles. All too often, we failed.

Informed time and time again, the Turkish authorities offered no meaningful support. As the list of Yazidi slaves held in Turkey grew, my rage whetted down to a razor of single-minded resolve. For every one of my people held captive, there was at least one ISIS terrorist lurking nearby like a human time bomb—and no one else had access to that information. If the lives of the Yazidis weren't worth anything to anyone, that intel was at least worth something to a lot of people.

"Infiltrators—coming into Europe—you sure?" Brownsword said.

"Like rats out of a sewer."

"Your contact got specifics?"

"Nothing but specifics—addresses, new names. They have their Yazidi slaves with them, and that's how we track them."

Days later, Brownsword told me to expect a call from an American who would take my intel and pass it along for verification. My idea was to offer the US government a deal: they get the terrorists, and we free the girls.

Long tongues of fragrant smoke climbed the crimson walls as we entered Lebanon's Lounge like shadows and took our seats against a far wall, alone. I was there with Maher, one of a handful of Yazidi cohorts who'd helped me move in and out of safe houses.

"Listen to me, Shaker, you need air. Everyone in the community thinks you're cracking up. I know a good shisha lounge," he said.

"Not a chance—I have to stay underground and wait. It's the only way." I was barefoot on the floor, clacking away at my Android.

Maher was sitting across from me, drinking from a can of Coke. The carbonated liquid sounded like a swarm of insects, and my guts churned like cement. I saw an image of Bowers in Mosul at the flour factory, running a sleeve across his sweaty face.

Flies, I heard Bowers say. *Flies on top of flies.*

I rummaged through a bag, pulled out a prescription bottle, and held it up. I took one pill and swallowed it, dry as paper. "All good."

"You need more than pills. Thought you were going to kill me last time I came in here with food—that was some crazy military move."

"I'm sorry about that." And I was. All Maher wanted to do was go out, drink some good Arabian chai. Be a normal person for a night.

"They have cushions on the floor," he said. "No chairs—just like home."

"Like home," I breathed.

"That phone is going to kill you."

Suddenly, I couldn't wait to get out of there.

SILKEN CUSHIONS LAY scattered like soft jewels; everywhere the hum of chatter and clinks of cups. Instantly, the perfumed warmth of Shingal covered me like a warm bath, and I let my tired psyche soak in it, grateful for the fleeting moment.

You see? Maher seemed to say, leaning back. The bulb of water gurgled as he sucked in drafts of fragrant smoke.

The tea was good and I drank it down so slowly. Knots buried deep along my spine loosened, and I glanced around. Maher had assured me that he'd had the placed scouted before I went in.

"You don't even know who to look for," I'd laughed, but my eyes were roving.

Less than an hour later, two men slinked over to the bar. Right away, I noticed one holding a piece of paper in his hand. At regular intervals now, I shifted my eyes to the pair, who had their wide backs turned. Leather jackets, bulky—easy to conceal a reliable piece in there. Several times, I watched them sip sodas and smoke, but they never turned around.

"Shaker," Maher said. "When you look away, those guys over there look at you. Every ten minutes. One's got a paper in his hands."

"Yeah," I said. Something wasn't right.

Cool and agile in his black jeans and faux suede loafers, Maher moved like an elegant predator across the dim lounge, passing along the bar before slipping into the restroom. Trapped against a wall on my silk raft, I tracked the men along my periphery and drank down a full cup of chai. As waitresses floated past through veils of shisha, I scanned escape routes: back doors into an alleyway, kitchen to nowhere certain, front entrance to the main street and plenty of human cover.

"Time to go," Maher said, sliding back down next to me. He took in a long last puff of tobacco and let it out slowly, shrouding us both in smoke. "That paper has your face on it."

But I already knew.

THE MEN FOLLOWED us out and would be hard to lose. One had arms like battering rams; when he turned his head, you could see the veins in his neck bulge like taut wires. Moving along the crowded front patio, I suddenly realized Maher was gone, and I looked over to glimpse his dark blue shoes racing across the intersection. Dodging into a side street, he disappeared.

Then a voice shouted over the din, "Hey, Shaker Jeffrey. How are you?"

I turned now, taking solace in the cover of the populated street. A few young drunkards shoved past and paid us no mind.

"You want something?" I asked, straightening the frayed lapels on my jacket.

"Nadia, she was so good to us," the second one said, stepping up to me. He had a gash like a claw mark across his pocked face. And he grinned—all gold caps. "I can still taste her." Then he went on and on talking trash in spit-laced Arabic.

"What are you talking about?" I kept saying. I'd expected a knife or a gun—not words.

"Nadia Murad? Your whoring girlfriend who thinks she's a celebrity. That was a nice protest you Yazidis put on in Berlin.

You and her lighting those little candles together. Your Baba Sheikh can baptize our *sabayas* all he wants, no one can be a virgin twice. Whatever you got from her, I broke it in first."

The man behind him laughed and nodded. "I had her too," he said.

Before I could react, another figure lumbered up behind me and whispered the name of my beloved like a wet curse into my ear. Right then, my limbs went to steel. In the next beat, a thunderclap of rage rushed out from my core. I whipped around, only to catch an open fist in the hollow of my cheek. The crack was hard and fast, and I stumbled back a pace as pain seared through my jaw. Now all three set upon me, and my arms went up to shield myself from a rabid onslaught of punches. Crouching way down, I scanned the melee for an opening. Maneuvering left and right, I found solid ground and countered with a few hard returns, one right after the other. Each fresh bash pummeled my knuckles to the consistency of crushed grapes; the chapped skin on my bottom lip tore open. Blood smeared my face.

Now, a full-scale battle of fists erupted in the streets, and all I could see were arms and balled up hands coming at me. Women screamed and men hollered. Through the propped-open doors of the lounge, smoke billowed. I could just make out the Assyrian woman behind the bar pressing a phone to her ear. By her red face and jabbering mouth, I knew that she was calling the *Polizei*.

When the blade came out, I didn't see it, just felt the tip slide along the shallow flesh of my abdomen as though it were made of butter. Animal instinct propelled me way back, but a thin crimson bloom erupted over my white shirt. Falling to the sidewalk, I heard the wail of sirens. Someone crouched over me with a stack of napkins and hollered for help. Speaking in German, I assured him again and again that the wound wasn't deep.

SEVERAL OFFICERS ARRESTED my attackers, and then questioned me in the back of the ambulance on the way to the hospital.

"The barmaid corroborates your story, so we won't keep you." The officer told me that the other men were illegals—no papers. He asked me if I knew who they were.

"ISIS," I said. "Probably came in from Syria."

"You sure about that?"

"They tried to kill me—that makes it pretty obvious."

"Not to us."

OVER THE NEXT months, agents would come after me time and again: on narrow side streets, in and out of trains, outside bus terminals; dark-clad Arab men with cell phones pinned to their ears followed my every move. They stole my laptop, hacked into my phone, watched me from cafés, and sent death threats to my family back in the camps.

But I remained undeterred.

The more they chased, the more resolved I became—even after narrowly escaping a gun pressed against my head. Those foot soldiers, and the people who sent them, wouldn't have been so bothered if I wasn't winning—at least that's what I thought. But the truth was, they were getting harder to outrun. Or maybe I was just slowing down. At some point, they would keep their promise and slit my throat, let me bleed out slowly while they filmed it all for my mother. I didn't want to die in Germany, but I wasn't going to stop.

There was nowhere else for me to go.

Chapter Twenty-Five

Through the Perilous Fight

THE SCALES OF WAR STARTED TO TIP FAST AGAINST ISIS IN THE spring of 2017, as American naval vessels anchored in the Gulf and fighter jets and drones skidding high over the Jazeera unleashed an avalanche of missiles straight across the beating heart of the caliphate. Australia, the United Kingdom, Belgium, the Netherlands, Denmark, and Jordan all took part in a relentless and colossal offensive of ordnance against the Islamic State's infrastructure, pounding away at their oil interests, bases, and strongholds. One after the other, dumbfounded enemy units surrendered their posts and retreated—often cowering under the cover of human shields—out of crumbling towns and burning villages that they would leave booby-trapped in lethal tangles of trip-wire bombs.

By the summer solstice, that demonic and once indomitable force had hemorrhaged well over half its territory, and saw revenue streams of black market crude all but choked off. As the besieged caliphate continued to bleed out, its fighters set aside their sacred lust for jihad and scuttled from the front lines.

Crouched and camouflaged along the smooth desert gullies, my Yazidi cohorts photographed scores of retreating militants, who stood in clusters at the sides of roads to take turns shaving off their telltale beards and change into ordinary civilian clothes, abandoning those black uniforms and flags in dirty heaps like shed skins over the sand. Then, those once ardent warriors filed slowly onto air-conditioned buses that ferried them as returning tin gods back into safe territory. One ISIS commander even ran for Iraqi parliament without any mention ever being made of his affiliations. Meanwhile, other more intrepid militants simply traversed the western frontiers, dovetailing into a ready camouflage of migrating hordes.

As other Yazidi associates stood watch along a half-dozen points scattered across the border, scores of militants were jumping the line right into Turkey. Once there, they linked up with ISIS facilitators who guided them into the comfort of established safe houses, often nestled in quiet suburban neighborhoods. Unwilling to give up the spoils of war, many of these terrorists had taken along their Yazidi *sabayas*, disguised under trembling chadors as submissive Arab wives, who in turn carted their own enslaved children.

Still well-funded and organized, ISIS operatives were now bribing Turkish officials and civil servants, who swiftly proffered the one thing that ensured each incoming terrorist a safe seat inside the Trojan horse of terror that would carry them right into wider Europe—a valid Turkish passport. Now, by the hundreds, unchecked, unknown, and daily, soldiers of the Islamic State were invading the continent. But there was one fatal flaw in the latest plan: those captive Yazidi slaves, who were still stealing cell phones and reaching Salman.

My ANDROID CHIMED through the dull weekend quiet. From the hard floor, I looked over and stood straight up, glimpsing the name I'd been waiting for—Alex Holstein—flashing across the screen.

"Brownsword briefed me up, but you can still take me through it," he said, a hint of New York lacing his voice. He sounded just like a cop on one of the American shows I sometimes watched when I couldn't sleep. "The situation has gotten worse, right? He mentioned passports."

"Easy," I said. I'd practiced that conversation over and over. "I told you guys many times. I want to make a deal with the Americans—"

"You reach out to Interpol?"

"Yes, a lot."

"So, it's not that simple."

"Yes, it is—it's very simple," I barked. In the background I could hear the chattering monotone of a radio over a low whine of static. Then the voices stopped and there was only the steady breathing of the man at the other end. Leaning against the mildewed wall of my basement room, I slid down to the floor. Conveying it all to a stranger on the phone was like trying to fill a glass with an ocean. "Here's the deal: I give the American government the exact locations, identities, and movements of ISIS in Turkey—hundreds of them—and they help me and my partners coordinate a rescue-op of the Yazidi women and children."

"You're right. That is simple—to guys like you and me."

"We can do it right now." Every night, I'd sat up for hours planning my part of the operation, from infiltration to extraction and transport into Germany. There was a whole network ready to go, and I told him so.

"Those IDs and the passport scheme are going to be game-changers. First thing we need to do is get you the right point of contact, who can haul all you've got up the chain and get it processed—fast."

"Isn't that you?"

"I'm the bridge—I take people across and fix them up—keep things moving."

"What do I do?"

"Keep fighting the fight." He sounded just like Brownsword. "You and your partner carry on compiling data, and wait. Help is coming. Meanwhile, there's a team already pushing your case for that special visa, the SIV, to the front of the line—and it's one crazy long line. A lot of people think it's a matter of national interest that we get you to the States."

"This mission first—or nothing." The truth was, I didn't believe I was ever getting out; of the thousands, I'd only ever heard of a handful of terps who'd received a visa. And even then, the pencil pushing had taken years.

"Right. I'm going to take what you just told me to a couple of guys—both called Mike. One is retired FBI. Joint Terrorism Task Force. Hunted al-Zarqawi back in the day. The other is former SEAL Team Six. I'll get it to the two Mikes—they'll know who to hit with this. And whoever that is will probably want to talk to you."

"We don't have time to wait to talk."

"Yeah, you don't have a lot of time period, Mikey—that's the cold truth."

When we got off the line, I just sat there, listening to the low rumble of traffic outside, and watched the light slowly fade and swallow shadows in the room. All through the vacant night, memories overtook me in frantic sounds and voices. The war had been long and full of losses and it was getting harder and harder to keep going and think straight. But I wasn't giving up. One step at a time, I was finding my way through a labyrinth. In the morning, I looked over to see that the door stood wide open—my laptop was gone.

I got up fast, grabbed Babo's picture, and left. So little sleep, and I was on the move all over again.

Chapter Twenty-Six

All the Faithful

IN THE MONTHS OF WAITING THAT FOLLOWED, MY BODY WITHERED down to a skeleton sheathed in wasted muscle, but I kept to the same unyielding pace. In my personal mission to thwart the enemy, I could not stop. I took to smoking shisha like a madman. Every now and again, I messaged my family on Facebook, sending out reassuring pictures of easy times, interesting landmarks, smiling people, and cultural events. Daki believed that the worst was over for our family; and as time carried us across 2017, we were scattered all over the earth, in camps or safe havens—but still alive.

Somehow, Bowers sensed that I was in a bad way, and without saying a word in advance, sent me money through Western Union. It wasn't the first time, and he sent more to my family in the camps. He could not have known what that meant for us. The man had seven children to feed, and yet he'd thought of feeding me and my own. Because of him, I had my first taste of good meat in weeks; afterward I kneeled down over the ground of my dank room to whisper up a prayer to God, and a *yaho* all the way to Idaho.

Meanwhile, as ISIS continued to lose terrain, more Yazidi cases poured in, and I crisscrossed Germany, often forgoing food and sleep, to meet them, always with a smile. So many were small children, only revealed as they crawled from the craters of bombed-out blocks, or wandering the liberated streets of Mosul and other towns like wraiths. Dozens of half-grinning boys emerged from the wreckage as though from their own graves, coated in the grime of war and drugged for so long they no longer knew their own names. Those forsaken Yazidi strays were all ours and would not be left to the unwitting world, or we were finished as a people—as human beings. Girls discarded as their captors fled the smoldering cities sometimes sat stunned for days in abandoned homes, at last praying to their own god again until we found them.

Once cross-border rescues had taken place, I would travel to perimeter towns and train stations, or even to meet smugglers' vans at the sides of roads, and ferry survivors in bundles to hospitals or sanctuary homes. Still in the dead of night, Salman and I met in the void to tally our growing list of captives. All the while, I kept in contact with Alex, and he with "the two Mikes," as we worked through what was called "processing."

As an added safety net, an American handler started checking on me most days. Sometimes she pinged more than once through an encrypted platform. She kept tabs on my well-being and the status of any forms or reports, ensured I was obtaining medical attention when warranted, and monitored my rescue work. We got to know each other well, but would never meet in person. Mainly, she was just a kind voice from the free world, and I was soon calling her *Xweşko*—Sister. Xweşko convinced me to take regular walks and seek out friends in their tiny asylum rooms. Sometimes, all we did was exchange YouTube videos, watch clips of *The Ellen DeGeneres Show*, and tell jokes to pass the dark times. Or we simply sat hours on end in our hemispheres and said nothing much at all.

Hope was my stalker now, its long tendrils sweet-talking agonies like an opiate. Not far behind, ISIS operatives lurked, tracking my steps like a pack of hunting dogs loping through the urban brush, waiting for the moment to close in. Somehow, I always managed to stay one step ahead.

From the United States, I was assured that a coordinated team was still working on my SIV case while monitoring the ongoing situation in Turkey. Xweşko relayed the directive that I employ social media to put out disinformation, and she provided a clandestine email platform. Every few days as instructed, I posted pictures of myself standing along the Rhine, in verdant parks, dressed to the nines at weddings, or of the beaming children of friends. Meanwhile, I was scrambling all over Lower Saxony, waiting to hear from Alex or one of the Mikes that the rescue deal was in full motion.

"The thing is," Alex said over the line, "there are so many moving parts. It's taken this long just to convince the State Department that you're in a lethal situation. Germany is considered a 'safe' country, so we had to rearrange their brains. There was a shit-ton of paperwork."

"I'm not getting out, Alex—sorry to tell you. It's OK. I'll keep going."

"Listen, one step at a time. You've cleared State with flying colors—and that was the big one. Now the ball's in Homeland Security's court. They've made you a top priority. The team is on this—they want you back, and back alive."

"What about the rescue—in Turkey—the girls?"

Wherever he was, I heard him let out a breath—then: "All we can do is inform the people who decide whether to take the safeties off—and that much we have done. So now, we just have to wait. Believe me, we're all as frustrated as you are."

Right there and then, I didn't believe him—or any of them.

SEVERAL TIMES I traveled to Berlin where agents interviewed me for hours; once they sent a "special American envoy" to conduct a full debrief. Everyone kept repeating the same mantra: it's all going to be fine. How I'd grown to hate that word—*fine*—almost as much as the word *team*. Still, Alex kept up the mantra: the team is pushing hard; the team is there for you; the team won't rest until you're on safe soil. . . .

Often now, I spent successive days in solitude tethered to my Android. Saw doctors when it got too hard to breathe; they kept doling out more pills. Eventually, I stopped sleeping almost entirely and just kept working, no longer keeping track of days. Despite all the outside assertions, there seemed no end in sight to the struggle. At least that's what I thought.

And maybe that's why one night I finally broke right down—to the cold cement floor, limbs splayed. Unable to move any longer, not wanting to. Just then, Dil-Mir came back to me, stepping in her flowered dress and Shingal-perfumed skin through the door to my room, a lamb in her arms.

I brought you your Daki, she said.

I stood up and beheld her loveliness, dark hair all loose. "I forgot about this one," I said and leaned over to caress the animal's fur.

It's my birthday, she said.

And I motioned to the small burning candle I'd lit for her in the corner.

Then I took a long veil that I'd kept secreted for months and ran the thin fabric over my hands. How many times had I thought of the moment she'd done the thing that had split our destiny in two forever? All night, I stayed up pacing the room, talking to her.

In between, my Babo came back, but only in a whisper:

You spend your packet at last, boy?

"Yes, Babo—I have."

As THE HOURS bled out into daybreak, I was ready. Then, in a well-practiced maneuver, I tied the veil into a tight loop, fixing it to the metal pipe running along the ceiling. The copper rung could take the weight of several men—let alone one Yazidi with nothing left in him. No more running—I'd done all I could. On my knees, I bent to extinguish the candle. As the smoke swirled, I asked all the faithful angels to save my soul.

And then, not a foot away, the Android buzzed. Empty veil hanging behind me, I looked over, reached, and glanced at the screen: Anne Norona with another case needing transport. And I could have let it all go, right then and there—they would have to find someone else now—but I'd already glimpsed the face of a boy hovering over the glass.

His name was Khiri.

IN AUGUST 2014, invading soldiers of the Islamic State had swarmed two-year-old Khiri's village in Shingal, taking him and his young mother to Syria as slaves. Until his rescue, Khiri had been used as a torture dummy—beaten to subdue the homicidal tempers of his captors, or to compel his mother to submit to whatever new perversion they came up with.

I collected frail Khiri from the pick-up point to take him in a bundle of blankets to the hospital in Berlin. A team of doctors was waiting. On the trip that we made by train, I held the tiny malnourished boy, who was no more substantial than an empty grain sack. At first, he clung to me while he drifted off to the gentle rocking of the train. I'd never seen a child so tired—more tired than I'd ever been.

Looking down at the fragile form dressed in a new blue T-shirt and pants, I took in the serrated indentations along the blistered skin where his ear had been—teeth marks. And then I studied the arms—scars like nail holes, where soldiers of the Islamic State had put out their cigarettes. Tenderly, I moved my palms along his bird-wing limbs, thin bones all knotted and askew.

Then I read the report again: Militants had taken turns swinging Khiri from the wrists, smashing his legs into cinderblock walls and breaking both femurs, and never setting the bones. There was worse still: wearing lace-up leather army boots, grown men had repeatedly kicked the boy in the abdomen at full force. Even after that, they used implements to maim his genitals—it would take multiple plastic surgeries to make the boy right again. And yet, Khiri slept in my lap, warm and breathing.

Who am I to abandon him? I thought.

Just then a message on my Android came in—Xweşko. She had some new information and wanted to talk. The fact was, I didn't want to talk to any of them—no food and no sleep and so little left of me. But she persisted, mentioning the word *team* like some magic Band-Aid someone had given her.

I was sick of the word *team* and told her so.

The screen stayed blank for a minute and I thought she was long gone, but then she started texting. One at a time, names emerged that I knew at a glance as brethren:

Sergeant Ronald Bowers

Captain Robert Brownsword

Lieutenant Colonel Jay Migone

Senator Marv Hagedorn

And by the last, I was on Mount Shingal again, thirsting among the multitudes left to die over the rocks—but those four men were right up there with me, listening, making frantic calls, mobilizing, keeping me strong even as I wailed for help. Now they were back, on a train in the middle of Germany as I delivered a broken Yazidi angel to safety. Their names lit my screen like lodestars.

As the air rushed from my lungs, I called Xweşko's line and asked her to explain what made no sense.

"That's your team—Team Shaker. There are many more of us, but they were the first. It started when they came to DC in August 2014, and no one even knew if you were going to make it out. Brownsword and Migone have gone back and forth to the Capitol pounding down doors. Bowers has been pulling in all kinds of help. Because of him and Hagedorn you now have senate and congressional offices joining in. Those guys aren't giving up. Neither can you. Not now."

It took several stunned minutes to contain all that was in me—for the moment, I could only answer: *Yaho.* OK. And the line cut out.

I couldn't fathom it. What had I ever done for any of them?

WHEN THE TRAIN pulled into Berlin, Khiri stirred and then looked right up at me. I was weeping.

"I've seen airplanes," he whispered.

"Me too," I answered, so surprised to hear the shy song of his voice. "This is a train."

"I know, you told me."

"Yes." I tried hard not to choke on my own breath.

"My name is Khiri." Then he held out the thumb he'd been sucking and pointed it at himself.

"I'm Shaker," I said, mirroring him.

"I hope to take lots of trains. Don't you?"

"Yes, I hope it—"

But I could hardly hear myself.

Then, without any reason, the boy smiled wide, showing a mouthful of swollen gums. In his lit-up eyes, over which the scenery out the window was passing, I saw my own ashen face staring down—and then I saw all of them: Dil-Mir. Dapîra. Saïd. The lost. And then the freed, every shining face staring out like bewildered newborns at the moment of their rescue: from rafts, vans, trains, buses, under bridges, out of forests, squalid tents, rusted-out cars, and heaps of rubble. Between Anne and me, and the legions of volunteers scattered all across the continents, we'd rescued untold thousands.

Finally, I saw my brothers-in-arms, starting with Sergeant White, and I understood that those still-living men simply had to keep me alive, or it might all have been for nothing—the blood and souls spilled over the sands. They needed to save me, just as I needed to save little Khiri. Together we were all fighting the same war. Ours was a campaign against inexorable evil.

And we must win.

Khiri closed his eyes again, and let his head rest against my beating heart.

Epilogue

Überleben

ON THE THIRD WEDNESDAY IN APRIL 2019, WHEN MY PEOPLE celebrated the festival of Charshama Sari Sali, the birth of the universe, I was in Germany—and still waiting in peril. By now, a few precious family members had asylum papers, along with a handful of old friends from Shingal. In recent weeks, as the Coalition Forces squeezed ISIS fighters from Syria, more Yazidi captives emerged from the abyss. Still, tens of thousands remain missing, the dead in the mass graves unidentified and unconsecrated, their tyrants at large—for now.

Recently, Senator Hagedorn let me know that the coordinates and intel I'd provided during the genocide played a critical role to "open the road" and establish a safe corridor used to get trapped Yazidis off the mountain.

"Without you being there, willing to communicate with a stranger, those people would have all been slaughtered," he said. "And don't forget the five hundred girls in the warehouse."

Whatever happens to me now, just for knowing that, my soul can rest in peace.

NOT LONG BEFORE the spring holiday, Alex called with news.

"You ever heard of a man named Colonel Jesse Johnson, Shaker? He's one of the most highly decorated veterans in the United States military, and I happen to be working on a book about his life. So, I told him all about you—and then I happened to mention that you met General Petraeus once . . . "

It turns out Colonel Jesse Johnson was General Petraeus's commanding officer with the 509th Airborne Battalion in Vicenza, Italy. Back then David Petraeus was a second lieutenant fresh out of West Point. Ever since, the two have stayed friends.

"The general won't remember me," I said. "No way."

"Well, Colonel Johnson reached out to him with your story and he got back to him in about a nanosecond. You're one of his vets—that's how he sees it."

Within hours, General Petraeus sent my case to a member of the board at an organization called No One Left Behind (NOLB) that has helped five thousand Afghan and Iraqi combat interpreters acquire visas to resettle in the United States. James Miervaldis served as an army reservist deployed to both Iraq and Afghanistan, spent three years working to get his own terp out, and knew the system better than most anyone.

As it happens, I am but one of over ten thousand stranded terps who have simply fallen prey to a hidden cancer of red tape: the Special Immigrant Visa (SIV) program actually expired in 2014. Not to mention, the system is designed to work independently of outside influences: congressional and senate recommendations, as well as letters from high-ranking officers in the military and intelligence, are disregarded. All of my work to promote the interests of the United States while risking my own life, deemed irrelevant. No one had figured any of this out until now.

At the same time, Senator James Elroy Risch, chairman of the Senate Intelligence Committee, has taken a personal interest in my situation and contacted the ambassador in Berlin, while advising and coordinating with both the State Department and the Department of Homeland Security. Unfortunately, the Department of Homeland Security recently claimed that I appeared to have "settled" in Germany and sent back my application. Apparently, someone pushing papers at DHS did not "get the memo" that I fled to Germany for security reasons and remain under threat in Europe at large. Senator Risch and NOLB have ensured that my case will move forward, and at the same time Team Shaker is growing exponentially. Now, it's not just about me: it's about all those who served the United States with honor, and just want to come home.

LONG AGO, MY Babo taught me that hardships lighten if you anchor them to moments of gratitude. I've had my share: the morning my sister Nadia gave birth against so many odds to a healthy baby boy in a refugee camp. When Anne Norona received the Woman of the Year award in Britain for her charitable work helping sick Yazidis; and then as she plucked my smiling cousin, Khairi Aezdeen, from his somber tent in the KRG and took him for a trip through England for a time. Khairi was also a combat terp, but gave up on the visa program years ago. These days he helps our people through Anne's NGO Yezidi Emergency Support (YES) and teaches at a camp school for girls. And above all, I am grateful for the moment I watched Nadia Murad receive the Nobel Peace Prize in Sweden, and held it up for every Yazidi like a mighty sword against the beast of the Islamic State.

IN THE MIDST of my frantic endangered life, I went to see a Yazidi friend in a home for the aged in Oldenburg.

"There's an old Jewish man down that corridor you need to see," my friend had told me, and pointed.

Lying back in a hospital bed, Werner stared out, waiting—now I know he was waiting for me.

"Shaker," he said, his hand making loops in the air. "Come, let me see you." I went to the side of the bed and stood there looking down at the frail figure lying there attached to an IV. In a moment, he took up my palm. "The path you walk, I've walked long before you," he said at last.

Then well into the eventide, we exchanged our histories. As a member of a rescue railroad, Werner and a fledgling army of resisters risked their lives to save an endangered generation of fellow Jews from certain extermination in the Nazi concentration camps.

When my turn came, I took a long breath and began with those murky predawn hours of August 3, 2014. Werner listened, all-knowing.

"It's over for me," he said. "But you're still in it. You can start to believe it's going to go on and on forever. I thought we'd never beat it."

"How did you make it through?"

Werner reached over and took my hand again, forming a soft bridge between us. "*Überleben*—to survive. There is only one way to do it. Time—you must learn to walk with time, dear Shaker."

"Yes," I breathed, and knew that it was true.

I must walk with time.

And I am. We Yazidis have diminished, but we are not gone from this earth.

Acknowledgments

IT BRINGS US great joy to thank the many individuals who have supported us and this book at every stage. We are grateful to the incredibly meticulous and intelligent team at Hachette/ Da Capo: Fred Francis, Bill Warhop, and Amanda Kain; and especially our gifted and compassionate editor Robert Pigeon, whose immediate and unwavering enthusiasm for this project was our rocket fuel.

To our wonderfully smart agent Sharlene Martin and her team at Martin Literary, including Anthony Flacco—thank you for guiding this book to the perfect home.

We are also grateful to the following journalists, activists, academics, and authors whose collective focus on war, terrorism, genocide, and the Yazidi people has been invaluable to this project: Christina Lamb, OBE, with *The Times of London;* Anne Speckhard, adjunct professor of psychiatry at Georgetown University Medical School; Matthew Barber, scholar of Yazidi history and culture at the University of Chicago; and David Simon, director of the Genocide Studies Program at Yale University. Many thanks to Akila Radhakrishnan, president, Global Justice Center; Phumzile Mlambo Ngcuka, executive director of UN Women; Pramila Patten, UN Special Representative of the Secretary-General on Sexual Violence in Conflict; and

Pari Ibrahim, executive director of the Free Yezidi Foundation. Also, thank you to Sebastian Junger, Andrea C. Hoffmann and Farida Khalaf, and Jenna Krajeski, whose exceptional books provided invaluable insights. And we would like to also pay tribute to the journalists with Ezidi24, who have done great work on behalf of the Yazidi people.

Our deep gratitude to Anne Norona, founder of Yezidi Emergency Support (YES) and tireless hero. Please help her continue her dangerous and lifesaving work as she sustains the most vulnerable and forgotten Yazidis: http://yezidiemergency support.org/.

For Khairi Aezdeen, former US combat interpreter and current Yazidi activist and volunteer. Thank you for the hours you spent telling your part of the story, and for your ongoing work to help all those left behind with you in the camps.

Thank you to James Miervaldis and every member of No One Left Behind, for their relentless collective efforts to bring US combat interpreters home, and for shepherding us through the labyrinthine Special Immigrant Visa process, while also providing invaluable information for the book.

Our gratitude to Becca Heller, cofounder and executive director of the International Refugee Assistance Program (IRAP), her fiercely intelligent associate attorney Julie Kornfeld, and their colleague Jonathan Riedel. Your work to advocate for refugees and to help displaced individuals like Shaker find paths to safety is awe-inspiring.

We must place writer, lobbyist, and pundit Alex Holstein in his own category for his brilliant and aggressive help marshaling so many elusive members of the intelligence community, the United States government, and the military into an indomitable army of support for Shaker, the Yazidi community, combat interpreters, and this work (he also took the time to read over every page).

Thank you, Mike Williams and "Mike B." for your courageous work and encouragement from the shadows.

Thank you to Colonel Jesse Johnson and General David Petraeus, two all-American heroes who deserve stars of their own on the flag. We owe these two men an enormous debt of respect and gratitude for their support of this work through their incredible efforts on behalf of Shaker, and all the combat interpreters left behind after wars came to an end.

Nadia Murad, Nobel Peace Prize laureate, human rights activist, survivor, and founder of Nadia's Initiative. Your courage has been a beacon for every survivor.

We are grateful for the exceptional and ongoing efforts of Senator James Elroy Risch, Senate Foreign Relations Committee chairman, and his staff for taking Shaker under their mighty wing. We will see you at Shaker's barbecue in Washington, DC.

The original members of Team Shaker were there from the very start, answering countless questions over endless hours, reading pages while also offering incredible life-saving support to Shaker and the Yazidi people. There is no doubt that without the tireless and selfless efforts of these four brave and selfless men, Shaker and so many would have perished at the hands of ISIS in 2014: Robert Brownsword, Jay Migone, Ronald Bowers, and Senator Marv Hagedorn.

Many thanks also to journalist and filmmaker Jason Stant with the Associated Press for his continuing friendship and support.

And to all the volunteers in the Mosquitos, and around the world fighting for humanity itself. You know who you are.

From our hearts, we thank you all.

From Shaker Jeffrey:

FIRST AND FOREMOST, I must pay tribute to our Yazidi high spiritual father, Baba Sheikh, for continuing to shepherd our people through the pain of yet another genocide. And after him, I must offer gratitude to my entire family, both the living and the lost: my mother and father, grandfathers and grandmothers, brothers and sisters, nieces, nephews, and cousins. Together and in the memory of those no longer with us, we will carry on fighting for the next generation of Yazidis, so that they may live and thrive in peace.

I am humbled by all those who have tried to help me and my people survive and get to safety. My brothers-in-arms: Bowers, Brownsword, Migone—thank you for being with me and keeping me going all this time. And to Senator Marv Hagedorn, whom I "met" on the mountain and who has never really left my side— you are my brother.

Thank you to General Gary Sayler, and the members of the United States government, who have done so much for me personally and for my people. And all the "fighting friends" I met on the mountain, whose names I would never know—together we worked in the pit of hell to save so many. You will always be in my heart.

I would like to personally thank my Yazidi sister, Nadia Murad, as without her courage so many of us would have none left. Our work together carried me across the darkness.

I must also pay tribute to the following heroes and steadfast friends: Nawaf Ashur, Dr. Andreas Gammel, Dr. Mirza Dinnay, Murad Ismael, Staff Sergeant Richard McNall, Sergeant First Class Catlin Tanner Eagleman, and all the brave and good members of Team Shady and Team Spider.

Many thanks also to Jonathan Howell, Christopher Faulkner, and Marvin Iavecchia, who were with me during the war and helped me get through it.

And a special thank-you to journalist Christina Lamb for traveling to meet our survivors, capturing their pain so movingly with her gifted pen, and sharing it with the world.

And thank you, *Kaça Babo*, daughter of my father, my sister Katharine, for finding the words.

From Katharine:

I AM SINCERELY grateful to Shaker's family in Iraq and his Yazidi counterparts for opening up their world to me with such patient generosity. The courage of each and every Yazidi kept this project going every step of the way.

I am sincerely thankful for the loyal friends and colleagues who have all guided, supported, and inspired my work in innumerable ways: Marlene Cooper, Dr. Christine and Mark Till, Libby Burton, T. C. Boyle, Elias Campbell, Dr. Ted Brown, Christl Reeh, Dr. Azil Resiew, Gloria Allred, Susan Schellenberg, Gail Regan and Nancy Regan, the Leofantis, Wongs, Fyalls, Seppanens, and Smiths.

And thank you to my first reader, editor, and loyal armchair partner, Matthew, and his girls. Not one word would have made it out without you.

I must thank and pay tribute to my family: Alex and our wonderful loving children, who waited so patiently as I toiled away again. I hope to have made you as proud of me as I am of you. And my gratitude goes to my mother, who faced down her own tyrants from a hospital bed—your unwavering decency and bravery through intense pain has inspired so many. Thank you to all my loving cousins, especially Aida Harris, who filled an abyss. And thank you to my steadfast big brother, John— always at another's side doing what is right and good.

And to dear *Brako* Shaker, my sweet brother. Thank you for gifting me with your darkest sorrows. Our long perilous journey together will only end when I can reach out at last and touch your hand.

Index